LOVING
~ AN ~
# IMPERFECT
# MAN

LOVING

⤶ AN ⤷

IMPERFECT

MAN

STOP WAITING FOR HIM TO MAKE YOU HAPPY AND START GETTING WHAT YOU WANT OUT OF LIFE

Ellen Sue Stern

POCKET BOOKS

New York   London   Toronto   Sydney   Tokyo   Singapore

POCKET BOOKS, a division of Simon & Schuster Inc.
1230 Avenue of the Americas, New York, NY 10020

Stern, Ellen Sue, 1954–
  Loving an imperfect man / Ellen Sue Stern.
    p. cm.
  ISBN 0-671-52516-6
  1. Love. 2. Man-woman relationships. 3. Mate selection.
  4. Perfectionism (Personality trait). 5. Self-acceptance.
  I. Title.
  HQ801.S826   1997
  306.7—dc20   96-41487
                                                    CIP

First Pocket Books hardcover printing February 1997

10 9 8 7 6 5 4 3 2 1

Text design by Stanley S. Drate/Folio Graphics Co. Inc.

Printed in the U.S.A.

For Louis Sky, with love, Nelle

ACKNOWLEDGMENTS

Writing this book has been one of the most difficult and the most rewarding experiences of my life. Throughout every step of the way, I have been loved, supported, encouraged, cheered, bolstered, and fed by a community of family and friends to whom I am eternally grateful. I am so blessed. In turn, I bless each of you, for your help in bringing this creation into being:

My wonderful parents, Frank and Rosalie Kiperstin, for your generous support, without which I would have had to get a "real job" and could never have written this book.

My daughter, Zoe Stern, for being my role model of a gutsy, honest, and confident young woman.

My son, Evan Stern, for being my soul-mate, playmate, and shining light.

My sister, Faith Schway, for your abiding love and belief in me.

Jill Edelstein, for being my shelter in the storm.

Mollie Moore-Goldstein, for teaching me about unconditional love.

Martha Morris, for knowing when to say: "Let's pray."

Gary Stern, for taking such good care of our children.

Bonnie Hoffman, for continually encouraging me.

Joel Hodroff, for reminding me when to soar and when to rest.

Rachel Solomon, for making me laugh.

Beverly Lewis, for being a constant source of friendship and wisdom.

Lyndsay Rosen, for being there when it counted.

Joey Morris, for teaching me about raw honesty.

Amelia Sheldon, for your enthusiasm and editorial input.

Claire Zion, for your initial belief in this book.

Scott Stevenson, for sharing the "zone" with me.

Paul Speltz, for lending the "Funky Princess," the little red Fiat.

Fredd Lee, for your faith and generosity.

Marjorie Shapiro, for extending your healing touch.

Bob Edelstein, for being my honorary big brother.

And last, but not least, Lance Pustin, for being the perfect imperfect man.

CONTENTS

1

STILL WISHING AND
HOPING HE'LL CHANGE   1

*Men just don't get it; I just wish he'd . . . ; We teach
what we need to learn; Falling in love with
ourselves*

2

LOVING OURSELVES:
A RADICAL NEW APPROACH   29

*The power of self-love; The damage of self-loathing;
Redefining perfection; A working road map; The
journey from fear to love*

3

THE FIRST LEAP:
CULTIVATING CLARITY   48

*Romantic sobriety; Overcoming our resistance; The
importance of grief; Disillusionment: A positive
process; Dealing with him; What are YOU giving?;
Compatibility; Chemistry; Affinity; Purpose and
Destiny*

4

THE SECOND LEAP: CULTIVATING INTEGRITY   76

Our highest vision of ourselves; Intention and action; Overcoming our resistance; Dealing with him; Making commitments

5

THE THIRD LEAP: CULTIVATING SELF-POSSESSION   93

Accepting our singularity; Are we really liberated?; Overcoming our resistance; Economic independence; Practical competence; Emotional autonomy; What men can teach us about autonomy; Spiritual foundation; Dealing with him; Sound investments; Emotional currency; Wise spending; Why can't he read my mind?; Fear of conflict; But can he deliver?

6

THE FOURTH LEAP: CULTIVATING STRENGTH   129

Strengthening ourselves; Overcoming our resistance; What men can teach us about "selfishness"; What we can teach men about giving; Nourishing ourselves; Nutrition assessment; Stretching our bodies; Sensuality; Eroticism; Safety and passion; What men can teach us about sex; What we can teach men about sex and love; Dealing with him; Nurturing ourselves; Creativity; Mothering; Nature; Beauty; Retreat and ritual; Cleaning up our act

7

THE FIFTH LEAP: CULTIVATING DISCERNMENT 174

*Making discerning choices; Beyond codependence;
Presence: A powerful alternative; Filling our
toolbox; Surrender: The balance between
attachment and detachment; Overcoming our
resistance; Measures of discernment; What men can
teach us about being rational; What we can teach
men about feelings; The concept of service; Dealing
with him*

8

THE SIXTH LEAP: CULTIVATING ACCEPTANCE 206

*Permeable boundaries; Holding on to anger;
Overcoming our resistance; Opening our wounds;
Identifying the source of our anger; Expressing our
feelings; Should you or shouldn't you?; Four steps
to productively expressing anger; Honoring our
needs; Dealing with him; What men can teach us
about keeping it simple; What we can teach men
about emotional processing; The nature of
forgiveness*

9

THE SEVENTH LEAP: CULTIVATING CREATIVITY 249

*Overcoming our resistance; Intention; Initiative;
Inspiration; Intelligence; Imagination; Your role:
Teacher; Your role: Student; Your role: Inventor;
Your role: Empathic; Your role: Social Director; Your
role: Seductress; Your role: Parent; Your role:
Cheerleader; Your role: Healer; A bittersweet
eleventh act*

10

THE EIGHTH LEAP: CULTIVATING REVERENCE

288

Making our relationship a sanctuary; Being a blessing; Intentional acts of kindness; Intentional acts of gratitude; Intentional acts of celebration

AFTERWORD

303

Still Wishing and Hoping
He'll Change

Last summer my fifteen-year-old friend Mollie fell in love. It was just like in the movies. I listened raptly as Mollie tried to find words to describe the indescribable. "He can see inside me," she confided, her eyes lit with joy. I listened for over an hour, then quietly asked, "Is there anything about him you *don't* like?" She stared at me as if I were insane. "Of course not," she replied. "He's perfect." I didn't know whether to burst her bubble or bite my tongue. I spared her the benefit of my wisdom, wistfully longing for a time when I was that young, that idealistic, so blinded by love as to be impervious to reality.

We've all been there, however long ago and far away it seems. There was a time when just being with our partner made us feel like the luckiest person in the world. Our passion exceeded our pessimism, our fulfillment outweighed our frustration, our appreciation of his finest qualities overshadowed our awareness of his flaws.

Wouldn't it be wonderful to feel this way again? To be

1

so deeply in love, so confident of the rightness of our union that we can truly say, "I'm perfectly happy with the man in my life." After spending the past decade working with thousands of women, I'm convinced that deep down in our hearts, this is what each of us wants. Not every minute of every day, and certainly not with the naivete of a love-struck teenager. We can't turn back the clock to age fifteen, though I frankly doubt most women, myself included, would opt for a second tumultuous round of adolescence. Nor can we rewind our current relationship back to the beginning, unraveling the intricate tapestry of experiences—some positive, some negative—that have brought us to where we are today.

There's no going back. There's no starting over. We're far too intimately acquainted with our partner's imperfections to be swept off our feet. We're old enough, wise enough, and experienced enough to know the difference between the first flush of romantic passion and the more complex realities of day-to-day coexistence. We may never feel quite so enchanted as we did in the beginning, still and yet, few of us would trade the sweet innocence of first love for the richer, more satisfying nourishment possible in a mature love relationship. Like the character Francesca in *The Bridges of Madison County*, we may fantasize about running away with the man of our dreams, but like Francesca, we remain committed to loving the one we're with.

Committed—but not necessarily satisfied. Despite years of working on relationship issues, most women still express a certain amount of discontent. Are our expectations too high? Are we pushing our partner to live up to an unreachable ideal? Most women, sooner or later, are accused of being overly demanding and impossible to please, often on the heels of our bringing up yet another "Honey, we need to talk about something" conversation with our mate. I wish I had a dollar for every man who has thrown up his hands in despair, uttering the famous words, "What do you WANT from me?!" In short, are *we* creating the problem by expecting more than is reasonably possible? Or, in the age-old words of philosophers, poets, and one too many men-who-feel-pressured, What DO women want?

Men Just Don't Get It

In my seminars I ask participants to make a wish list of what it would take to be more satisfied with their partner. Here are their Top Ten Wishes:

1. I wish he were more emotionally responsive.
2. I wish he were more helpful and supportive.
3. I wish he would appreciate how hard I work and how much I do.
4. I wish he were more romantic.
5. I wish he weren't so oblivious.
6. I wish he were more caring and considerate.
7. I wish he'd grow up and act like a man.
8. I wish he weren't so selfish.
9. I wish he were more affectionate.
—And the universal wish that's become shorthand for summing up all of the above:
10. I WISH HE'D GET IT.

When we say we want men to "get it," here's what we mean: We want our partner to care enough about us and the relationship to make a concerted effort in the areas in which we've explicitly asked for change. (Ideally, they'd know what we want and need without it being spelled out, but that's too much to expect.) Although the specifics vary from woman to woman, universally speaking, we want to be accepted, appreciated, acknowledged, and adored. We want support, understanding, and respect. We want companionship, intimacy, an erotic connection, and a shared vision in which we are mutually invested. Most of all, we want to be taken seriously in our efforts to create the relationship we envision.

Many of us are starting to run out of ideas—we're also starting to run out of patience—and some of us are starting to run out of time. Most women describe their relationship as "up and down"; things coast along smoothly for a while, interrupted by irritating incidents or outbursts. We may rate our relationship as "pretty good, given what's out there"; our partner may earn relatively high marks compared to the general population of men, which may or may not be saying much, depending on how we're feeling at any given moment. Some of us struggle with serious chronic issues that repeatedly pop up. And some of us are dangerously close to the end of our rope, questioning the long-term viability of our relationship and wondering if it's worth it to go on trying to improve it.

In contrast, men usually describe their relationship as "fine." Pushed to elaborate, most men say something along the lines, "I'd just like her to leave me alone," which translated, means, "I want her to accept me as I am." The contrast between men and women's apparent level of satisfaction is supported by dramatic statistics: Over three quarters of marital counseling and approximately seventy percent of divorce proceedings are initiated by women. Either women are more proactive about getting help or getting out, or men are just more easily satisfied.

Whether we're at the FINE ONE DAY–NOT SO FINE THE NEXT DAY stage, CHRONICALLY FRUSTRATED stage, or FED-UP stage, one thing is true: Whatever the ways and to whatever degree we've asked for changes without seeing significant signs of improvement, we are understandably confused and are asking ourselves these three basic questions:

- What's reasonable to expect in an intimate relationship?
- Should I back off and try to accept him as he is?
- Is there anything more I can do?

If any or all of these questions are uppermost in your mind, you're in good company. My first seminar on the topic of loving an imperfect man convinced me that I needed to hurry up and write this book. I had hoped at least twenty or thirty women would show up on that chilly, gray November night in Philadelphia. Instead, I watched hundreds of women file into the auditorium—individual women, groups of two or three friends, mothers and daughters, the last stragglers settling into folding chairs quickly set up in back—women from diverse backgrounds, seeking answers, hoping for some key to the mystery of loving the special man in their life.

Although I was momentarily overwhelmed by the response, I wasn't *that* surprised. The vast majority of women in Philadelphia, in every other city across America, and perhaps throughout the world emphatically say "Yes!" when asked, "Are you in love with an imperfect man?" The planet is populated with imperfect men and the women who love them. I'm one, you're one; most of your friends, coworkers, and casual acquaintances may count themselves firmly and squarely in this category.

I started my seminar by asking, "Raise your hand if you're involved with a perfect man." No hands went up. Had anyone raised their hand, they would have won a cash reward and the opportunity to run the seminar while I took notes. Next I asked, "Raise your hand if you've ever met a perfect man." One hand tentatively went up in the air: "I once saw a movie called *Falling in Love*," the woman in the audience said. "The main character seemed perfect. . . ." Then her voice trailed off as she added, "Of course, it *was* a movie and he *was* married to someone else." Finally, I asked, "Raise your hand if, despite your partner's imperfections, you love him and want to make your relationship better." There was a unanimous show of hands.

If you're reading this book, it's because you haven't given up. The good news is, despite our frustration, we along with the majority of women are still committed, still hopeful, still invested in the possibility of improving our relationship. We may think he's imperfect (he is), we may have tried everything humanly possible to change him (we have), we may feel confused about what to do next (we are), but we *haven't given up*. And we mustn't give up—if for no other reason than the fact that love is rare and once we've found it, it's well worth fighting for.

There's no statute of limitations when it comes to love. The depth of desire that initially drew us to our partner and inspired us to say I do, whether in marriage or a less formalized context, hasn't disappeared. It's merely gone underground, overshadowed by the immense challenge of maintaining a long-term relationship. Yet for each of us, there was a moment in time when we felt just that way. It may have been on our third date when we suddenly realized, "Oh, my god, this may be the right guy." It may have been on our wedding day when we looked into our beloved's eyes with perfect confidence that we could sustain our connection through thick and thin. It may have been at the birth of our first child when after hours of grueling labor with our partner at our side, we felt our love renewed through the sacred act of cocreation.

For many of us, we've experienced that feeling resurface in otherwise ordinary moments: he's down on his hands and knees fixing the kitchen sink; he surprises us by bragging to friends about our recent promotion; he charms the pants off us by singing "It's a Beautiful Day in the Neighborhood" while bathing the children. Suddenly, out of the blue, we are stuck by that spark and remember why we love him. These moments are what keep us invested; providing the hope and energy that fuels our ongoing commitment.

But moments aren't enough. Regardless of the ways in which we are satisfied, we continue to question whether the man we're involved with has what it takes to *consistently* maintain the loving partnership we crave—not because it's impossible to satisfy us, not because we expect our partner to cater to our every need, and not because we expect miracles. We don't expect to be madly in love every minute of the day; we know that's unrealistic; besides, who's got the energy to muster that constant level of emotional intensity regardless of the rush? We're not looking for perfection; we just want a new, improved version of our mate. As the character Hope in the television series *thirtysomething* said when her husband, Michael, asked if she was going to leave him for another man, "I don't want another man. I just want a better you."

What constitutes "better" for us varies from individual to individual, depending on what we feel is missing in our relationship. We know we can't have everything, but we still haven't decided, once and for all, whether what we have is enough. We're constantly taking inventory: He's a terrific father, but he's at a dead end in his career. He makes a great living, but his sexual technique leaves something to be desired. He's socially adept, calls his

aging mother every single day, but is utterly oblivious to
the piles of his underwear on the bedroom floor. We try
to count our blessings, to appreciate our mate's positive
and endearing qualities. But no matter how many times
we make our pro-and-con list, we're still left wondering
how to accept the ways in which our partner falls short
of our expectations.

Sometimes this question is framed as an earnest inquiry, "Should I just try to accept that this is as good as it
gets?" Other times it's phrased as defeat, "What's the
point of trying since nothing ever changes?" Or, in some
cases it's phrased sarcastically, "If they can send a man
to the moon, why can't they send them all?" Whether
expressed as confusion, resignation, or a patronizing dig,
this question arises out of women's heartfelt search for
answers. Make no mistake about it: These are *not* angry,
cynical, male-bashing separatists. These are *not* desperately "needy" women with an unsatiable hunger for reassurance and support. These are *not* battered abuse
victims in need of protection. On the contrary, like yourself, these are smart, secure, successful women who are
serious about creating a healthier, happier relationship
with the man in their life. Is it time to learn to live with
what we have? Or is there something more we can do to
feel more satisfied and fulfilled?

On the surface it seems as if accepting our mate's imperfections and learning to live with reality is the only sane
option. After all, we have control only over ourselves; as
"The Serenity Prayer" reminds us, "God, give us the
grace to accept with serenity the things that cannot be
changed, courage to change the things which should be
changed, and the wisdom to distinguish one from the
other."

We don't have the power to change anyone else. That's a fundamental truth. Knowing this, however, hasn't kept us from trying. And trying. And trying. We've knocked ourselves out trying every conceivable strategy, expending enormous sums of energy in the pursuit of remaking our partner. We've spent tons of time, emotion, and money "working" on our relationships. We've read dozens of self-help books, often leaving them open on his pillow with the relevant passages highlighted. We've attended twelve-step recovery groups and personal growth seminars, spilled our guts to friends and therapists—dragged our mate along when it seemed appropriate, in an effort to convince him of the value. We've tried loving him less, loving him more, dancing with our anger, facing our codependence, decoding his alien language, and accepting that it all comes down to the fact that we're from Venus, he's from Mars. We've urged, encouraged, nudged, explained, complained, advised, fixed, analyzed, healed, inspired, and—when all else failed—threatened, retreated, or withdrew until the next round. We've been mother, teacher, guru, cheerleader, mentor, CEO, and rabbi, all in the spirit of helping our partner become the man we know he's capable of being. Women should win the Noble Prize for heroic effort above and beyond the call of duty on this front. The collective energy expended by women is enough to move mountains; meanwhile we can't even get him to pick up his socks, pick up the kids, pick up some flowers on the way home from work, (fill in the blank), without reminding and rewarding him each and every time.

No wonder women are weary. No wonder we're angry, resentful, and disappointed at how hard we've tried and how little seems to have changed. At times our efforts have paid off. We may have invited our mate to a fruitful therapy session or initiated a constructive conversation that resulted in his taking on more household responsibilities. In all fairness, a fair amount of progress has occurred in the relationship between men and women. I'm impressed and encouraged by the forward strides made by a good number of contemporary men: men who are happily parenting rather than reluctantly "baby-sitting" their children, men who are taking on their share of domestic tasks, men who are willing to work on their own growth and healing and be active partners in intimate relationships. That having been said, the fact remains: the changes we request are often met with a fair amount of resistance and very little staying power. We mention that the laundry needs folding; he glances at the overflowing hamper, scratches his head and says, "I still have clean underwear in my drawer." Or he rises to the occasion for a day, two days, maybe as long as a week, then regresses until we remind him again. Then he angrily responds, "I SAID I'd do the laundry! Why don't you give me a goddamned break!" The worst part is that it's a thankless task. All we want is to have a wonderful relationship, and somehow we end up in the lousy position of being the Laundry Gestapo instead of the helpmate and ally we'd much rather be.

While we don't have the power to change our partner, we *do* have the power to change our own approach. We can start to do this by looking at the gap between our expectations and reality.

I Just Wish He'd . . .

Our confusion between desires and expectations is a core part of the problem. Here's the distinction: Everything we *want* is okay to want—as long as we take full responsibility for pursuing our desires. Everything we *expect* is conditional upon our partner's capacity and willingness to deliver, which is where we get jammed up. Consider this scenario: Let's say we long for a deeper level of emotional intimacy with our mate. We want to honestly share our feelings; we'd be thrilled if he'd do the same. There's nothing wrong with what we want. In fact, our desire is honorable, well-intended, and inspired by our vision of a closer connection. Or, on a more practical level, perhaps we want our mate to assume a more active coparenting role. Again, our wish may be perfectly reasonable. Beside our own need for support, we genuinely believe that our children would benefit from greater involvement with their father. So far, so good. Knowing what we want and believing that our desires are justified enables us to act on them. We, in turn, empower ourselves by exercising our options. We do so when we reveal our innermost feelings or come up with creative ways to foster a closer relationship between our children and their father. Whether our partner responds in kind is out of our control. That's an expectation.

Identifying and pursuing our desires is central to our integrity and self-respect. However, expecting our partner to be forthcoming puts the onus on him to determine our happiness. When we want something from our mate and he can't, doesn't, or won't come through with it, we either blame him for disappointing us or turn our anger inward, blaming ourselves for wanting what's beyond our reach. Instead of separating what we can control and what we can't, we push our partner to meet our expectations or reconcile ourselves to settling for less than we want.

But aren't there some things we have the right to expect? Or, as women often say, "Why shouldn't I expect him to . . . ?" We all have certain belief systems about what we *should* be able to expect from our partner. These expectations are based on a fairly complex combination of factors, including romantic fantasies, cultural norms, and our perceptions of other intimate relationships we've seen up close. What they're usually *not* based on is a real and honest picture of the actual person we're intimately involved with. Whether Prince Charming rode up on a white horse, whether Ward Cleaver brought home a steady paycheck so June could stay home and bake cookies, whether our father always gave our mother roses on their anniversary, or whether our best friend's husband is on the nursery school committee is totally irrelevant. We can want any or all of these things, but ultimately, all that matters is what it's possible to have with the particular man we've chosen as our mate. For better or for worse, he is who he is. Fantasy Man is just that—a fantasy. Comparing our partner to fairy-tale figures, one-dimensional TV caricatures, our father, or someone else's husband is silly and counterproductive. Assuredly, up close, our fantasies would shatter in the face of reality: Prince Charming doesn't exist. Ward Cleaver expected dinner on the table and might have balked if June had gotten a job. Our father was difficult and demanding. Our best friend's husband is having an affair. Whether we compare our partner to our therapist, our boss, our son's geography teacher, or the man behind the meat counter, soon enough we would see that each of them has his own particular issues that will surface, and we realize that we are simply dreaming about trading one set of challenges for another.

Our expectations are also based on our interpretation of what it means to be loving. Human beings tend to telegraph desires by giving what we want to get back. We instinctively express our love in the way we want to be loved. We treat our mate in the way that we want to be treated. We offer what we want to receive.

For instance, if we believe that loving means going out of our way to do little things for our partner, we'll expect him to do the same. If we demonstrate our love through emotional support, we're apt to judge the degree of his commitment with similar criteria in mind. If affection is our primary way of saying "I love you," we're likely to lavish hugs and kisses on our partner, hoping he'll return the gesture.

Naturally we assume that our mate will—and should—reciprocate in kind. But this formula is fraught with disaster. Since no two people express their love in the same way, it's dangerous to base our expectations of our mate on how we conduct ourselves in the relationship. There are numerous reasons why shows of affection may not come easily to our mate, and love isn't one of them. He may have grown up in a family in which affection was held in check. He may be shy or withdrawn, or his concept of masculinity may inhibit him from openly expressing affection.

Believing that "if he loved me, he'd show it the same way I do" is as unreasonable as thinking the sun should shine just because it's our birthday. We can pray for sunshine—and wouldn't it be nice nature cooperated—but whether there's sunshine or rain has nothing to do with the fact that it's March 13 and we're deserving of a sunny celebration. Likewise, how our partner expresses his love is disconnected from our desire and deservedness. He may show his feelings in other, equally meaningful ways, such as moonlighting in order to pay the mortgage, taking our car for a tune-up, or showing up for dinner at our parents' when he'd rather watch the Final Four. It's unfair to our mate and unfair to ourselves to expect his expression of love to mirror our own. We diminish his freedom of expression, *and* we deny ourselves his unique, authentic gifts.

Finally, our expectations are based on our perception of who our partner is and what *we* think he is capable of. These impressions are usually formed in the initial stages of our relationship, when we first fall in love. Here's how it works. Falling in love is a singularly magical, mystical experience during which we're offered a momentary glimpse of our mate's perfection. We recognize our partner's pure essence in all its goodness and light. Whether we're temporarily blinded by this light or luxuriate for a few hours, days, or weeks in this state, it is at this point that we see the best, most beautiful core of his being, and we are awed by the sight. That's whom we fall in love with—the proverbial "rose-colored," highly romanticized, larger-than-life image we've been treated to.

This phenomenon is sometimes described as an energy exchange in which the feelings of love we project toward our partner emboldens and illuminates him. It's as if our love for him enhances his finest qualities, bringing out the absolute best in him. This is often referred to as the infatuation stage of a relationship. It is the period during which, like my teenage friend, Mollie, we're so bedazzled that we only see what's positive about our partner. This image stays with us, and it is upon that which we build our highest expectations of our mate.

This stage is also sometimes referred to as blind love. We're so infatuated we can't see our new love realistically. But maybe just the opposite is true. Perhaps that instant when we see our partner's pure essence—the truest, most authentic part of him—is when our vision is the clearest and most illuminated. Either way, it's a double-edged sword. On the one hand, this transcendent experience entices us. We want more. On the other hand, it creates an impossible standard for our mate to live up to.

Sooner or later reality sets in. A man I know recently fell in love. A few days into his romance he called to excitedly relate something wonderful his new girlfriend had said: "She told me, 'Don't ever change.' " He was sure he'd died and gone to heaven; I was sure it was only a matter of time before she would change her tune. Six months later he was grumbling over all the ways this same woman was critical of him. The woman who had once thought he was perfect now had a long laundry list of ways she'd like him to improve.

Inevitably, as our relationship develops, our partner's flaws come into focus, revealing the gap between his essence and reality. Deep down he's incredibly tender, yet much of the time he's guarded and defensive. He has passionate aspirations—he dreams of writing a novel, being a teacher, learning to fly—yet he's stuck in a boring job and isn't doing anything about it. He'd be an incredible father, but he's scared of the commitment. He cares deeply about his parents, but it wouldn't occur to him to pick up the phone and call them once in a while.

Our perception is altered as we struggle to reconcile the gap between our picture of our partner's perfect essence and his real-life behavior. But no one—not even Mother Teresa—manifests their perfect essence all of the time. Every human being is a work in progress; we are all struggling to overcome our fears so that we can fully achieve our potential. None of us are all the way there; each of us is a poignant combination of strength and fragility, courage and terror, inspiration and despair. We mess up; we blow it; we fail ourselves and others in myriad ways. No matter how perfect we may be on the inside, we have some distance to go in order to become everything we're capable of in our daily lives.

This may sound very familiar to you. But knowing all of this doesn't keep us from trying to close the gap. Most of us have trouble accepting both our mates and our own imperfections; we're constantly trying to improve upon ourselves, to be more accomplished, more attractive, more whatever we think is lacking in ourselves. Likewise, we want to perfect our partner. We see his potential. We can easily envision how much better both of our lives could be *if* he'd make a few small changes in the right direction. So we get in there and start working on him as if he's a project. He'd look better with a trim, so we schedule a haircut appointment. He needs to slow down; we register him for a yoga class. He's meant for bigger and better things, so we rewrite his résumé and circle job openings in the paper.

Somebody has to do it, right? So why not the one person who loves and cares about him the most? Why not? *Because it's not our job.* Our efforts to improve our relationship have failed for one main reason: they revolve around trying to change our mate, which is a way of trying to control what is beyond our control.

Now, before you say, "Control! I'm just trying to help because I *care* so much!" consider what is actually going on. We *think* we're being caring, not controlling, because our intentions are motivated by our desire to help. But here's the catch: He's not interested. We may think that improving his relationship with his mother would be good for him, but that doesn't necessarily mean he does. We may feel that his career would take off if he just learned to be a little more assertive, but that may not be his style. We may truly believe that his getting in touch with his feelings would be healing and a process that would allow him to grow, but it's simply not on his agenda. In other words, what matters to us doesn't necessarily matter to him.

In fact, rather than thanking us for our help, he is more likely to withdraw, recoil, or berate us for getting on his case. It's not that he doesn't care that we care; he just doesn't want to hear it because he hears what we're saying as criticism or judgment. For example:

We suggest:	He hears:
"Let's role-play before you go in and ask for that raise."	"I don't trust you to handle it."
"It's easier to burp the baby if you hold her over your right shoulder."	"I think you're a bad father."
"Don't you think we should work on our intimacy issues?"	"I think you're an inadequate lover."

When it comes to men, we can safely assume that any unsolicited advice will be interpreted as, "Nothing I do is good enough." And it isn't. If we're to be perfectly honest, our overtures are motivated by our underlying desire to change him in the ways we want. They may be positive changes; they may well be in his own best interest. But, as long as they're based on our agenda, they'll be met with resistance rather than receptivity.

Another reason our efforts backfire is that trying to change our partner is inherently disrespectful. Every human being has his or her own path and his or her own pace. Loving our mate means letting him navigate his path in his own time frame and in his own style. When we co-opt this process or try to rush it along, we rob our partner of his fundamental birthright to find his own way. The only time it's useful for us to intervene is when we are invited to do so. If our partner requests our insight, input, and direction, fair enough. If not, we mustn't patronize him by assuming we know what he needs better than he does.

There is, however, one way to offer our wisdom to him that sometimes works, although it's a little risky. Since men often won't initiate a conversation, especially regarding areas of perceived weakness, it can be useful to ask, "Do you want any feedback or suggestions?" which gives him the chance to say yes or no. In doing so, we have to be prepared to hear no and not interpret it as rejection. If the answer is yes, we must be extremely sensitive in our approach. The ancient practice of Zen Buddhism advises that we speak only when we have something to say that is True, Kind, and Useful. These criteria are a good gauge of when it is and isn't appropriate to speak up.

This reality is very tough for us to accept for two reasons. First, our love for our mate makes us want to help him in any way we can. It's frustrating and painful to watch someone we love make wrong turns, self-destructive choices, or stagnate when we know they can soar. Second, our partner's willingness or unwillingness to change directly affects the quality of our lives. To whatever degree he seems stuck—whether he refuses to deal with his feelings, ignores his responsibilities, or engages in self-destructive behavior—we're affected. So letting go seems impossible. If we lower our vigilance, we think, *nothing* will change, which is why we keep trying and trying.

Ultimately, trying to change our partner doesn't work because it's self-destructive. Not for *him*, but for ourselves. Over the past ten years scores of women have identified themselves as codependent, which loosely interpreted means we're overly involved in our mate's issues at the expense of our own. This is an addictive and self-destructive habit. And we're still doing it. After years

of "working" on our codependence, we're still overly focused on trying to fix our mate.

Why can't we stop? Because we're getting too much
out of the equation. We derive a great deal of our meaning and self-worth from our steady involvement in helping (fixing, changing, healing) our partner. Doing for
others gives us a reason for being. In my Indispensable
Woman workshops, I ask participants to list some of the
rewards they get by making themselves indispensable.
Identity always comes up. One woman put it aptly when
she said, "I know who I am by looking at my list." When
we withdraw our attention from our mate, we're forced
to take a good, hard look at ourselves. The more we focus
on him, the less we focus on ourselves. The less we focus
on ourselves, the less we have to face our own issues. The
less we have to face or own issues, the less we have to do
our own healing. The less we have to do our own healing,
the less hurt we have to feel. In short, focusing on him
allows us to absolve ourselves of doing the real work that
can truly make a difference—the work of healing ourselves and becoming whole, which I'm deeply committed
to, both professionally and personally.

We Teach What We Need to Learn

I always start my seminars with these words, "My friend
Bonnie says, 'When I have a problem, I have a problem.
When Ellen Sue has a problem, she writes a book.'" This
book is no different from my others. The issue of loving
an imperfect man is one I've been struggling with nearly
all my life.

One of my earliest memories is twirling around in a
tutu at probably four or five, trying to get my father's attention. He was distracted, oblivious to my frantic twirl-

ing until I crashed into the stereo cabinet. That got his attention. He drove me bleeding to the hospital for stitches. I still have a faint scar just above my eyebrow from this episode.

At thirteen I turned my attention to boys, spending most of my bat-mitzvah party in the bathroom putting electric curlers in my hair. At sixteen I fell in love. I was obsessed with a boy named Martin. He could quote all of *Waiting for Godot*, listened to John Coltrane, wore purple bell-bottoms and—as if that wasn't enough—had a family who sat around over dinner having intellectual and political discussions. Every word I spoke, every T-shirt I wore, even the friends I chose were subject to his approval, which he meted out sparingly. I spent four years turning myself inside out to please him. Through my senior year of high school and all four years of college I was focused on trying to get and keep his love, love I didn't feel worthy of and always felt at risk of losing.

At twenty-two I decided it was time to be a bride. I married my best friend, a sweet, gentle man named David. Our "Goodbye Columbus" wedding was an extravaganza with matching bridesmaids and a lavish sit-down dinner for over three-hundred guests. My now yellowing photographs show a scared-looking girl-woman who looked as if she was wondering what she was getting herself into. Two years later our marriage ended in an amicable divorce.

I had been separated less than a month when I ran into Gary, a high-school friend, whom I immediately started dating and married within six months. Gary was talented, intelligent, and provocative. We shared the important things in life: a similar aesthetic, political views, career aspirations, and the commitment to create a healthy family. Together we raised two beautiful children, developed successful careers, made a home, and became part of an extended community. From all appearances we had a "perfect marriage." In fact, it took nearly twelve years of therapy, several expensive romantic retreats, and every ounce of emotional energy for both of us to face the truth: we loved each other, but Gary was gay. No amount of trying would change that fact. Our marriage needed to end.

I lost a lot. In return, I gained the freedom to refocus on myself. But instead of taking time to grieve, heal, regroup, and reexamine my own life, within a month I fell in love. Starved for the passion I'd been missing, I plunged into an intense love affair with Joey, a forty-four-year-old man who'd never been married, never had children, and had lived in the same apartment for fourteen years with his autistic cat. No problem. Instead of heeding the red flags, I shifted into high gear. We got married. I'd teach him how to be a husband and a father. He could have his own private study—off-limits to the kids. The cat's litter box could be in my bedroom closet so she wouldn't be traumatized by having to go downstairs. It didn't work. Every attempt to turn the intimate triangle of myself and my children into a perfect square ended in screaming fights, frustrated children, and a resentful husband who couldn't stand the chaos of our lives. He refused my requests for marital counseling and made it abundantly clear that if he'd known *this* was what he was signing up for, he'd never have said "I do." I pushed and pushed until I collapsed. First pneumonia, then last-ditch bonding vacation with him and the children in Jamaica, and finally a tarantula bite forced me to come to my senses. On my fortieth birthday I asked for a divorce. I promised myself I would never again drain myself trying to remake a man. I was entering my prime. It was time to put myself first.

Now, if I were a therapist listening to a client telling

this story, I'd say, "Good for you! With all this insight, you're in great shape to stop making the same mistakes!" But, no. Instead, I placed my first and only personals ad, which read, "THINKING MAN'S SEX OBJECT." I got forty-two calls—the usual array of seedy salesmen, aging hippies, closet bisexuals, boys I'd dated in high school, and married men looking for a fling. How do people do it? I had two kids to care for, a book overdo, and I was spending god knows how much time doing boring phone interviews of these guys, dressing up for disappointing lunch dates, then having more awkward phone calls saying, "You're really nice; you're just not my type."

Then I met Number Forty-Two. Louis dazzled me the moment he walked through the door. Here was a forty-six-year-old, politically correct, emotionally evolved Jewish boy from Philly with a cabin in Vermont, a graduate degree from a Warrior Weekend, and the bluest eyes I'd ever seen. He'd read Marge Piercy, listened to the Indigo Girls, made small talk with the salespeople when I schlepped him shopping, and awakened erotic desires within me that I hadn't even known existed.

The first three months were ecstatic. He wanted to know everything about me. He gave me his grandmother's engagement ring for my birthday. He drove my children to school when I was sick. For the first time in my life I felt totally loved. I had completely revealed myself and it wasn't only good enough, it was terrific.

Then the ambivalence started. By forty, you'd think we'd recognize the signs. He would cancel a date to stay home and do laundry and make comments like, "I need a little space," or "I'm worried I can't give you everything you need," or "I understand if you need to date other people," which made me want to act out just to force the issue.

Instead of backing off a bit or opening myself to the

idea of dating around, I dug my heels in trying to regain his love. He said he was depressed; I gave him names of therapists. He said he needed space; I showed up on his doorstep. He wondered aloud if he was afraid of commitment; I "lovingly" engaged him in a vulnerable conversation about his mother's death and his fear of abandonment. None of this helped. So I did what I always do—planned another vacation. (Is there a theme here? Vacation addiction?) I spent two weeks at his cabin in Vermont with him in hopes that if my brilliant insights didn't seduce him, my great new wardrobe from Banana Republic would. It was a mistake. Within a few days of returning home, Louis showed up on my doorstep. I braced myself to hear what he had to say: "I need to tell you something. I'm not sure if I'm in love with you."

I was devastated. It was as if my lifeline had been pulled and my oxygen tank ripped open so I couldn't breathe. Louis had seen me and wasn't in love with me after all. I fled to my bedroom and crumbled in a heap in front of my full-length mirror. I wasn't angry at him, thinking, "Why *should* he love someone like me?" Rather, I felt consumed with shame—shame at having exposed myself and shame at having been duped. But mostly, shame at having believed I was good enough to be worthy of love. I stared into the mirror, tears streaming down my face. Then, something incredible happened.

I saw myself. My eyes met the eyes in the mirror in an instant of perfect connection. I was transfixed, staring into the wide green pools looking straight at me, daring me to look away. In a whisper I said, "I see you." My fingers reached for the strands of hair framing my brow. "I feel you." My whisper got louder as I said, "I hear you." I looked around my room, at framed photographs of my children on my nightstand, copies of the books I'd written on my bookshelf, gifts from friends arranged around the room I'd designed in Caribbean colors, filled with art I'd chosen, my grandmother's quilt, and my favorite antique silver lamp. A warm, radiant flood of energy slowly filled me up, starting at my toes and rising to the top of my head. I closed my eyes; then I slowly opened them and stared back at myself in the mirror. I smiled, with a deep sense of what had transpired. I had fallen in love with myself. I had found the missing piece.

Falling in Love with Ourselves

Loving ourselves is the key to loving and living with an imperfect man. That's what this book is about. We've spent far too many years trying to love him better, when, in fact, we need to do a better job of loving ourselves. Ten years ago a best-seller took the world by storm. Millions of women devoured Robin Norwood's infamous book, *Women Who Love Too Much*. It's message was how to stop engaging in self-destructive (and, in some cases, abusive) relationships in which we are putting out far more than we should. It was—and remains—a groundbreaking work. But the title has always disturbed me. How can anyone love *too* much? How can we be too loving in relationships that sorely need more love, in a world where love is the fundamental agent of healing?

There is simply no such thing as too much love. There is, however, such a thing as not loving *ourselves* enough. Getting in touch with our innate worth creates a powerful shift in how we perceive and relate to our partner. My personal epiphany dramatically altered my relationship with Louis. I suddenly saw myself as complete, with or without his love. His ambivalence no longer seemed a reflection of my self-worth and, as a result, what he could or couldn't give stopped being such a big deal. I chose to remain in the relationship, but instead of wanting him to fulfill my expectations, I resolved to love and accept him for who he is—an imperfect human being—nothing more, nothing less. And I resolved to reinvest my energy toward becoming the strong, powerful, worthy woman that I saw reflected in the mirror.

I'd like to tell you that this experience permanently transformed me, but I'd be stretching the truth. Learning to love ourselves is a lifelong process. Some days we feel gorgeous and grounded; other days we're consumed with self-doubt. But any experience of seeing ourselves as worthy and whole unto ourselves—however fleeting—is incredibly empowering. It reinforces our foundation. It strengthens our commitment to our health, happiness, and well-being. It inspires us to be our very best.

Making the fundamental shift from focusing on what's "wrong" with him to what's right and worthy and lovable about ourselves frees us in a variety of ways. First, we stop struggling to help him fulfill his potential and start focusing on our own growth and healing. We also stop being stuck in the muck of our anger and disappointment and start learning how to forgive and go on. We stop allowing ourselves to be disregarded and start insisting on being treated with respect. We stop worrying about whether we're settling and start making sound choices based on our needs and desires. We stop resenting our partner's lack of reciprocity and start giving what we can truly live with. We stop agonizing about his imperfections and start appreciating his gifts. We stop blaming him for what's missing and start figuring out ways to get what we need both within and beyond our relationship. And the best part is none of this depends on waiting for our mate to change. We can dramatically transform our own lives—and redefine our relationship—whether or not he participates in the process. For years we've been trying to improve our relationship, but, we're still left asking, What about him? Loving ourselves has less to do with him—and more to do with our willingness to make positive changes on our own behalf.

None of this is possible if we continue to focus our energy on changing our partner. All of this is possible if we make a commitment to love ourselves.

Loving ourselves may seem like a simple concept, one that's neither groundbreaking nor original. After all, how many times have we heard it said, "You have to love yourself before you can love anyone else?" However, the simplest truths are the most profound. And they're the ones that are the toughest to learn and incorporate into our lives. As Robert Fulghum reminds us in *All I Really Need to Know I Learned in Kindergarten*, we are continually learning and relearning the basics, such as saying please and thank you, the importance of the buddy system and remembering to hold hands when we cross the street. The same is true for the basic concept of loving ourselves. We may be all grown up—successful in our careers, terrific parents, competent and capable in important ways—and still never have learned the simplest, most essential lesson.

It's time to return to the classroom of life and commit ourselves to a graduate-level course entitled, Learning to Love Ourselves. Going through this process requires commitment and courage, a willingness to rigorously face our own issues, diversify our resources, develop more fully, and make profound changes in our lives. It asks that we cultivate a number of so-called lofty—but absolutely necessary—spiritual qualities that will make us more loving, peaceful, and purposeful individuals.

This may sound like a lot to ask. It is. Our willingness to embrace the challenge depends on what we think we have to gain. If you can genuinely say, "I'm satisfied with my overall relationship the way it is," then there's no need to read on. If, however, you can envision your relationship becoming happier and healthier, then there's every reason to try a new approach.

This may also sound as if I'm asking women to try harder and take on more. I am. When I first broached this idea with a group of women, several responded with, "Why me? Haven't I already done enough?" The answer is yes. We've done enough. In fact, we've done too much without adequate reward. The solution isn't to do less, but rather to invest our energy in ways that will truly pay off—in healing, strengthening, nurturing, and empowering ourselves. There's more to do—only this time it's for *us*. Doing this for ourselves will enhance the quality of our lives regardless of how our relationship is ultimately affected.

I've also been asked, "Why should women become more evolved? Isn't it time for men to do a little work?" Again, my answer is yes. Women are incredibly evolved, which is *exactly* why we should make the next leap. It's been said that at this point in history it is up to women to heal the planet, whether it be through mothering, mentoring, changing the emotional climate of the workplace, creating compassionate politics, or taking our intimate relationships to new levels of fulfillment. If we're truly more evolved than men, let's see what we're made of and what we can do if we set our minds to it.

As for men, it is incumbent upon them to evolve to their fullest with the help of any and all available resources. I am writing this book to and for women because I am a woman and because I believe women are ready to take the next big leap. Although my choice of language and examples are based on my heterosexual orientation and lack of experience in lesbian relationships, much of the content is applicable to gay and straight women alike. Hopefully men will also benefit from this book. Ideally we will share it with our partners or they will read it on their own. The changes that will come as a result of women embarking on the path ahead will likely lead our partners to take a good, hard look at themselves. When one partner in a relationship makes significant shifts, usually the entire dynamic is affected. The process of our loving ourselves holds inherent rewards for our partners, who may respond by taking their own positive steps forward. But that decision is not up to us; that's up to them. Meanwhile I continue to pray that men continue on their path toward growth and healing.

Just as I haven't written this book for men, it also isn't for women in abusive relationships. If you are in one, if your mate is physically or emotionally abusive, turn your attention to seeking professional help. Your mate isn't imperfect—he's dangerous, which is patently unacceptable and demands immediate attention. This book also isn't for women who are on the fence. The path I'm offering isn't for any woman who is committed to remaining stuck, who is looking for justification to hang on to her anger, who smugly believes that women are genetically superior to men, or who wants to blame her mate—or herself—for what's gone wrong. This book isn't for sissies, blamers, victims, or control fiends. It's for powerful women ready to make eight life-changing leaps.

Loving Ourselves:
A RADICAL NEW APPROACH

One of my favorite Joni Mitchell songs has these words in it: "And I love you best when I forget about me." I'm not sure if it's meant as romantic sentiment or an ironic statement of how women deny ourselves love when tending to a relationship. Either way, it's true—and this truth is at the root of our difficulties with our partners.

We enter into relationships intent upon loving our partner to the best of our ability. We strive to understand who they are and what they need. We offer support, companionship, intimacy, and pleasure. We build them up when they're down, comfort them when they're hurting, encourage their ambitions and share their sorrow and their joy.

Oftentimes we succeed. At other times we seriously question our ability to meet what may well be one of life's greatest challenges, loving another human being. And for good reason. Loving is hard, as is evidenced by the overwhelming number of divorces, breakups, and destructive relationships, and the general difficulty of maintaining long-term intimacy. Few human endeavors ask as much. In a loving relationship we're called upon to reveal our innermost feelings, be trusting and trustworthy, see through another's eyes, integrate lifestyles, tolerate annoyances, reconcile differences, and merge friends, family, and finances, while remaining consistently likable and lovable.

Our success rests on the degree to which we love ourselves. This is the one area we've ignored in our efforts to improve our relationship, as exemplified by Marcy's story. "The first three years of our marriage were pretty amazing," says Marcy, a forty-year-old graphic artist and mother of two teenage daughters. "Paul and I both had great jobs, we had loads of friends, and we loved just being together. Sex was beyond my wildest imagination, and I can't even remember arguing about anything. But shortly after our Kelly was born, things changed. Paul lost his job and was unemployed for over a year. Having a new baby was exhausting. We started getting on each other's nerves, our sex life went to hell, and I even went to a counselor to talk about whether I should consider a divorce."

Like many of us, when Marcy began experiencing problems in her marriage, she went into high gear. She saw a therapist and joined a women's group. She devoured self-help books, dragged Paul to a relationship seminar, and tried desperately to engage him in productive dialogues about intimacy and communication. The harder she tried, the more frustrated she felt. Her therapy revolved around finding ways to break through Paul's resistance, which would have been useful had he been a willing participant. Reading relationship books made her feel alternately inspired and defeated. She tried to put their suggestions and strategies into practice and when nothing dramatically improved, she either blamed herself for being ineffective or assumed that her relationship was unsalvageable. A church-sponsored Marriage Encounter weekend provided a brief flicker of hope for them, but, in the end, neither she nor Paul were able to permanently rekindle their connection.

By the time I met Marcy, she was extremely discouraged. "What should I do?" she implored. "I've tried everything everyone recommends, and nothing is getting better." My heart ached for Marcy. She loved her husband and was bending over backward, truly giving the relationship her all. But it wasn't working. She was on the wrong road, the same road that you and I have traveled, and she was getting nowhere.

I gently rerouted Marcy by encouraging her to refocus on herself and take a look at where SHE wanted to go and how SHE'D like to get there. I urged her to concentrate on nurturing herself, evaluating her goals, pursuing her passions, and strengthening her own personal support systems. In Marcy's single-minded pursuit of healing her marriage by focusing on her mate, she did herself a dual disservice. First, she was less and less attentive to her physical, emotional, and spiritual needs. And, second, with each new strategy that failed, her self-esteem plummeted, until she felt lost and hopeless.

The Power of Self-Love

We needn't feel hopeless just because the road we've taken up until now hasn't brought us to our desired destination. Our end goal has been noble, but our means of navigation have led us astray. We thought we were on the right path, and our conviction that we were moving in the right direction kept us going, even as we hit endless obstacles and roadblocks.

It's time to embark on a new and different road, one directed toward giving more love to ourselves. Loving ourselves isn't an intellectual concept; it's concretely manifested in our attitudes and actions. It's basic to how we see the world and how we approach each and every relationship.

That we should love others has long been drummed into our consciousness, beginning with our learning the Ten Commandments, which counsel us to love thy God, love thy parents, and love thy neighbor. There's no mention of loving thyself, nor are we taught to do so in any other realm of our life. In our families, at school, at work, and within our community, the importance of being loving and caring toward other people is drummed into us. Yet there is hardly any emphasis on being good to ourselves, respecting our feelings, attending to our own needs and desires. It isn't until we're fairly grown up that we begin to form relationships that foster self-love. If we're lucky, we may make a dear friend or find a supportive teacher or a tender lover who encourages us to love, honor, and respect ourselves. Unfortunately, most of the messages we receive from our culture, our religious upbringing, and our community are more negative than positive, more focused on noticing what's wrong with us than on nurturing what's good and worthy and right.

It may be difficult for us to understand how our lack of self-love has diminished our capacity to improve our relationship. This is partly because in order to even think about loving ourselves, we have to hold ourselves in higher esteem. One beautiful thing about women is that we are quick to place a high value on the people in our lives. What's frightening is how little we value ourselves. We deprive ourselves of solitude, support, and necessary nourishment We squander our energy, give indiscriminately, capitulate unduly, and allow others to take advantage of us. We erode our self-worth by holding on to our anger. We seek what's beyond our mate's ability to give instead of diversifying our resources. We put our hopes and dreams on hold. We second-guess our judgment, censor our opinions, and diminish the importance of our issues for fear of making waves. We refuse to take ourselves seriously, which is just the thing we criticize in our partner. In all these ways, we are sorely lacking in self-love. Either we don't think much of ourselves or we think this is what it takes to preserve our relationship. We see our sacrifice as the necessary trade-off for whatever love and intimacy we get.

The only way to reverse this pattern we have fallen into is through our attitudes and actions. The two are interconnected. Our attitudes, or what we believe to be true, underly our actions. Our actions alter our attitudes. For example, if we believe that our role as women is to serve other people, even at our own expense, then we will act accordingly. We will put aside our needs and make ourselves the last priority. As we consistently place ourselves at the bottom of the list, we begin to see ourselves as lowly and undeserving, which reinforces our attitude that we are unworthy. If, however, we believe that we're entitled, even required, to be good to ourselves, our actions reflect this attitude. We carry ourselves with pride. We make quality time to do what's important. We pay attention to our health, our friendships, our aspirations, and our personal growth, which in turn builds in us a strong and healthy attitude of high self-worth.

Our relationship with ourselves dramatically influences the fate of our relationship with our mate. To whatever degree we believe that we are unworthy, we will push him to prove his devotion. If we're insecure, we'll interpret his actions as proof that he doesn't love us. If we're wounded, we lash out at him or blame him for failing to comfort and reassure us. If we're unhappy with ourselves, we keep wishing he was different instead of appreciating him for who he is.

The Damage of Self-loathing

The belief that we are inherently unlovable is deeply ingrained in each and every one of us, women and men alike. The emotional injuries we sustained in childhood combined with cultural and religious messages of conditional love have damaged our self-worth. Many of us see ourselves as stupid, boring, unattractive, or unappealing. Somewhere along the line we got the idea that whoever we are, we just aren't good enough, and the idea stuck. It's easily accessed any time we question our worthiness.

My insecurity has long been attached to my physical appearance. In high school my sister, Faith, was a beauty queen. I, on the other hand, was smart, chunky, and bespeckled. At age forty-two, I can objectively see myself in the mirror as slender and pretty. But I easily regress to that old view of myself, most often when dressing for a date.

During my twelve years of marriage to Gary, I endlessly subjected both of us to miserable scenes in my pursuit of the perfect evening attire. I would try on an outfit, pose stiffly before him, and ask, "Do I look okay?" He'd give me his cursory once-over, nod, and say, "You look fine." I'd retreat to the bedroom and try on outfit after outfit, asking his opinion, until my clothes were in a heap, he was disgusted, and I was ready to put on a bathrobe and let the baby-sitter go. Poor Gary couldn't figure out the right answer (Try: "You're the most gorgeous woman on the planet")—not that I'd have believed a word of it if he had said it. My conviction, calcified in adolescence, negated anything positive he may have said and genuinely meant. All I could hear was the steady refrain of my self-loathing.

Our lack of self-love cripples our best intentions; repairing our emotional injuries and constructing a more positive view of ourselves enables us to carry them out. When we feel good about ourselves, we're more accepting and appreciative of our mate. When we feel confident, we're more skillful at negotiating and problem solving. When we're self-accepting, we're more forgiving. When we're well-nourished, we're more giving. When we're secure, we're more spacious. When we feel beautiful, we're more sexually available. When we're growing, expanding, and excited about our own lives, we have that much more to bring to everything in our lives.

Even on the most superficial level, we can see how this plays out in our relationship. Let's say it's been a lousy day. We woke up with a migraine, a pile of bills, and an overdrawn checkbook. Our boss snubbed us, our son has strep, our perm is a disaster, and the day-care worker just gave notice. We walk in to the house after all of this, feeling like we've been run over by a truck and encounter our mate, who's upset over having lost an important account at work. We know how we should behave, but we're running on empty. We listen halfheartedly to his dilemma. Our fear gets the best of us and we aggravate his anxiety by worrying aloud about how we're going to pay the rent. We suggest that maybe he could have tried harder or been more effective in his pursuit of the account. We remind him that we have plenty of problems of our own. Though we want to be loving, we're just too depleted and defeated to rise to the occasion.

In contrast, let's say we've had a red-letter day. Work

———————————— ᔛ ————————————

was a breeze, an old friend got in touch, our son won the spelling bee, and the silk shirt we've been eyeing finally went on clearance. We walk in the door at the end of the day humming. We're calm, positive, with emotional change to spare. From this space of serenity and optimism, we know just what to do. We put our arms around our mate and ask him about his day. We listen carefully, extend empathy, offer constructive suggestions and abundant encouragement.

Sometimes we have it to give, and sometimes it takes everything we've got to just be civil. It's unreasonable of us to expect ourselves to always to rise above our fears, anxiety, distractions, and concerns to be loving and attentive toward our mate. We don't always feel good about ourselves. We're not always hopeful, happy, and secure in who we are. In fact, plenty of the time we're critical, disdainful, and intolerant toward ourselves. We feel blah about our lives. We fail to meet challenges or achieve goals. We perpetuate unhealthy patterns and self-destructive behavior. We make wrong choices, bad moves, and act selfish or mean toward the people we care about the most.

All of this makes us feel crummy and unlovable. But we're neither. Our hearts are in the right place. We all want to be strong, noble, generous, and loving. But we're not the Buddha. We're limited by our humanity, by our ongoing struggle to love and accept ourselves as we are. It takes years, perhaps our entire lifetime, to achieve unconditional love toward ourselves, which is the prerequisite for unconditionally loving our mate.

In the best of all possible worlds, we would be totally healed and whole before entering into an intimate relationship. If we were all totally evolved, I wouldn't need to write this book and you wouldn't be reading it. In a state of bliss we'd be perfectly happy with our partner. We'd feel no anger, judgment, or impatience. We'd forgive all because we'd have nothing to forgive. Total self-acceptance would enable us to completely accept our partner as he is. Total serenity would enable us to be at peace with what we have. Total unconditional love of ourselves and our partner would fill us with gratitude, appreciation, and awe.

Redefining Perfection

This is a wonderful fantasy and a worthwhile goal, but it's not about to happen. If it could, what challenge would remain? As Rabbi Manis Freedman, in his book *Why Don't People Blush Anymore?* says, "If your partner was perfect, you wouldn't have to have any talent or intelligence." Perfection is typically defined as flawless. When we talk about a "perfect" relationship, we usually mean one that's easy, flowing, completely fulfilling, and problem free. Similarly, we'd describe a "perfect mate" as one who is infallible and unconditionally loving, who always meets the mark and comes through in every possible way.

That's not what we're looking for here. Throughout this book we will explore the concept of a perfect relationship through a new lens, redefining the concept of perfection in the following way: Perfection doesn't mean easy or flawless. Rather, perfection means that which is challenging, that which stretches us to be our biggest, best selves.

Defining perfection as *opportunity* sheds a different light on what's hard about our relationships. Just as the Chinese character for *crisis* is the same as the character for *opportunity*, those experiences that are challenging are usually the ones that yield the greatest reward. For example, we've all been through difficult, perhaps even horrible, experiences. In the midst of them we may have felt despairing, angry at God for the hand we'd been dealt. But in retrospect, we often look back on the worst crises as rich and life-changing crossroads. The same is true in our love relationships. The absence of problems doesn't translate into a perfect relationships. As M. Scott Peck, in the opening of his famous book *The Road Less Traveled*, writes: "Life is difficult. Once you know this, life isn't so difficult at all." Life *is* difficult, but at the risk of rewriting three of literature's most profound words, I'd replace the word "difficult" with the word "challenging." Difficult conveys crisis. Challenge conveys opportunity, which is at the core of a "perfect relationship"—not one with zero problems, but one filled with ample opportunity to grow.

Apparently we're not meant to be fully evolved before we engage in loving relationships. Nor are we meant to be handed a partner who's reached enlightenment. And there's a good reason for this. Intimate relationships provide the opportunity, the spiritual classroom, in which we heal and become whole. Here is where we learn to love and to be loved, to face demons, confront difficulties, forgive grievances, and forge partnerships. This is exactly why relationships are so hard. We have to willingly expose our weakness and vulnerability. We have to willingly venture outside of our emotional comfort zone in order to grow.

Saying yes to a relationship is the first step we take in this journey. The commitment to engage in a serious intimate relationship demonstrates our willingness to learn how to love ourselves and another. We may take this for granted, especially if we've been involved in this relationship for several years. But it's no small feat to enter into a relationship of this magnitude. We should acknowledge ourselves for having the courage and the guts. Part of loving ourselves is giving credit where credit is due. For every initiative we've taken toward confronting issues, resolving conflicts, and building trust and intimacy, we deserve congratulations for going the distance. We've worked damn hard, and we're ready to take the next step.

To move forward we need to redefine what actual work is called for at this juncture. We've seen how our traditional definition of "working" on our relationship has yielded limited results at best. What we loosely refer to as "women's work" within the context of relationships is heavy on self-sacrifice, on helping, supporting, and nurturing our mate. But the real work of life and love is quite different. We must realize that our caring for others is contingent on our caring for ourselves. We must understand that, until we attend to our own healing and growth, we are limited in what we can offer. Consequently, we must redefine what constitutes constructive work, or effort that serves our best interest and promotes self-love.

In discussing this topic, I'm often confronted by women who say, "I pride myself on how much I care. I don't want to stop giving as much as I give." And we needn't. In fact, the greater our self-love, the greater our capacity to give. Depletion erodes our resources. When we're rested, replenished, and feel good about ourselves, we naturally have so much more to offer. In a recharged state we have good energy, greater tolerance, and more generosity of spirit. The more we give ourselves, the more we have to give others.

To shift into focusing more on our own needs, we must change both our attitude and our actions. We must adopt the attitude that we are worthy of love, and we must actively strive to make ourselves a much higher priority on our personal to-do list.

This is easier said than done. I can think of at least a half-dozen reasons why we resist. Take your pick:

I don't have time.
I'm too stressed out.
Other people need me.
They'll get mad.
I don't want to be selfish.
I can wait.

Let's take each of these apart. As for time, most of us are stretched to the max. We don't think we have time to focus on ourselves, yet we somehow manage to make time for others. Are we less important?

We're incredibly stressed out. But instead of finding ways to reduce our stress, we keep going and going and going like the Eveready battery. What will it take for us to stop?

Lots of people depend on us: our partner, children, friends, parents, and others. We can keep putting their needs ahead of our own, or we can find a balance between giving and receiving.

And yes, they may temporarily resent it. But if they truly love us, they will understand the importance of our being good to ourselves. Which isn't selfish. We think that caring for ourselves is a crime. It's not. It's loving. It's responsible. It's a way of enhancing our ability to give.

This goal of self-love truly cannot wait to be fulfilled. We mustn't put our needs, our desires, our growth, and our development on hold one minute longer by continuing to travel a road that isn't taking us where we want to go. A new road beckons: I offer you this map.

A Working Road Map

Before embarking on this new path, let's take a moment to review where we are. We've seen how focusing on our partner instead of ourselves has dead-ended us in our search for a better relationship. We've seen how loving ourselves more is an alternative path and that refocusing on ourselves is the first step on this path. Now what?

As in any journey, a map is essential. A good map tells us what direction to follow as well as the quickest, clearest route to our destination. We've defined our destination and direction. We hope to reach a place of greater satisfaction in our relationship. We know that we're moving in the direction of developing greater love for ourselves. Now, we need to determine the best route for our journey.

How do we proceed? We proceed by making the commitment to cultivate the following eight spiritual qualities in ourselves:

Clarity
Integrity
Self-possession
Strength
Discernment
Acceptance
Creativity
Reverence

Each of the following chapters focuses on the practical, emotional, and spiritual development of each of these qualities.

Clarity means being absolutely honest about where we are and what we want in our relationship. *Integrity* means living in accordance with our most deeply held values and beliefs. *Self-possession* means healing and becoming whole. *Strength* means fully developing our physical, mental, and emotional resources. *Discernment* means making wise and well-informed choices. *Creativity* means discovering new and imaginative approaches to our relationship. *Reverence* means seeing our union as sacred and holy.

The cultivation of these qualities can be used as a path to personal growth; individually and collectively they enhance our lives and improve our capacity to love and accept our mate. We have to know what we want in order to make commitments we can stand by. We need to develop independence and autonomy so that we can find the balance between giving to our mate and nourishing and nurturing ourselves. We need to become strong and healthy in order to heal ourselves, so that we can accept our differences with our mate. Doing so frees us to find creative ways to improve our relationship that allow us to feel grateful for what we have.

How does our cultivating spiritual qualities translate into tangible changes in our relationship? Wouldn't it be more useful to concentrate on more concrete tools, such as communication techniques and other behavior strategies? No. Working on that level is insufficient. As many of us have seen after years of experimentation, behavioral changes have only limited results unless they're an outgrowth of deeper emotional and spiritual shifts. For example, it's not enough to attend assertiveness training and take a bolder stand if we don't also strengthen our inner foundation. It's not enough to improve communication if we don't have a clear understanding of what we're trying to express. It's not enough to release our anger if we don't also heal our pain and reconcile our grievances.

To illustrate the importance of going more deeply into our issues let's revisit Marcy and Paul. Money was one of the topics upon which they repeatedly got stuck. As you recall, Paul was out of work for over a year, which coincided with the birth of their first daughter. Paul was depressed, they had trouble making ends meet, and couldn't find a way to comfort and support one another. They tried sitting down and making a budget. They tried talking and arguing about how money was being spent. They blamed each other and became increasingly estranged.

I suggested that Marcy temporarily put aside her judgments and pay attention to her feelings. She was frightened and much of her fear was rooted in the past. Her father had lost his job when she was twelve. As a result, her family had to move to a small apartment and she wasn't able to go to camp that summer. She often fell asleep at night overhearing heated arguments between her parents. When she approached them, wanting to know what was going on, they shooed her away, saying "You needn't worry your pretty little head about it," which made her worry all the more. Marcy needed to be in the loop and she wanted to help, neither of which was allowed in her family.

One of the best things about being a grown-up is that we get to do it our way. Instead of being at the mercy of our parents' values, beliefs, and well-intentioned, but not necessarily healthy, choices, we have the chance to approach issues differently. In her marriage, unlike her childhood, Marcy had the ability to get the information she needed. She was able to express her fear and ask for support. She was able to make choices about her and Paul's economic situation. And, most important, she was able to see how her unhealed wounds were adding stress and conflict to her relationship at a time when her marriage called for both her and Paul to stretch.

Working at a deeper, more foundational level makes it possible to actually change our behavior. Anyone who's ever been in therapy can attest to this. It's typical for people to go into therapy wanting to make a change, usually within the context of a relationship. We want greater intimacy with our mate. We want to stop fighting with our children. We want to get along better with our parents, our friends, or our boss. We hope for some magic formula that will relieve our pain. And there isn't any. We quickly discover that we're in for some serious, hard work.

The same is true here. Cultivating spiritual qualities and translating them into behavioral strategies is plain old hard work and the only work that will create real and lasting change. What makes this work so difficult is fear. We're afraid that the process of learning to love ourselves will force us to face our unfinished business, confront what isn't working in our lives, and challenge us to make difficult changes. Likewise, we fear that in focusing on cultivating these qualities, we'll put our relationship at risk, that we'll have less time for our partner, that we'll discover we're compromising our values or our vision and that we'll want too much, ask for too much, or realize that our relationship isn't meeting our deepest needs.

We can limit what's possible—for ourselves personally and in our relationship—by allowing fear to tyrannize us. Or we can do what's loving and empowering. The road we're embarking on is one that will take us from fear to love. Fear is what keeps us from moving forward, and love is what inspires and supports our transformation. Making the shift from fear to love requires us to take a number of big leaps: A Leap of Faith—that we will remain safe and that our relationship will remain intact. A Leap of Hope—that our efforts will pay off. A Leap of Courage—that we have what it takes to break through fear and get to the other side.

The Journey from Fear to Love

A Course in Miracles, a spiritual course most recently explored in Marianne Williamson's book *A Return to*

Love teaches us how fear undermines us and love frees us. I heard it said best at the funeral of author Melody Beattie's son Shane. Shane tragically died in a skiing accident at age fourteen. At the funeral, comic and twelve-step recovery author, Louie Anderson, spoke about the power of love, with these simple words: "Everything is either fear or love. Anything that isn't fear is love. Anything that isn't love is fear."

This concept is at the core of every "problem" we experience in our lives and in our relationships. Every time we are anxious, impatient, angry, or controlling, it is because we are afraid. Fear feeds on a feeling of scarcity: There's not enough time. There's not enough money. There's not enough love. Likewise, every time we are our best selves, it is because we are coming from a place of love, a feeling of safety and abundance. As long as we are driven by fear, we remain imprisoned. We feel disappointed, angry, or frustrated with our mate. When we shift from fear to love, we are suddenly empowered. We stand firmly on a foundation of abundance, confident that we have enough time, enough resources, enough strength, imagination, and wisdom to make the right choices regarding our relationship.

This fairly typical scenario underscores how fear plays out in relationships: You drag yourself home after spending twelve hours at the office meeting an urgent deadline. The breakfast dishes are still in the sink; your school-age kids are fighting over the VCR; you haven't taken your coat off when your husband turns to you and says, "What's for dinner?" Your first impulse is to throw your briefcase at him and storm out of the house. Can't he see that you're ready to drop? Is it too much to expect him to give you a minute to change clothes? To referee the children? To throw a frozen pizza in the oven or, God forbid, take you out to dinner? What you feel is anger.

Rightful anger, to be sure. But what's underneath the anger is fear. We fear that our home is going to hell, our kids are going to kill each other, and we're going to kill our husband if he doesn't notice that if anybody asks us to do one more thing, we just might collapse.

What's useful about looking at our response as fear rather than as anger is that while anger keeps us barricaded and bruised, fear takes us deeper into our feelings of vulnerability. Anger and fear feel very different. Try this experiment: Say out loud, "I'm angry." Notice what that feels like. Now, take a deep breath and say, "I'm scared." When we get down to our fear, we are able to move to the next step, which is to identify what we need. For example, I need more help, I need more time, I need more appreciation. Once we name what we need, we can figure out what it's possible to get from ourselves, our mate, and other people in our lives. Are there ways in which *we* can reduce our stress level, say, by taking a mental-health day, having a massage, hiring a baby-sitter? Is there anything we can calmly ask our mate for, such as doing the breakfast dishes or watching the kids for an hour while we nap? What other resources exist? There are friends we can talk to, the McDonald's drive-through, a weekly support group where we can go to prioritize our overwhelming demands.

Letting ourselves feel our feelings and identify what we need are acts of self-love. Whenever we take action on our own behalf, we have shifted from fear to love, from an attitude of scarcity to an attitude of abundance. We learn that we *do* have enough—be it time, energy, or love—and, if not, we get busy making up the difference. We do what it takes to get what we deserve.

Figuring out what we want and need is the natural precursor to shifting from fear to love. Cultivating clarity is the first big leap toward increasing our love for ourselves and our partner. We take an honest and searching look at the quality of our life and our relationship to assess what's working well and what needs attention. But first, a few words of caution: In making the commitment to embark on this difficult and challenging road, we must be careful to not push ourselves too hard. We must harness our perfectionism so that it doesn't get the best of us. Small steps are sufficient. Expecting giant leaps of ourselves only adds to our stress. This isn't a marathon. Slowly, gently, we begin to refocus and rebuild our strengths, starting first with cultivating clarity.

3

The First Leap:
CULTIVATING CLARITY

There's a little bit of Alice in each of us. We encounter apparitions, decipher riddles, and slip through rabbit holes trying to find our way into Wonderland. We're too small, too big, too lost, or too bewildered to unlock the magic key to happiness. The opening is just within our reach, but happiness eludes us because we lack the clarity to know what we truly want.

I know a woman who's been married fifteen years. Some would say she has a fantastic marriage. Her husband is a successful physician; which allows them to travel extensively and enjoy an affluent lifestyle. Their three children are happy and well-adjusted. They count themselves lucky to have numerous close friends and a supportive extended family. The woman is forty-five years old and owns a thriving consulting business. She dresses stylishly, works out regularly, and looks ten years younger than her age.

When I ask this woman how her marriage is going, she

always says, "Great!" with a smile on her face and an upbeat lilt to her voice. But, like Alice, she finds happiness elusive. Every six months, almost to the day, she calls to tell me she's had it. Her litany of complaints reveals a sobering image of a painfully cracked reality beneath a glittering veneer. Her husband barely speaks to her other than to discuss schedules and plans. He rarely touches her except in bed, where she obliges his considerable sexual appetite, despite her total apathy toward their lovemaking. She is desperately lonely, and, in a stage whisper, she confides that she is thinking of leaving him, although she feels trapped by her age and financial dependency, despite a college degree and fifteen years in the workforce. She sounds absolutely resolved to get out and has started to initiate action. She's called an attorney, is secretly perusing her husband's savings accounts and financial status, and has hired a private investigator to follow him in case there's anything funny going on. She suspects an affair, but has no proof. I am alarmed. I cheer her on in her efforts to liberate herself from an obviously unworkable situation. But first I recommend marital counseling, a suggestion that is met with silence and then followed by the words, "He'd never go." "What about you? You can—and should—go for yourself," I say. She isn't interested. Pumped with purpose and the adrenaline of self-righteousness, she says she'll keep me posted on her progress. I wait to hear from her. After three days I call to inquire how she's doing. "Fine," she replies, "everything's much better." She and her husband are planning a cruise to the Bahamas, and she's upped her workout routine to be in top bikini form. "But what about . . ." I stutter, then realize, having gone through this routine numerous times, that my words are wasted. In her mind, everything *is* fine, at least for the next six months, at which time I can count on another phone call informing me her marriage has hit the skids. Until then, she'll slide through the days and months, sometimes hopeful, sometimes hopeless, but always able to rationalize away her pain.

This woman is in trouble, and the root of her trouble is lack of clarity. It would seem, at first glance, that her problem is simply that she's in a "bad marriage" by many peoples' standards. But clearly, in some fashion, it works fine for her. What she's getting apparently balances out whatever sacrifices she's making, however monumental they may seem to you or me. Like each of us, she has made trade-offs: loneliness, emotional estrangement, lack of tenderness and affection, for economic security, social status, and a way to avoid her worst fear—being single and alone. In her eyes, she has a workable marriage and I would never be so arrogant as to suggest otherwise. For her, it *is* fine, and that's all anyone can ask for. Except for one thing—her doubts will continue, ensuring recurrent outbursts. I have to wonder, underneath it all, how does she really feel? Has she convinced herself that her marriage is palatable? Or does she lie awake at nights racked by confusion, struggling between the disparate realities that are tearing her apart? Most of all, what will it take for her to find inner certainty that the choices she's making are ones she can truly, permanently live with?

Most of us wonder whether or not we can be permanently happy with our partner. We feel confused about how much our partner is capable of. We don't know how much to ask for, how long to wait, or how to measure improvement. We don't know if we're getting anywhere and if what we have is enough. We're not even sure why we're unhappy—whether it's us, whether it's him, or whether it's just life.

Most of us exist in a state of relative insanity, which is at the root of our discontent. I am not using the term *insanity* as a clinical diagnosis of severe mental illness, but rather to describe the normal human capacity for denial. For these purposes, let's define *sanity* as "being honest about what is" and *insanity* as "lying to ourselves about what is."

Happiness rests on our ability to achieve sanity. Sanity depends on clarity—on the degree to which we are firmly rooted in reality. Clarity requires truthfulness—our capacity to muster the guts it takes to be perfectly honest with ourselves about the quality of our relationship and the quality of our life.

We don't think of ourselves as insane. After all, we go to work, manage relationships, and carry on our daily responsibilities with a fair amount of ease. Yet much of the time we feel "crazy." We're not sure about what we want or how to attain it. One week we're happy with our partners, the next week we're calling a therapist. Our questions and doubts fill us with anxiety. We neither trust our own instincts nor act in accordance with our seemingly inaccessible inner truth.

What's missing is *clarity*: A strong and clear picture of who we are, what we hope for, what we have, and what we need to work on in order to create peace and happiness in our lives. Clarity is essential on several levels. When we're clear about who we are, we are able to know how we really feel. When we're in touch with our feelings, we can envision what we want. When we identify what we want—defining our personal goals, ambitions, and purpose, we can act as forceful agents of our own destiny.

Cultivating clarity is extremely challenging because it

demands our willingness to tell the truth. Sometimes the truth is hard to face. We tend to deny or distort the truth instead of leveling with ourselves and others. Facing reality—without airbrushing it, glossing over it, or rearranging it to our liking—forces us to see it as it really is and often is the first step in *doing* something about it. Taking a close look at our lives and pondering change is scary. Most of us would rather pretend that our marriage is solid, our sex life exciting, and our partnership equitable than face the possibility of having to make hard changes in order to improve what we have.

Being honest is different from having a positive attitude, putting the best face on difficulties—for example, accentuating our partner's shining attributes or reminding ourselves that everyone has a bad day—is a way of making the most of what we have. Interestingly, we may also have trouble being truthful about the positive aspects of our relationship. Instead of celebrating the ways in which our partner fulfills, excites, and supports us, we may downplay or diminish his contributions. This sounds crazy, but actually, there's a reason why we do this. Our incapacity to honestly assess and acknowledge what's good in our relationship reinforces our focus on what's lacking. If we were to fully acknowledge all the ways in which our relationship is satisfying, we'd lose some of our steam for complaining about what's missing.

When we are dishonest with ourselves, clarity is impossible. Dishonesty is a way of imprisoning ourselves, whereas honesty is liberating. "The truth will set you free" are six of the finest words ever written. Honesty frees us in a number of ways. It liberates us from living in a state of denial, which only reinforces the status quo. If we deny the reality of our relationship—either the good or the bad—we are stagnant, nothing changes, nothing improves. If we ignore the truth, we are powerless to make choices that could alter our reality. When we're honest about the particular issues facing us, we can take positive steps toward their resolution. For example, if we pretend that we're getting along great with our husband when, in fact, we argue with him constantly and secretly question whether our marriage is falling apart, our marriage will go steadily downhill because we won't take steps such as improving communication or seeking counseling, that could potentially make things better.

A few years ago I experienced this phenomena first-hand, not within my romantic relationship, but rather within the context of my personal finances. The book I was working on was a year past its deadline, my cash flow was barely trickling, and my bills were piling up until I couldn't bear to open the envelopes. Intimidating messages from bill collectors threatened imminent disaster. I was living in a state of constant terror that the phone would be disconnected, the water turned off, and that we'd face eviction if I was late on one more month's rent. For weeks the piles of bills mounted as I sank into an increasingly paranoid and terrified state. My denial was my defense. I rationalized that not opening the envelopes would, in fact, eradicate their existence. I bought lottery tickets and prayed for miracles. When all else failed, I reminded myself there were no longer any debtors prisons.

Finally, I couldn't stand it any longer. I took a deep breath and proceeded to face the music by, literally, facing reality. I spread the bills out on my bed and opened them one by one. I calculated the bottom line, made payment arrangements, and wrote checks. I contracted for extra editing work to increase my income and decrease my debt. It was the only way out and it was a huge relief. Once I honestly faced the magnitude of the mess I was in, I was free to solve the problem. Once I got "sober" I found the solutions.

Romantic Sobriety

Sobriety is an outgrowth of clarity. When we're clear about reality and honest about ourselves and our relationship, we are demonstrating romantic sobriety. The term *sobriety* is most often used in the field of chemical dependence to describe the state of being completely free of any mood-altering substances. When we're chemically-altered (stoned, drunk, or engaged in addictive activity), our perception of reality is skewed. We see through the illusory haze of our altered consciousness. So it is with sobriety in every other aspect of life. Being sober, or conscious, means seeing reality clearly—seeing what is without distortion of any kind.

This is how we must look at our relationship. Our illusions, delusions, and fantasies create an altered state in which it's impossible to see our partner and our relationship for what they truly are. We cling to illusions that our partner is more willing, giving, or capable than he is. We operate under the delusion that we can change him at will. We entertain fantasies that someday he will magically turn into the man we want him to be.

Our lack of romantic sobriety keeps us trapped in a state of denial. We may as well be stoned or intoxicated, as long as we're unwilling or unable to open our eyes, our minds, and our hearts to what *is*. Most of us have fleeting moments of sobriety when we let the truth in, usually at times when we no longer have the energy to maintain the illusions. A heated argument leaves us feeling inconsolable or a failed effort at intimacy makes us momentarily aware of our estrangement. We may call a close friend or therapist and confess our doubts and fears. We may reach out to initiate a candid conversation with our mate or throw a tantrum to get him to notice the depth of our despair. For an instant we may feel shaken by the sobering truth, which usually passes once everything settles down and we regain our equilibrium and return to a state of denial.

Just like maintaining sobriety from alcohol or chemicals, romantic sobriety requires a firm, ongoing commitment to take an honest, sober inventory of the status of our relationship.

Overcoming Our Resistance

Our fear of facing problems in our relationship is a serious obstacle to cultivating clarity. I can't count the number of times I've listened to women complain about problems in their relationship, and yet, when I gently ask: "What do you want to do about it?" a wall goes up. They begin to waver, rationalize, and downplay their concerns. Suddenly they can't tell me enough good things about their partner, and all the reasons why they're lucky to be with him. They may even become enraged or aggressive, accusing me of pushing them to ruin a perfectly good marriage.

What's going on? Why the resistance to clarifying issues? Well, it's like opening Pandora's box. We fear the contents may come spewing out, overwhelming us with terror, forcing us to take action. There are so many "What ifs . . ." What if we discover that our relationship isn't everything we hoped for? What if we uncover hidden feelings of anger, resentment, or longing? What if our revelations expose the need to reevaluate our relationship or, harder yet, bring us face to face with the need to reexamine ourselves?

Our willingness to take the risk depends on what we're protecting and what we have to gain. To whatever degree we can envision a positive outcome, be it, relief, problem solving or greater intimacy, it's worthwhile to clarify our feelings. However, there may be aspects of our relationship and our life that we feel too vulnerable to reveal. For instance, we may not be ready to confront our husband's alcoholism, our credit-card debt, or our tepid sexual relationship. This is natural. Everything in it's own good time. To start down the path to clarity we need to establish a certain degree of safety. Be assured that clarifying our feelings doesn't necessarily mean we have to do anything about them in the immediate future, but it provides good solid information about where we are right now.

We begin by honestly assessing our feelings. Our feelings are keys to the truth; assessing them is one inroad toward knowing what's truly going on within our life and within our relationship. Telling the truth about how we feel is perhaps the toughest part of cultivating clarity. It takes guts to let down our defenses and experience our fear, sadness, and disappointment. But the rewards are abundant. Whenever we allow the truth to emerge, the sadness to penetrate, and the tears to flow, we are flooded with relief. Breaking through our denial and accepting the truth is an important way of loving ourselves, of letting ourselves be authentic and free.

The following exercise can serve as a guide for clarifying your feelings about your relationship in the present. It's always useful to begin in the here and now, to start with what is true in this moment, at this point in your relationship. Don't worry about whether *your* truth is the absolute truth, since the only truth we have is what we feel inside at any given moment. Our feelings are constantly in flux. All we can hope for is to be as in touch as

⤛

we can be with our present reality. For now, complete the following sentences as honestly as possible.

Most of the time, being with my partner makes me feel

_____.

⤛

The one word I would use to describe my relationship is

_____.

⤛

What I like most about my partner is _____

_____.

⤛

What I dislike most about my partner is _____

_____.

⤛

I feel sad when my partner _____

_____.

⤛

I feel angry when my partner _____

_____.

⤛

I feel disappointed when my partner _____

_____.

⤛

I feel loved when my partner _____

_____.

⤛

Right now I would rate my relationship as _____

_____.

Ꮫ

If you asked me if I still love me, I'd say _____

_____.

Ꮫ

If you asked me if I'm still in love with him, I'd say _____

_____.

Once you've completed this exercise, notice how you react to your responses. Do any of them surprise you? Make you feel scared? Sad? Confused? Encouraged? Hopeful? Did you hesitate to answer any of the questions? Is there anyone with whom you might choose to share your responses?

It can be immensely helpful to clarify your feelings in the company of a trusted friend or counselor. I recommend against confiding in your partner at this point, since he has a vested interest and is unlikely to be objective. But respectful feedback from a trusted person outside the relationship, if we're willing to hear it, can keep us honest; loving and supportive input can challenge our interpretations and give us a fresh way of looking at our feelings. The goal here is to be as real, as honest, and as sober as we can be in assessing how we truly feel.

Once we know how we feel, we can move on to creating our vision for the sort of relationship we want. After five, ten, fifteen years with the same partner, it's somewhat difficult to clarify our hopes and dreams. When we first became involved, we may have known exactly what we wanted: a best friend, a father for our children, a playmate and partner, the love affair of the century. Over time, our vision is compromised by the realities of life: economics, career moves, family responsibilities, the reality of who each of us has turned out to be. What we want changes as we change, as our priorities are redirected, as we come to know ourselves, our partner, and the parameters of our relationship more clearly.

Despite this, we can and must create a workable vision of our ideal relationship. We must know what we want before we can get what we want. What we want is a highly personal and individual choice that reflects our deepest held values and desires. One woman wants a loving companion above all else, another would happily trade comfort for erotic passion, still another holds financial security as sacred, while another considers healthy co-parenting as her highest priority. Just the other night, while lying in bed eating M & M's and watching *Star Trek* with my boyfriend, Louis, I recalled that as a teenager, my "perfect relationship vision" was of marriage being like a slumber party, only with a boy. What is your vision? Remember, *there is no right vision*. Whatever *you* hold dear is what counts, as long as you make a conscious choice, which will depend on your figuring out what you want most in life.

We look to both the past and the future in order to clarify our vision. First, we take a trip back in time, to the beginning of our relationship. We recall the initial feelings that drew us to our partner, and that helps us remember why we're here and what we truly hope for. We close our eyes and recapture our earlier feelings toward our mate. The moment we fell in love. The qualities that attracted us. The feeling of certainty that inspired us to choose him as a partner.

In retrospect, one woman is convinced that she married her husband because of his obvious devotion to his mother. "I could see how much he respected women and knew he would treat me accordingly." Another woman was bowled over by attending a company Christmas party with her fiancé. Coworkers made a point of telling her how confident and competent he was in the workplace, which made her feel proud and certain that she'd chosen a strong, powerful man as her mate. A divorced, single mother was struck by the way her boyfriend played catch with her four-year-old son, saying, "Right then and there I knew I wanted him in my life."

Sometimes our attraction is based on more subtle and intangible qualities; the tenor of his voice, certain endearing gestures, the way he looks in a crisp white shirt inexplicably draw us in. On one of our first dates, Gary waltzed into my apartment and, in a debonaire move reminiscent of Cary Grant, tossed his hat across the room, where it landed neatly on my coatrack. Now this guy really knows how to make an entrance!

Think back and recall what originally attracted you to your partner, then complete the following sentence:

I was attracted to his ——————————————.

Our initial attraction and the first flush of falling in love made us see him as a prospective partner. But it's our belief in our mutual hopes and dreams that enabled us to make a serious commitment. We may have envisioned bringing up children, starting a family business, or traveling to faraway places. Our desire for loving companionship, shared aspirations, financial prosperity, or erotic passion may have cemented our commitment. Recall your initial hopes and dreams to the best of your ability and then complete this sentence:

I wanted our relationship to be about ——————————.

〜

Next we move on to exploring our present and future vision, which, naturally, has changed some over the years. Our vision is constantly evolving, so that it's only possible to know what we want right now as we work to envision the future we hope to create. With that in mind, complete the following sentences:

What I want most in life is _____.

〜

What I want most from my partner is _____.

〜

My highest priority is _____.

〜

I'd be happy if _____.

〜

My idea of a perfect relationship is _____.

If romantic sobriety is the goal, and if there's no such thing as a perfect relationship, why bother to answer the last question? For two reasons. First, because our utopion ideal gives us clues to our feelings about our less-than-utopion reality. If we secretly long for a marriage of perfect harmony, we compare reality to that ideal. If our secret image of a perfect man involves long-stemmed roses, we're likely to feel cheated when our birthday comes and goes without so much as a dandelion. Second, though we recognize our ideal or perfect relationship as a fantasy, on some level, we're still hoping that someday our dream will be realized. While we may know it's a fantasy on one hand, we still go on hoping that our partner will engage us in a deep conversation about our feelings, or spend hours on foreplay, or surprise us by taking the kids camping for the weekend, giving us a luxurious three days to do anything our hearts' desire. In short, how we feel about what we have is still determined by fantasies of perfection and our illusion that with enough effort on our part, they may ultimately be realized.

The Importance of Grief

When we open our eyes and take a good hard look at what we've got, we may experience a certain amount of sorrow. Even as we count our blessings, we grieve over our lost opportunities, broken dreams, and unfulfilled fantasies. We grieve over the harsh words, the unfinished arguments, the times of distance and estrangement, the moments when, despite our good intentions, we failed to be our best self. Mostly we grieve over our unfulfilled fantasies as we struggle to reconcile ourselves to the ways in which our partner may never fulfill our image of who we want him to be.

Grieving is the only path that will lead you from disappointment to acceptance. There's no way around it; you have to go through it. The grieving process is highly personal; different individuals use different means of coming to terms with sorrow: weeping, writing in a journal, talking to a friend or therapist, or even taking out our wedding pictures to reflect on the sweetest, most romantic hopes and dreams that never came to pass. This process is a necessary release in order to liberate ourselves from the shackles of our disappointment and needn't be a depressing, drawn-out experience.

Freedom lies on the other side. When we reconcile ourselves to our losses, our heart opens and lightens. We begin to see the reality of our relationship—what we have and what we need to work on. We're prepared to strip away the illusions in order to see our partner and our relationship with clarity. Seeing what is and grieving for what isn't enables us to reconcile our expectations with reality.

Disillusionment: A Positive Process

The word disillusionment usually has a negative connotation. We say we feel disillusioned when we feel let down or cheated, when life doesn't give us what we hoped for, when reality destroys the hopes, dreams, and illusions we're hanging on to. When we say we're disillusioned in our relationship, we usually mean that our partner has disappointed us, that he hasn't turned out to be who we believed he was. We were attracted to his strength, but as the years pass, we've seen that in times of trouble, he often shrinks from challenges. We loved how affectionate he was, but over time, he's become increasingly withdrawn. We believed he had a great future in store, but his career and his earning power haven't panned out the way we had hoped.

Most of us come to expect disillusionment as an inevitable part of being in a relationship. We assume that over time anyone is bound to disappoint us and to have trouble living up to his or her original promise. Yes, usually we discover everyone eventually is a bit different from how they initially appeared to us. But disillusionment is only inevitable if we define it in a negative way.

The realization begins in childhood, when our image of our parents as larger-than-life forces fades before our eyes and as we gradually come to see them as fallible human beings. Our closest friends become real to us as we become familiar with their weaknesses and vulnerabilities. The perfect beings our children appear to be at birth emerge into unique and quirky individuals as they grow, yet that doesn't make us love them any less. In fact, we usually find we love them more. This ability to love the real person that emerges over time is what separates real love from superficial attraction. The stranger we gaze at across a bar and take home with us for fantasy material will never disappoint us because he will never lose his illusory qualities. For one night we can make him into anything our imagination desires without the fear of facing the more complicated realities that arise over time.

Our stubborn refusal to see and accept our partner for who he is creates our disillusionment and our subsequent feelings of distress. But there is another way to approach the concept of disillusionment. We can see disillusionment as a positive process of stripping away the facade in order to reveal the real human being within. It's like eating an artichoke; we have to patiently peel away each leathery leaf in order to savor the succulent heart hidden within. The same is true our beloved. Only by stripping away the illusions—seeing and loving the real person beneath can we begin to experience a deeper, more abiding affection.

However, to do this, we must cultivate clarity, which requires our willingness to pursue romantic sobriety. Our capacity to see our partner clearly depends, once again, on being rigorously honest with ourselves. We must be willing to ask ourselves, and answer honestly, some tough questions about the nature and quality of our relationship. It can be confusing when we try to determine whether or not our relationship is meeting our needs. We're not sure what standards to apply or how much emphasis to place on particular qualities. Is it more important to have a friend or a lover? Passion or comfort? Intimacy, economic security, mutual goals, or someone we can talk to about anything and everything?

Again, these determinations are purely individual. Each of us receives different gifts in our relationship, and each of us has our own unique priorities. What is irrelevant to one woman makes another's heart sing. The following twenty questions will help you assess what you are and aren't getting in *your* relationship:

1. Are you proud of your partner?
2. Are you learning important lessons in your relationship?
3. Can you depend on him for physical support?
4. Can you depend on him for emotional support?
5. Can you depend on him for financial support?
6. Are you physically attracted to your partner?
7. Is your sexual relationship fulfilling?
8. Do you trust him?
9. Do you enjoy his company?
10. Is your relationship challenging?
11. Is your relationship comfortable?
12. Is your relationship stimulating?
13. Are you having fun?
14. Do you share mutual goals?
15. Do you share mutual friends?
16. Are your values compatible?
17. Can you work out your differences?
18. Do you consider him an equal partner?
19. Are you free to be yourself?
20. Can you imagine happily spending the rest of your life with this man?

This exercise is meant to help you measure your satisfaction with various aspects of your relationship. Each is important, some more than others for you, depending on what you particularly value. Knowing what lessons we're learning in our relationship helps us to understand why we're in it. We need to be honest about whether we enjoy our partner's company, whether he's fun, comfortable, trustworthy, challenging, and stimulating to be with. It's important to assess the degree of emotional, physical, and economic support we're receiving or missing. Seeing the ways in which we're compatible and whether our values and goals match up shows us the ways we mesh with our partner as well as the ways in which we diverge. Can we successfully work out conflicts and create an equitable partnership? Do we feel free to be ourselves, free to express our passion and eroticism? Most of all, does the idea of a lifetime or long-term relationship with our mate fill us with trepidation or joy?

This exercise also reveals both the ways in which you feel delighted and the ways in which you feel disappointed with your partner. You may discover a bit of both. Every relationship has its share of compatibility and incompatibility, aspects that work easily and well, along with areas of difficulty and conflict. Pay attention to all of your responses, noticing where your relationship is strong and thriving and where it needs attention. For instance, you might discover that you greatly appreciate your husband's emotional support, but you still have nagging doubts about his long-term earning potential. You may trust him implicitly, but are still waiting for him to take on his share of responsibilities. This exercise may also reveal new information about where you are. For example, after months of worrying that your libido had gone permanently underground, you may realize that you're still plenty attracted to your mate, but unresolved conflicts are getting in the way of romance. The goal here is to gain a firm handle on how your relationship is and isn't satisfying you in various ways.

Dealing with Him

Should we, and if so, how best to communicate our new-found clarity to our partner are tricky questions. We want to let him in on what we're learning, and it's tempting to verbalize each new insight with the excitement of a child opening a birthday gift.

Be careful. Some insights are better temporarily kept to ourselves or discussed with a close friend or counselor. You may be thrilled that you've figured out what your marriage is missing, but don't expect your mate to jump up and down at the news. Be sensitive to him and kind to yourself. If you can share some of the clarity you've gained in a respectful way, saying just enough to reassure your partner that what you're learning will enhance your relationship, then go ahead. Doing so may evoke a stimulating and productive dialogue from which both of you will benefit.

There is another way to express our newfound clarity, and that's through our actions and commitments. We can take what we're learning and use it in our relationship without making it the main topic of conversation.

What Are YOU Giving?

Just as it's important to be rigorously honest about what we are and aren't receiving from our partner, it's necessary to ask what we are contributing to our relationship. A number of years ago, when in the painful process of separating from my first husband, I realized that most of my pain had to with what I was and wasn't GIVING rather than what I was and wasn't GETTING in my marriage. I knew what I was capable of, and for whatever reason—lack of love, compatibility, maturity, or perhaps, inspiration—the sweet lovely young man I'd married simply wasn't getting the best of who I was at that time.

Giving feels good, even many times it's more satisfying than receiving. In many ways, the degree to which we feel free to give is a measure of our relationship's success. Ask any person in the midst of a divorce to describe their own behavior and they're likely to say, "I'm angry, with-drawn, and feeling pretty stingy with my time, energy, and affection." Ask the same question of anyone whose relationship is going well and they may tell you they're overflowing with generosity. Take a moment now to an-swer the following questions regarding what you're cur-rently giving in your relationship:

1. Are you emotionally available?
2. Are you physically affectionate?
3. Are you trustworthy?
4. Are you interested in your partner's work?
5. Are you open with your feelings?
6. Are you sexually responsive?
7. Are you doing your share?
8. Are you intellectually stimulating?
9. Are you willing to work out conflicts?
10. Are you encouraging and supportive?

Knowing what we're giving reveals a great deal about the quality of our relationship. It gives us clues as to whether we feel spacious and secure, whether our heart is open and our spirit is overflowing with love.

Purely and simply, we all want to give. Determining that isn't complicated in the least. What muddies the pic-ture is our confusion over our feelings toward our mate and our beliefs about whether or not our needs are being met. Our love, our generosity, and our most fundamental commitment to our partner is subject to our confu-sion—or clarity—when assessing the quality of four dif-ferent aspects of our relationship: compatibility, chemistry, affinity, and destiny.

Compatibility

Compatibility is a way of describing how well we get along with our partner. How much do we have in common?

How well do we coexist? Is our time together fun, interesting, and stimulating? Do we feel comfortable and secure?

Some couples are naturally more compatible than others. They rarely fight, find it easy to share space, and have an equitable working relationship. They enjoy each other's company and are comfortable and secure in their day-to-day dealings. Other couples struggle to find common ground, have more disparate lifestyles, or are adversarial by nature. This doesn't necessarily imply a lack of compatibility; it just necessitates a little more effort and cooperation for them to interact as a couple.

Take a moment now to rate your compatibility level on a scale of 1 to 10. How do you feel about your compatibility quotient?

I'd give our compatiblity a _____.

Chemistry

Individuals who seem less compatible often have a higher level of that ineffable, magical alchemy we sometimes call chemistry. There's no way to concretely measure chemistry, it's just something we feel. Chemistry is at work when we experience a deep sense of rapport and attraction to another human being. When we first meet, we may marvel at our instant connection. We may feel as if we've found a long-lost friend, exclaiming that "I feel as if I've known you forever." These feelings may carry over into the bedroom. Sexual chemistry is like finding the perfect dancing partner. Without much practice at all our timing is synchronized, our movements gracefully aligned, and our bodies fit together like matching pieces of a puzzle.

Some couples have more chemistry and attraction

than others. Ozzie and Harriet seemed comfortable but not necessarily passionately in love. Elizabeth Taylor and Richard Burton were at each other's throats, but they couldn't keep their hands off one another. Most relationships fall somewhere in the middle. At times we feel more like comfortable roommates, other times we can't get enough. There are certain trade-offs between comfort and chemistry. Comfort can disintegrate into complacency if we don't make an effort to constantly rekindle romance. With high chemistry tumult and turmoil can take over if we let passion rule.

Our needs for comfort versus passion differ from individual to individual. Some of us are content with our partner being our best friend and closest companion, happy with occasional sparks of passion. Some of us gladly trade a certain amount of stability for a more fiery and passionate connection. Some of us are wildly attracted to our partner; we love looking at him and get shivers when he touches us. But in every relationship, attraction and passion ebb and flow. The same muscular forearms, striking cheekbones, and winning smile can make us weak in the knees one moment and leave us cold another, depending on how well we're getting along. Rate your general attraction level on scale from 1 to 10. How do you feel about your attraction quotient?

I'd give our attraction a _____.

Affinity

While we can measure compatibility in concrete terms, the affinity level in our relationship is harder to define. We often describe affinity as a feeling of like-mindedness, shared sensibilities, or the belief that we have found a kindred spirit in our mate. Affinity affords us a feeling of confidence regarding the rightness of our union. Even if we're at odds or in conflict, our deeper sense of affinity assures us that we are on a mutual path and meant to be together.

Just as levels of compatibility and attraction among couples fall along a continuum, affinity varies from couple to couple. Our level of affinity comes into play in a variety of areas, such as the fundamental interests and issues that the two of us are drawn to, our personal and relationship goals, and our shared creative pursuits and consuming passions to which we're deeply committed.

I've seen relationships lacking affinity thrive and others in which affinity abounded end. Lack of affinity can weaken our relationship or greatly enhance it, depending on how willing we are to appreciate and embrace our differences. My greatest affinity is for human connection. I can spend hours talking to friends or even strangers, fascinated by the inner workings of the human psyche. My partner would rather watch a squirrel gather nuts than sit in a café talking. He finds animals and all aspects of nature vastly more interesting and alluring than the company of human beings. On a recent vacation to Jamaica, we grappled with our seeming lack of affinity, each making strides toward appreciating what moves the other. He spent more time chatting with new acquaintances than he would have left to his own devices, and I spent three hours of our last day admiring a magnificent ironwood tree he'd found in the woods.

Rate your affinity with your partner on a scale of 1 to 10. How do you feel about your affinity quotient?

I'd give our affinity a _____.

Finally, we can evaluate our relationship from the perspective of destiny, asking ourselves whether this is the person with whom we're meant to be, perhaps for the rest of our days.

Purpose and Destiny

Knowing—much less fulfilling—our destiny is a lifelong task. From the moment we are old enough to perceive ourselves as separate individuals, we seek to discover our purpose on this planet. As children, this takes the form of play. We play house, stumbling around on our mother's high-heels, fantasizing that we'll be a teacher, a mother, a nuclear physicist when we're all grown-up. In adolescence and young adulthood we grope for identity, experimenting in relationships, trying on various academic or career hats to see what fits. And, as adults, we are continually faced with the burning questions: Why am I here? For what purpose was I placed on this earth?

Our intimate partner plays a key role in our destiny. It is no accident that we found one another; now the challenge is to figure out why. There are as many reasons why as there are relationships. One woman's husband has been a steadfast source of support as she's healed her wounds from an abusive childhood. Another woman, a single mother by choice, sees her boyfriend as the one and only person with whom she should have brought a child into the world. Ideally, our mate is our spiritual partner, our teacher and guide who helps us grow. And, ideally, our partner will travel the distance with us and we will ripen and age together.

But not necessarily. In primitive times, human beings, if they were lucky, lived until age forty, maybe fifty. Today we live a lot longer. My blessed grandparents were around to see my children born and my parents are thriving well beyond their seventies. When our life span was shorter, it made perfect sense that we mated and remained with the same partner until we died. Now that middle age is creeping toward fifty and eighty is still considered sprightly, our concept of life partnership must be adjusted. While some of us may be fortunate enough to remain with the same partner throughout our lives, many may enjoy significant relationships with more than one man. We may choose different traveling companions at different stages of the journey, each fulfilling a piece of our destiny.

I was twenty-five years old when I married Gary. I fully expected us to grow old together. In the five years since our divorce, I've grieved over our parting, railed at the injustice of his being gay and of our not being able to someday celebrate our fiftieth wedding anniversary. But never once have I regretted my choice to marry him. Our union was meant to be. At that stage of my life, he was my perfect partner. Together we built careers, raised two beautiful children, and created a community of family and friends. It is no longer our destiny to walk side by side. At forty-two I am meant to create along different lines, to forge unforeseen partnerships, to walk a new path. Still and yet, knowing everything I know, if I had it to do again, I wouldn't change a thing.

The process of uncovering our destiny is paradoxical, simultaneously mysterious and obvious. We can spend our entire life searching for our purpose, trying to decipher whether we're in the right place, wandering like Alice through the winding labyrinth of Wonderland. Or we can trust our instinct to guide us in this deceptively simple search by answering these two questions:

- What kind of person do I aspire to be?
- Is my relationship challenging me to be my best, biggest self?

～

Let's tackle the second question first. We know whether our relationship is inspiring us to heal, grow, and develop by the lessons we are learning from it. Remember, a "perfect" relationship is one in which we are learning and growing and one that isn't necessarily smooth and easy. Whatever the lessons, be they tolerance, acceptance, patience, or compassion, and in whatever ways our partner serves as a catalyst for growth, we are in the right relationship at this stage of our life.

What lessons are you learning in your relationship? They can range from the elementary to the extremely complex. We may be learning to share physical space, what our partner likes for dinner, what channel of the six o'clock news he prefers. Other lessons are far more difficult. How to trust our partner when we've been hurt before. How to face the insecurities that arise when he seems distant or unaffectionate. How to compromise, deal with money, overcome sexual problems, or become more accepting and compassionate. Some lessons are welcome and others we have to force ourselves to sit still and pay attention to.

Our attention span and willingness to learn depend on whether or not the particular lessons in our relationship are compelling to us and we feel they are furthering our development. Our husband's temper may test our patience, something we consider valuable and important for our own growth. Our partner's chronic career confusion may be an opportunity for us to confront our materialism or our judgmentalness, or provide an opening for us to help him sort out his goals. His higher libido may challenge us to heal sexual scars, and his lack of involvement with his parents may inspire us to spend more quality time with our own.

Discovering the lessons inherent in our relationship helps us know whether our union is destined. In the following space, rate your destiny quotient on a scale of 1 to 10. To what degree are you confident that you and your partner belong together?

I give our destiny quotient a _____.

Knowing that destiny has brought us together, how-ever, doesn't necessarily give us the tools to create the relationship we envision. Clarity alone isn't enough with-out the integrity to carry out our destiny. Loving our-selves also means having the courage of our convictions, the guts to be true to our values and our vision.

The Second Leap:
CULTIVATING INTEGRITY

ntegrity is another powerful expression of self-love. When we have integrity, we live in accordance with our most deeply held values—we're true to who we are and what we genuinely want for ourselves and our loved ones. When we're acting with integrity, we feel grounded and good about who we are. When we compromise our integrity, we often feel uncomfortable because we're being false to ourselves, which limits our ability to love.

Although it may be hard to admit, most of us compromise our integrity from time to time in our relationship. We agree to do something in spite of the fact that it violates our values or ethics. We back down on an issue we care deeply about or give in on a serious matter because it's easier than fighting for what we believe. We may compromise our self-worth by allowing ourselves to be mistreated, or we may sell out in any number of ways in order to avoid conflict.

We don't compromise our integrity because we're

weak; we do so because we're caught in a situation in which we don't see a workable alternative. For example, we may have made a commitment to stop drinking, and we're at a party with our husband and friends. Alcohol is flowing, and we feel pressured to join in the fun. We're torn. We want to honor our commitment, but we figure it won't hurt to have just one glass of wine. Another example: We haven't been feeling particularly receptive to lovemaking. After thinking about it, we realize that we need to feel closer and more intimate in order to be aroused. More foreplay would help. So would some sweet and romantic pillow talk. He's not the type. His style is faster, more aggressive, and the only three words we ever get out of him are, "Did you come?" We crawl into bed determined to tell him what we need. He strokes our forehead, pulls us toward him, and passionately kisses us as one hand reaches under our panties. We try to get into it; we want to please him; maybe if we fantasized a little . . . We could always fake it . . . No! . . . Wait . . . Our integrity is on the line.

There are also times when we choose to compromise because doing so serves us and/or our relationship. We may put our career on hold to support our partner while he finishes graduate school. We may accept his going hunting even though we're politically opposed. We may push ourselves to be sexual with our mate when we'd rather fold laundry because we know lovemaking creates a softness and sweetness unlike anything else.

We're often faced with making choices based on ordering our values and priorities. When we make one choice over another, even if it's not our first choice, we are still acting in accordance with our values. Making a conscious, thoughtful decision after weighing all the benefits and the costs is one way of demonstrating integrity. We do what we think is right at the time, taking into account all the factors involved. In contrast, when we compromise our integrity, it's usually because we've decided that it's too difficult to do what we know is right. We make a deal with ourselves to temporarily ignore our inner truth.

The costs of compromising our integrity are high and often extend far beyond the immediate circumstances. This is especially true in our intimate relationship. Every time we compromise our integrity, we cut off a little piece ourselves. Our authenticity is threatened and our self-respect at risk. Compromising our integrity is, perhaps, the most profound manifestation of a lack of self-love. If we can't be who we really are and stand up for what we truly believe in, then what chance do we have of building a relationship based on love, trust, and respect?

In order to cultivate integrity, we need to have a clear and steadfast notion of who we truly want to be, both in our relationship and in our lives. This is *not* about who we want to be in order to fulfill anyone else's expectations, but rather who we want to become in order to carry ourselves proudly.

Living up to our best vision of ourselves fills us with inner strength and self-respect. Even when we're embroiled in relationship problems and even if our partner is acting weird or icky, we take great comfort in knowing we're firmly grounded in integrity. We all know when we're not. At times we succumb to less honorable instincts by engaging in behavior that is below our standards. We know we're acting out, but we can't seem to help ourselves. Here are some typical ways we lower ourselves in order to cope with anger and frustration:

> Pouting: We stick out our lower lip and sulk in a corner until he notices.
> Comparing: We rave about our best friend's husband.
> Retaliating: We give him a dose of his own medicine.

Bludgeoning: We keep beating him over the head until he gets the message.

Withholding: We withdraw attention, affection, or sex.

Therapizing: We explain how screwed up he is.

Threatening: We let him know what we'll do if he doesn't shape up.

Capitulating: We give in but never let him forget it.

Making Him Jealous: We remind him he's not the only fish in the sea.

These tactics are beneath us. They may drive home the point, but, in the end, they diminish our self-respect. We may be rightfully angry at any number of things he does to irritate or disappoint us, but as long as we're filled with integrity, we at least know that we're doing everything we can. We are empowered by the courage of our convictions, by being the best human being we are capable of being.

Kara describes how paying attention to her own level of integrity has made a huge difference in her relationship with her live-in lover, Adam, who is given to fairly regular rage fits. "I used to freak out when Adam starting having irrational outbursts," says Kara. "He'd come home from the office after having an argument with his boss and take it out on me. I felt for him. His boss is incredibly controlling and disrespectful, often treating Adam like some dumb kid just out of college instead of an upcoming partner in the firm. I could tell that Adam felt humiliated, but instead of talking about it so that I could comfort him, he'd pick stupid fights. He'd start yelling about all the unopened mail on the kitchen table, or he'd rave at me about some little thing I'd done to annoy him that had nothing to do with anything. Once he even accused me of cheating on him—a total figment of his imagination—and stomped out the door after flinging a shoe across the room and hitting the dog in the head." Kara was upset, intimidated, even frightened by Adam's outbursts. She'd try to reason with him, and when that didn't work, she'd sit shaking on the couch, trying to figure out ways to protect herself. Eventually Adam would calm down and Kara would slowly begin to let down her defenses and trust him again.

Kara dreaded and hated Adam's tantrums. But what she hated just as much was the position they put her in. She resented the energy drain of trying to rationally communicate with someone acting utterly irrational. She disliked how vulnerable and weak she felt in the line of fire. She felt ashamed of her inability to defend herself and, mostly, despised how the whole situation left her feeling angry and powerless.

Kara was clear about her feelings, needs, and desires. But she repeatedly compromised her integrity by allowing herself to be drawn into and become the victim of Adam's rage. Many of the problems we experience in our relationship can be remedied by having more integrity, by being sure we're being our best self, regardless of how our partner is behaving. Typically, when we're angry, frustrated, or disappointed, we blame our partner for putting us in this position. We react by trying to change him, which is a losing proposition. In these situations we can preserve our integrity by ACTing instead of REACTing. We can do this by looking honestly at how much of our distress comes from having failed ourselves—by allowing ourselves to be stepped on, by refusing to speak up on our own behalf, by backing down when we need to persevere, by pushing when it doesn't serve us, and by compromising our values. It pains us to be needy, bitchy, whiny, pushy, angry, or weak when we know we are capable of so much more. When it comes right down to it, it is our own behavior that ultimately imprisons or empowers us. During the summer of our estrangement, as angry as I was at my boyfriend, Louis, for jerking me around with his on again, off again affection, I was angrier still at seeing myself disintegrate into a former shadow of myself, full of insecurity and desperation.

Think for a moment about the last time you were upset with your partner. Most likely he acted in a way that felt disrespectful to you, he might have been either doing something objectionable or not doing something you'd asked him to. You got pissed off, bummed out, or just plain sick and tired of having to deal with his junk. You may have sulked in a corner, binged on chocolate, read him the riot act, run to the mall, or delivered your Relationship 101 lecture for the hundredth time. Whatever tactic you used to cope with your feelings, chances are, it didn't make you feel better. It may even have made you feel worse. Yes, he may have gotten the point, but at what price?

Every choice we make has both a cost and a payoff. When we allow our partner's actions to determine our reactions, we pay the heavy price of being disappointed with ourselves. We get to be right, but at the cost of our own integrity. In contrast, when we act courageously on our own behalf, we run the risk of angering our partner, by establishing boundaries or speaking our piece, but what we gain is the deep certainty that we are being true to ourselves, which is a priceless commodity. Kara, for example, has a variety of good options for dealing with her husband's outbursts. Instead of debating, shrinking, or armoring herself, she might try some of the following integrity-filled strategies. She can respond to Adam by saying, "I understand that you're feeling terribly upset by your boss, but please don't lash out at me." She must say this only once; repeating it is just another way of getting hooked in her husband's destructive drama. She could also say, "Excuse me, but I won't be with you when you're acting this way." If necessary, she can also leave the premises for a while until he calms down. She might also suggest that the two of them see a marriage counselor to deal with this recurring issue. If he's unwilling, she can certainly go on her own.

Kara could also lash back, threaten, or even call the police the next time Adam seems out of control. Any of these tactics might be effective, but she won't feel good about her approach or its consequences. Her goal is to improve her marriage while keeping herself safe. Letting Adam know how his behavior affects her and setting clear boundaries enables her to take care of herself without lowering herself to his level.

As Kara discovered, being strategic enabled her to take a more powerful stance. She knew she had to do something because being the passive victim of her husband's rage clearly violated her integrity. But it was equally important for her to make a strategic decision that fit with her values.

Our integrity informs our choice of strategy. Even when our values are clear, we still have to determine whether the means justify the ends. For example, millions of Americans were opposed to the Vietnam War. They were united by their belief in the inherent immorality of our country's interest and involvement. But different antiwar sympathizers chose different strategies to express their dissent. Some burned the American flag, others joined protest marches, some fled to Canada to become conscientious objectors, others organized sit-ins or other forms of nonviolent civil disobedience, and there were those who took a more radical route, supporting SDS, Weathermen, or other militant factions.

At times we may compromise our integrity to preserve what we believe is the greater good. For example, a person who values honesty above all else lies to the Nazis in order to shelter Anne Frank. An otherwise apolitical and nonviolent woman supports an attack on Planned Parenthood because of her overriding, heartfelt opposition to abortion. These dramatic examples illustrate extreme situations in which we're forced to grapple with our integrity in order to live with ourselves. But whether we're in Nazi Germany or our own home, the challenge is the same—to make choices that are in line with our integrity.

Sometimes we're trapped between a rock and a hard place. Our commitment to preserving our integrity clashes with our efforts and desire to keep the peace in our relationship. For instance, our values may dictate the importance of caring for our elderly parents, even to the extent of inviting them to live with us when they're unable to care for themselves. We've always said that if and when the time came, we were committed to following this course of action. But our husband is against the idea. The idea of living with our eight-five-year-old mother, who happens to be extremely crotchety, sometimes to the point of being abusive, seems to him like a fate worse than death. Our husband is understandably concerned about the financial and emotional stress this will place on our marriage. He begs us to consider a nursing home to avoid wreaking havoc in our home. What do we do? Do we honor our husband's request or do we stick to our original commitment?

These sorts of value conflicts force us to deeply examine our fundamental beliefs. Often we're forced to make an excruciating choice. Does our commitment to our aging mother exceed our commitment to our mate? Is our mother capable of getting adequate care in a nursing home? Is our husband capable of compromising? Can we live with ourselves if we turn our mother away? Can our marriage survive the possible trauma of going against our husband's wishes? What matters here is to honor our integrity. No matter the cost, what counts, above all else, is to know and act upon our highest vision of who we hope to be.

Our Highest Vision of Ourselves

Each of us holds a higher vision of ourselves. We aspire to be more caring, more compassionate, more creative, capable, or loving. We know when we're being our best selves. We have had plenty of experiences in which we've tapped our inner resources, been gutsy, courageous, risen to the occasion, and made ourselves proud. We may have experienced our highest self while staying up all night nursing an ailing child. Others of us may have reached our pinnacle in the political arena, fighting for a cause we passionately believe in. Or when thinking of the moments most filled with integrity, they are the countless times in our relationship when we've set aside petty concerns, extended ourselves beyond what was called for, and found it in ourselves to forgive in order to create goodwill and unity. In these moments of integrity, we may or may not be acting out of a conscious vision of who we want to be. Our actions may feel spontaneous and natural, flowing from our deep sense of all we stand for. Other times we have to work and struggle to figure out the best course to follow in order to manifest our own personal brand of integrity. That's when it helps to have a vision, a working definition of who we truly want to be in our lives and in our relationship.

Our vision, much like other aspects of our personal growth, is constantly unfolding. We are continually exploring, defining, and refining our concept of our highest self. But, at any given moment, we have some idea of what that person would be like. We may draw our ideal vision from a combination of the qualities we most prize in ourselves and those we admire in others. For instance, we may be aware that generosity is one of our finest natural resources and, we may add that to certain qualities we may respect in others we respect and would like to emulate. Perhaps we've always admired our mother's fortitude, our best friend's patience, our son's cheery disposition and optimistic outlook. We integrate these various positive qualities into a working image of who we aspire to be.

I have always admired my parent's partnership. For over forty years they have participated equally in parenting, worked side-by-side in business, and created a rich circle of family and friends with whom they share times of sorrow and celebrate occasions of joy. I have watched as each tenderly cared for the other through serious illness. My mother sat vigil through my father's three coronary bypass surgeries, and my father washed my mother's bald head during the period when she fought and won a valiant battle with ovarian cancer. My parents endlessly bickering over trivial matters: the best route to a certain restaurant, the fact that she pours three-quarters of a cup of coffee instead of filling it to the top. But they are completely devoted to each other as friends, lovers, and partners in the truest sense.

The word integrity comes from the root "integral"— that which is central, fundamental, and core to our being. Part of cultivating integrity is knowing what is integral to us. It is being aware of the values that make up the core of what we treasure and honor. Being in touch

〜

with our integral values—patience, flexibility, openness, gentleness, courage, and compassion—enables us to create our vision of our highest self.

To help you identify what's integral to you, complete the following sentences:

What I respect most about myself is _____.

〜

What I respect most about others _____.

〜

I am proudest of my ability to _____.

〜

My highest values are _____.

〜

I know I'm being true to myself when I'm _____.

〜

My goal is to become more _____.

Creating a vision gives us something to aim toward. We cannot always live up to our vision, but we can hold it before us as a beacon of what's possible.

Intention and Action

Intention and action are the ying and yang of integrity, harmonious sides of the same coin. Intention refers to our inner commitment to live according to our inner truth. Action describes the steps we take to manifest our inner truth through our acts. Intention without action immobilize us; action lacking intention inhibits our ability to create change.

Our intentions are pure. We want to be good and loving and generous toward our partner. We want to heal our wounds and forgive our grievances. We want to give the best of what we've got. Intentions are noble, and they guide us toward our end desires. But unless we act according to our intentions, we are stymied in our efforts, no matter how noble or inspired or well-meaning they might be. We can have the clarity to know what issues in our relationship require attention, we can have a heartfelt desire to solve them, but until we take active steps toward that end, everything stays the same. That's why, despite years and years of good intentions, we remain still frustrated over the very same problems that continue to limit our relationship.

For this reason, once we've created our vision, we must move on to develop the intention and action that will enable us to move closer to our ideal. Intention is trickier than it seems. It's easy to have all sorts of good intentions, like I intend to lose fifteen pounds, I'll stop smoking, I'll be a better listener, I'll spend more time with my kids. Many, if not most, of our intentions weaken or crumble when put to the test of commitment. What separates true intentions from casual, fickle promises is commitment. We really would like to go on a diet, get the nicotine patch, stop talking and start listening, or spend the half-hour it takes to read our children a bedtime story. It's not that we're insincere with some intentions; it's just that, in the end, we don't have the commitment to carry them through.

Overcoming Our Resistance

Why do we resist following through on our commitments? In our relationship, fear creates an obstacle to our best intentions regardless of how committed we feel. We waffle, ignore, or are ambivalent about our intentions because we are ambivalent about what's possible. As long as we can't envision a better outcome, our intentions remain weak. Just as our intention to go on a diet depends on our ability to imagine ourselves more attractive and our intention to stop smoking requires a solid vision of becoming healthier, our best intentions in our relationship are limited by the level of intimacy we can envision.

The same is true of our actions. Even when our intentions are solid, fortified by commitment and vision, we may resist taking action. We fear that our actions may cause negative repercussions. If we act on our intention to tackle sticky issues, might we anger or alienate our partner? If we take steps to create greater intimacy, will we be vulnerable to the possibility of rejection? These are real risks—challenges that can only be met by having the courage of our convictions.

Integrity isn't negotiable. We either have it or we don't. There's no such thing as being sort of honest, somewhat courageous, a little bit true to ourselves. We can cultivate integrity at our own pace and in the particular areas we're ready to deal with, but we can't do it in a half-hearted manner. We must be willing to take a stand with every ounce of guts we can muster, to be steadfast in the face of fear and adversity. There are a few tools we can use to strengthen our integrity, and these are knowing how we feel, knowing what we want, and being true to how we feel and what we want.

My fourteen-year-old daughter, Zoe, recently spent her spring break visiting her boyfriend Avram in Vermont. I was in favor of the trip and was fine about her going all the way until the night before she left. It was then that I suddenly wondered if I'd lost my mind. What in the world was I thinking allowing my little girl to spend a week with some teenage boy halfway across the country? I panicked and packed "benite," her worn and tattered baby blanket, beneath her Gap jeans, Alanis Morisette CDs, and the eyeliner she'd spirited from my makeup kit. I slipped a postcard inside her backpack on which I wrote: "Know what you feel. Know what you want. Be true to yourself. And call Mama anytime you want."

I made it through the week and she had a fabulous time. Although she might not have needed the reminder, my words served her well, as she shared an incident in which she had explained her boundaries to this lovely fourteen-year-old boy, who responsed by kissing her hand, placing it on his heart, and telling her, "The only place you need to touch me is here."

I'm glad my daughter is learning about integrity now, before she becomes involved in more intense and complicated intimate relationships. I wish I had known what she knows when I was a teenager or, for that matter, in my twenties and thirties. At that time, I was far too shaky to know my feelings and act on them with integrity. I was afraid of hurting boys' feelings, often said yes when I meant no, and made plenty of mistakes because I was not able to stand up for what was right. Today I am far more capable of setting boundaries and sticking to them. But I've made my share of errors along the way, as we all do.

Cultivating integrity demands our honesty about the ways in which we are and aren't being true to ourselves. One way to begin is by returning to the questions you answered earlier. Go back through each one and notice where your actions reflect integrity and where they are weak or shaky. In doing this exercise, you are likely to uncover ways in which you honor your integrity and other ways in which you compromise your integrity. Next to each entry, write or imagine writing an *H* for honoring your integrity or a *C* for compromising your integrity. For example, you may discover that you are usually quite honest with your partner, but that you often give in when you anticipate conflict. Or you may realize that despite your intention to be more supportive of his career, in actuality, you sometimes make disparaging or demoralizing comments. The gap between our intentions and our actions reveals the specific areas we need to focus on.

Dealing with Him

Ultimately our fear of making waves in our relationship is the biggest obstacle to maintaining integrity. Will he get mad if we stand up for ourselves? Will he be threatened if we pursue our vision? Will acting according to our inner truth or in our own best interest jeopardize the stability of our relationship? These are risks. But we mustn't allow them to make us compromise our integrity. When we lose our integrity, our self-worth erodes. Being true to our integrity without upsetting the applecart does take a certain amount of aplomb. Moreover, we need to first be firm in our own conviction; then we must be respectful in how we assert ourselves. A storehouse of residual anger can make our convictions sound like punishing threats, our commitments like campaign platforms or bulletins from the front. Remember that cultivating integrity is *not* about being right; it's about being righteous. A warrior doesn't wave her bounty in her enemy's face; she simply takes pride in winning her own battles.

Making Commitments

Now it's time to make new commitments that will foster greater integrity. Commitments are best expressed as promises we intend to keep to the best of our ability. For example, we might say, "I will work on creating better boundaries." Or, "I'm ready to be more honest about where I'm really at." Or, "I commit to being more tolerant and accepting toward my partner." Commitments are a form of affirmation, a powerful way of saying yes to ourselves, of activating our intentions and our actions. In making these commitments, we mustn't pressure ourselves to do more than what is reasonable and healthy. Effort is more important than outcome. It's important to give ourselves latitude and permission to backslide. Living with integrity doesn't mean being perfectly honorable every moment, but rather making the commitment to hold ourselves to the highest possible standard as often as we can.

For this final exercise, think about being the best person you can possibly be in your life. Next think about being the best person you can possibly be in your relationship. Holding this highest vision of yourself, make one real commitment to do something to change your relationship, calling on both your clarity and integrity. It might be something like, I commit to being more patient with my husband. Or, I commit to being more assertive about my needs. Now complete the following sentence:

I commit to _____.

As we continue to cultivate integrity, we develop a clearer idea of which aspects present particular challenges in our lives. Do we need to be more honest? Take a firmer stand? Have the courage of our convictions? Be more consistent in living according to our values?

However much work your personal evolution requires

of you to cultivate aspects of integrity, know that the effort is well worth the rewards. Having integrity is like standing on solid ground. It's a way of fully growing into our skin, embracing our authentic selves, and becoming whole and self-possessed.

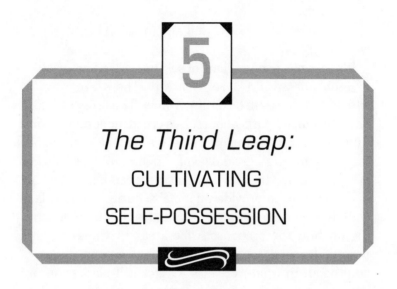

The Third Leap:
CULTIVATING
SELF-POSSESSION

"**L**ove consists in this, that two solitudes protect and touch and greet each other." These words by the famous German poet, Rilke, point out the importance of cultivating *self-possession,* the process of becoming separate, whole and complete unto ourselves.

We cultivate the quality of self-possession with two goals in mind: To fully embody ourselves—mind, body, heart, and soul—and to achieve a level of sanctuary within ourselves that keeps us safe and protected.

Self-possession holds an important key to improving the quality of our intimate relationship: When we fully possess ourselves, we come to our relationship whole and secure. When we are whole, we naturally make choices that allow us to invest appropriately, negotiate respectfully, create healthy boundaries, and stand on firm ground regardless of anyone else's responses. We respect ourselves far too much to ever put ourselves in a position of physical or emotional danger. We honor ourselves enough to treat ourselves well and insist on being treated well by others.

It's easy to see how a lack of self-possession contributes to problems within a relationship. There are ways in which each of is still becoming whole. The broken, shaky, or undeveloped parts of ourselves create dependence and thus, conflict with our partner. We may be emotionally fragile, requiring a great deal of support and reassurance. We may be lacking in economic independence, looking to our partner to provide financial security. We may lack confidence or competence in practical matters, depending on him to compensate for areas in which we still haven't learned to fully handle the responsibilities of adulthood. In whatever ways we lack self-possession, we expect our partner to provide for our unmet needs. When he isn't willing or able, we question whether he is the right partner and whether we are in the right relationship. Instead, we should ask ourselves this question: What steps must I take to cultivate self-possession so that I can come to this relationship as a whole person?

Accepting Our Singularity

The process of cultivating self-possession involves two primary tasks. The first is accepting our singularity, and the second is taking full responsibility for ourselves.

In some ways it is bitter medicine to accept that we are separate and alone. Many years ago, as I was preparing to marry for the second time, a conversation with a close friend brought this truth home to me. Twenty-six and still looking for Mr. Right, she was clearly frustrated, maybe even a tad bit resentful over my seeming good luck at planning another wedding. She said, "I'm sick and tired of being single." Without thinking about it, I replied,

"But, honey, we're all single when it comes right down to it. We may get married, live together, even bring children into the world, but ultimately, each of us is alone. We're born alone, we die alone, and when all is said and done, we're solely responsible for our own lives."

They were harsh words, and my friend wasn't thrilled by my philosophical meanderings, especially as she shelled out two-hundred bucks for yet another bridesmaid dress doomed to take up residence in the back of her closet. But I meant them. Today, having said "I do" three times, I mean them ever more. I've realized that regardless of how close and intimate and secure we are within our relationship, ultimately each of us is a separate, singular individual.

This is hard to accept. But learning how to embrace our separateness and to stand on our own two feet is the first quality we need to cultivate in order to create a stronger relationship.

Are We Really Liberated?

We pride ourselves on being independent and liberated, and in so many ways we are. In the past thirty years, since Betty Friedan's famous book *The Feminine Mystique* helped launch the women's movement, we have made tremendous strides toward economic equality, opportunity in the workplace, and a dynamic reinterpretation of our roles as women both inside and outside the home. We are free to pursue our dreams and ambitions, no longer shackled to preconceived sexist notions of what women are capable of. We determine how high we fly. We determine our destiny.

Contrast this newfound power with where we are in our intimate relationship. In almost every other area, career, motherhood, social, and avocational, contemporary women are autonomous. We're strong, successful, powerful agents acting on our own behalf. But when it comes to our marriage or relationship, many of us remain emotionally imprisoned. Independent as we are in every other sphere, we still feel shaky and dependent when it comes to dealing with our mate.

This may not be readily apparent. In our intimate relationship we may think we're running the show. After all, we're the one constantly bringing issues to the table in the hopes of fulfilling our agenda. We say what we want; we assertively ask for changes and relentlessly pursue our vision of a better relationship. On the surface we may appear to be in charge. But how in charge are we if we're still stuck in chronic anger and disappointment, waiting for our partner to come through? As long as we keep allowing our mate's behavior to affect our self-esteem, as long as we keep waiting for him to change in order for us to be satisfied, we place the power squarely in his hands. To whatever degree our happiness is contingent upon his changing, we remain dependent. This is one reason why we feel so stuck.

Here's how this works. You've spent six months proving yourself at work. Your hard-earned promotion will be announced at the company Christmas party, to which both you and your husband are invited. You ask him to join you, he declines, reminding you that he hates making small talk at those stuffy company parties where he doesn't know anybody. You're angry and disappointed. Doesn't he know how important this is to you? You wonder if you're making something out of nothing; maybe this promotion isn't such a big deal. Your excitement wanes as you try to convince him to come. He says, "Fine, if it's that important," and you say, "Well, I guess I can go alone." You show up halfheartedly, having allowed your partner to diminish your excitement and ruin your evening.

It's a shame when our mate lets us down to such an extent: But it's also a shame that we allow our intimate partner—the one person whose approval matters most—to cut us down to size. We're much bigger and more independent in most other areas of our lives. A quick look at how we conduct ourselves in our relationship with our mate compared to how we carry ourselves in other significant relationships illustrates the remaining challenge in our quest toward liberation. At work we've learned to carry ourselves with dignity and negotiate with a firm hand. As mothers, we're usually quite confident, trusting ourselves to make wise and loving choices in the extremely tough task of raising another human being. With our friends, even with our parents, we've achieved a certain level of autonomy and self-respect: We know our boundaries and make a concerted effort to honor them. But it all falls apart with the man we love. Too often we feel needy and insecure, seeking his approval and acknowledgment. Instead of trusting our instincts, we question our judgments and fold under duress. We regress, furious at ourselves for feeling weak and dependent, yet unable to stop giving him the upper hand.

How can we be liberated in so many ways, yet stuck in the same old patterns in our relationship? There are a number of understandable reasons for this discrepancy. For starters, our dependency on men is deeply acculturated. From time immemorial, women have been conditioned to base our value and self-esteem on external approval from men. Even the most evolved feminists struggle with lingering remnants of this societal conditioning. In addition, sexual intimacy creates in us a unique sort of vulnerability. Opening ourselves to emotional and erotic intimacy both empowers and exposes us. We reveal the deepest recesses of our being, allowing ourselves to be soft and be seen with our guard down. In doing so, we open ourselves up and can be hurt as a result. In revealing ourselves we allow for the possibility of loss or rejection, which consciously or unconsciously, increases our need for reassurance from our mate. For all these reasons, our love relationship is the place where we're most needy and least able to sustain the autonomy and independence we feel in other areas of life. Add to this our romantic fairy-tale fantasies of perfect union, and it's easy to see how and why our feelings of independence falter when our partner fails to meet our expectations.

We want to be taken care of, made to feel secure, and, oftentimes, rescued. The issues Colette Dowling addressed in her book *The Cinderella Complex*, one of the first women's self-help books on the market, still applies to many of us. Even as we prize our independence, thrive in careers, and take care of ourselves in numerous ways, there is a part of our female psyche that still fantasizes about fitting into the glass slipper like a glove. We needn't apologize for our desire to be taken care of, but we do have to recognize that our need may only be partially fulfilled. In reality, we're responsible for ourselves. Although our partner may support and care for us in myriad ways, it's not his job to meet our every need. We are ultimately responsible for our own fulfillment. Whatever he contributes is great, but ultimately the responsibility for our happiness sits squarely on our shoulders.

This is hard to accept, especially within the context of romantic union. Most of us connect love with merging, with the expectation that our beloved is here to make our lives easier, happier, and more secure. And we are fully prepared to give the same. Our subconscious "little girl" fantasies that "someday our prince may come" imply that we will be magically swept off to the castle, where we'll be given royal treatment. We'll be pampered, adored, and taken care of to our hearts' delight. Even our not-so-romanticized notions of love include the expectation that, almost by definition, intimacy means joining—the merging of two into one.

At times we are as one: We work together in perfect rhythm and harmony. We come together in erotic ecstasy and spiritual union. There are times when we *do* take care of each other, offering financial support, emotional guidance, or practical assistance to one another. Being self-possessed doesn't mean that we never help out or depend on our mates. A solid partnership depends on reciprocity and on each partner giving everything they've got and asking for what they genuinely need. When we consider our relationships, we should keep in mind the words of Karl Marx: "From each according to his abilities, to each according to his needs." Ideally, we each give to the best of our ability, balancing one another's areas of strength and weakness.

None of us is always able to tackle life alone. When we must, we do our best, whether it's entertaining ourselves, supporting ourselves, raising children alone, or developing our career without a partner at our side. One of the luxuries of being in an intimate relationship is that it enables us to lean a little when we need to, to depend on another human who has a vested interest in our well-being. But this arrangement works best when we *know* that if, for whatever reason, we had to, we could do it alone. Our confidence in our ability to stand on our own two feet makes a huge difference in how we carry ourselves and conduct ourselves in our relationships.

Cultivating self-possession involves confronting the paradox that each of us is singular, separate, and alone and yet we are also all connected and interconnected. On the one hand, each of us exists in a separate physical body and is ultimately responsible for our own lives. Yet we also exist in relationship to others, depending on those around us for survival and sustenance. In fact, some spiritual and philosophical beliefs go a step further and maintain that on a pure energy level, we are all one, we are all parts of a whole.

Intimate relationships are a microcosm of the paradox between singularity and connectedness. Each of us is required to stand alone while simultaneously working toward partnership and mutuality. As with all paradoxes, the right path lies in the middle. Finding the balance between singularity and solidarity is a daily spiritual practice. Our relationship thrives when we truly know when to stand alone and when to reach out to our partner.

Cultivating self-possession helps us to achieve this balance. Self-possession occurs on five different levels:

Mentally, we accept the reality that we are a singular human being, totally responsible for our own lives.

Economically, we develop independent means of support.

Practically, we develop competence in order to fully take care of ourselves.

Emotionally, we face our emptiness, heal our wounds, and discover what we're made of.

Spiritually, we experience our connection to the universe and develop a firm foundation of strength and serenity.

Overcoming Our Resistance

It's intellectually easy to say, "I alone, accept full responsibility for my life." Taking care of ourselves is part and parcel of being a grown-up; it simply comes with the territory, whether we like it or not.

Yet, in so many ways, we shrink from assuming this responsibility. We avoid facing our pain and healing our unresolved issues. We settle for complacency instead of aspiring toward ecstasy. We remain dependent, let things slide, and forgo opportunities for personal growth and development.

Our struggle to become separate and whole begins at birth, when our umbilical cord is severed. Until that moment, we float in a blissful, symbiotic state of perfect union in which we are one with our mothers. We carry our primal memory of this complete unity with another as we gradually are forced to accept the painful truth: Mother, the source of our survival, not only isn't a part of our body and our being, she also isn't always at our beck and call. We cry to be fed, held, and cuddled, railing against the injustice of our unmet needs.

We never stop longing for a reunion with that perfect partner. We never fully recover from the painful realization that no matter how much love there is in our lives, we are fundamentally separate and alone. It's the basic truth of life. And the older we get, the more obvious and real this truth becomes. Even as we prize our independence or feel capable of taking care of ourselves, we still yearn for the comfort of merging with another human being who will love, treasure, and care for our needs.

What frightens us? We're afraid of the possibility of having to totally fend for ourselves. There is something inherently painful about accepting our singularity. Just try saying aloud the words "I am alone" and notice how frightening this feels. Yet once we grieve for the loss of our fantasy of perfect unity, knowing that we are fundamentally alone can be profoundly empowering.

There are moments when we sense how separate and

alone we actually are. Usually it's when we're faced with a momentous challenge and know that success or failure lies strictly in our hands. When we experience a severe loss; suddenly, despite overtures of empathy and support, we are painfully aware that we are alone in our grief. When something happens to remind us that, even with a loved one at our side, we realize we are each here on a solo journey, on our own separate path, fully responsible for our own lives.

It is only recently that I truly experienced what it means to be alone. Last year I suffered from a short, but sobering episode of depression. My life fell apart. Shaking in a corner, I couldn't eat, sleep, write, or care for my children. The simplest tasks were paralyzing. I'd open the cupboard and stare at a can of soup, unable to figure out how to open it, much less why I'd want it. I couldn't figure out why people were smiling. My usual diversions lost their allure. The beautiful tree outside my window turned into the same old tree outside my window. I thought of suicide, not because I wanted to die, but because I couldn't imagine living this way forever. My friends rallied, begging to help in every imaginable way. My frantic parents sent me a ticket to Florida to visit them, my children tried to be helpful, and my lover was steadfast despite my total self-absorption and attempts to push away his affection. I desperately needed help and yet I knew there wasn't a way for anyone to help. I have never felt more alone in my life. It was up to me to climb my way out of this private hell, which is exactly what I did.

This experience forever altered my understanding of myself and of the purpose of relationships. Whereas before I consciously or unconsciously looked for a man to take care of me and fill my emptiness, I now see that my partner is here to enhance my life, not to ensure my safety, security, or survival. Understand, in numerous ways I have always been extremely independent and competent. I savor my freedom, pay my own bills, come and go as I please, and have an active social life of my own. But deep down, I always craved reassurance that there was someone out there—a husband or committed lover—who could be counted on to be my strength and my salvation.

Now I understand that I am my strength and my salvation. This realization fills me with peace and promise. To become fully self-possessed is a matter of assuming full responsibility for my life, which is well within my power. I needn't wait for a man or anyone else to be the source; I simply need to tap the deep well of strength and serenity within myself to become fully independent, fully self-possessed.

Economic Independence

Financial dependence is the single main reason women give for remaining in unhappy relationships. Those of us for whom motherhood is a full-time, on-the-premises vocation may trade economic independence for the freedom to stay home with our children. Those of us in the workplace still face inequality and lack of opportunity. Twenty-five years into the women's movement, we're still making sixty-eight cents to every dollar a man makes in the same position. A mere one percent of CEOs in this country are women. As we approach the twenty-first century, the possibility of a woman president or vice-president still seems light-years away.

Our lack of confidence in our ability to support ourselves and/or our children undermines our power. We've seen too many divorced female friends and coworkers struggle to make ends meet. We've agonized over the plight of welfare mothers or women settling for inadequate child care in order to keep a roof over their children's heads. But, depending on our mate for support or having to ask for money diminishes our self-worth. The fear of financial loss due to divorce or the terror of being a single mother unable to provide a secure lifestyle prevents us from seeing ourselves as an equal partner.

Hopefully, our relationship will endure and we will not have to be the sole source of our household's income or our children's support. But we must know—in our heart of hearts—that if we were ever to end up alone, we are able to make it on our own. Economic independence is a must. If we're presently employed, it's important to do what we can to be on the right career track, one that both fulfills us and meets our minimum financial needs. If we're home with children, we must be sure that, if necessary, we have marketable skills that can translate into economic freedom. If we've negotiated an arrangement in which our partner is the sole or majority wage earner, we must be sure that it's an equitable agreement.

We must also take responsibility for handling money matters in all aspects of our lives. The in-depth interviews I conducted in writing one of my recent books, *Living with Loss: Daily Meditations for Grieving Widows*, made me aware of the importance of being well-informed on personal financial matters. Three quarters of the women I spoke with deeply regretted their lack of interest and involvement in financial concerns prior to their husband's death. Usually due to generational expectations, most of the widows I spoke to had never worked outside the home. Many didn't have a credit line or a checking account in their own name. A number of them didn't even know how much money their husband made or the extent of their assets and debts. When I told one of these women the topic of this, my next book, Lynn, a seventy-two-year-old widow, made me promise to urge all women, whether married or single, to educate themselves, pursue a career, and be well-aware of their financial status.

Being able to support ourselves, whether we choose to or have to, is a way of investing in ourselves and our future. We can't be independent in other areas if we're dependent on our partner for financial necessities. Our independence here is both a matter of pride and a matter of survival.

Practical Competence

Likewise, as many of the widows I interviewed pointed out, it's important to be competent in practical matters. There are so many things many of us still depend on men for: to shovel the snow, put up the storm windows, fix the leak in the roof and the drain in the bathtub. There are those among us who do some or all of the tasks stereotypically delegated to men, and they should be commended.

I am not one of these women. For reasons of laziness (why do something someone else can do more easily?) I made it all the way to forty without ever mastering any of the above tasks. Fortunately or unfortunately, I married men who assumed it was their responsibility to carry wood, fix furnaces, take the car in for a tune-up, and do dozens of other things I happily assumed "men just do." After all, I rationalized, I do more than my share. I made all the social arrangements, gave birth to two children, and worked full-time. Why should I worry about changing the oil?

Here's why. Two years into my recent divorce, I was driving along the highway on a wintry night when my car began to sputter, shake, and grind to a halt. It was eighteen below zero and snowing. I'd noticed a red light flashing on the dashboard for a few months, and it had crossed my mind to ask the gas station attendant to check it, but I'd never quite gotten around to it. I sat in the car wishing for a car phone or for a highway patrolman or a nice man with well-developed biceps who wasn't a rapist or ax-murderer to pull over and offer his help. Cars whizzed by as I contemplated my options, which were freeze to death or find the nearest phone. In my miniskirt, bomber jacket, and distressed leather boots with their fashionably high three–inch heels, I stumbled along the shoulder, up the freeway ramp, and into a service station where I called AAA, and then my boyfriend, who thankfully came to rescue me. The pricetag for this little evening was $1200. Having neglected to change the oil, I threw a rod and had to buy a new engine for a three-year-old car with less than 20,000 miles on it. My complete disregard for practical matters taught me the importance of taking care of my stuff.

It's great to have someone to help, and it's fair and equitable for each partner in a relationship to contribute to the union according to their particular areas of competence. But this doesn't exempt us from knowing how to adequately handle normal adult responsibilities. Furthermore, developing competence increases our confidence and self-worth. I still wish my boyfriend would take my car to Jiffy Lube. I keep hinting and he keeps reminding me that I can do it myself, which is ultimately more loving than letting me off the hook.

Emotional Autonomy

We remain dependent on our men, whether it's economically, practically, or emotionally, because of the wounds that diminish our ability to love ourselves. These wounds are places we have inside where we feel helpless and vulnerable, where our lack of self-possession makes us need too much reassurance or blame our feelings of emptiness on our mate. Low self-worth makes us interpret his actions as a statement of his love or lack thereof. He's in a bad mood and we assume it has something to do with us. He's lukewarm about our vacation plans and we think it means he's ambivalent about our romance. He's chronically late picking up the kids from day care and we interpret his irresponsibility as a lack of commitment.

There must be something *we're* doing wrong! If our relationship were working, we'd be able to distract or cajole him into a better mood. If he were really in love with us, he'd be counting the days till our vacation. If he were truly devoted, he'd care enough to be on time picking up the kids.

In fact, his actions may or may not have anything to do with how much he loves us or how committed he is to the relationship. Maybe he's just having a bad day. Maybe he's too absorbed in work—or worried about money—to get excited about a vacation. Maybe he's stressed out or overscheduled, making it hard for him to meet his responsibility to pick up the children on time. Our unhealed wounds make it impossible for us to see our partner clearly. As the writer Anais Nin wrote, "We don't see things as they are. We see things as *we* are."

Intellectual and emotional myopia, our inability to see beyond ourselves, is part of the human condition. We live inside our own head, and our perceptions are skewed by the limitations of our personal experience. If we were totally evolved, we would have the capacity to see everyone and everything we encounter from every vantage point. We would be capable of seeing through the eyes of others, rather than seeing solely through our own eyes. Our human myopia is the source of original sin. In the Garden of Eden there was no separation from God or one another. We were all one and our experiences and interpretations of life were filtered through unity, rather than through the separate lenses of human isolation.

After the metaphorical fall from grace, we are challenged to see through new eyes, to transcend our myopia, which keeps us from things as they are. When the scales drop from our eyes, we see how we remain stuck by attaching symbolic meaning to our mate's behavior. It's a way of blaming him instead of taking responsibility for healing our own emptiness. As long as we believe that *he's* the problem, we avoid working on our own issues.

Facing our emptiness can be terrifying, as Sasha, a forty-seven-year-old high school teacher discovered upon going into therapy. She admits, "For the first five years of my relationship with Zach, I was pretty sure that my unhappiness was caused by his lack of commitment. I wanted to have a baby and he refused. The more we argued about it, the angrier I got about his unwillingness to make a serious commitment to our marriage. I accused him of being scared and selfish. I gave him time frames and ultimatums. And I started to seriously contemplate the possibility that our marriage wasn't solid enough for us to break through this impasse and create a lasting future together." The harder Sasha pushed, the more Zach withdrew. Although becoming a father wasn't a high priority for him, he wasn't entirely closed to the idea either. What he didn't want was to play out a role in his wife's preconceived plans. If they were going to have a baby, he wanted their decision to be a natural and mutual outgrowth of their love.

In therapy, Sasha was asked to temporarily put aside her fears and judgments of Zach and, instead, focus on her own feelings. First, she got in touch with her anger over Zach's refusal to "give" her what she wanted. This was a familiar feeling, which restimulated past experiences in which her father had consistently withheld his affection, creating a pool of rage that Sasha had never been able to deal with. Next, she became deeply saddened as she felt the full measure of her emptiness, which she secretly hoped would be ameliorated through carrying, birthing, and mothering a child. As Sasha experienced the depth of her emptiness, she wept for all the times she had felt alone and neglected. Finally, she tapped her deepest longing to create life, to nurture and love a child, and to share in this awesome endeavor with the man she loved. Her entire presence changed as she felt the pure longing of her best intentions. She was visibly transformed—her eyes lit up, her posture straightened—as she embraced the possibility of fulfilling her hopes and dreams.

As a result of facing her issues, Sasha agreed to put her agenda on hold for a year. She continued to want to have a child, but her sense of urgency abated as a result of looking honestly at her unhealed wounds.

Healing ourselves is the first step we take toward gaining emotional autonomy. Healing requires us to trust our own feelings, which is sometimes described colloquially as "trusting our gut." Many factors conspire against women trusting our gut. For one thing, we were raised in a culture in which female intuition and women's truth isn't awarded much value. We may have grown up in families where our father's and brothers' opinions carried more weight than our mother's, sisters', and our own. In school we may have sat silently in the classroom watching as our male schoolmates were called on more often, rewarded for speaking up, when we were subtly taught to subdue our voice. In the workplace we may receive the message that our input is less valuable than that of our male colleagues. All of this we carry into our intimate relationship.

The net result is the tendency to doubt, censor, and mistrust our own take on what's going on within and around us. These ingrained messages and highly influential life experiences must be reversed in order for us to fully trust our feelings. We have many of the tools to do this. Our instincts are well developed and our emotions close at hand. We simply need to practice honoring our emotions and expressing them honestly.

We usually know when we're not honoring our emotions. We feel anxious, uncomfortable, and ill at ease. Our insides and our outside don't match. We may be smiling on the outside, while inside we're miserable or agreeing to something that hits us the wrong way or acting conciliatory when we're angry or conflicted. These are red flags, signs that we're out of touch with how we truly feel. When we come up against this sort of dissonance, we must stop, take a step back, and ask ourselves, "How am I really feeling right now? What do I know—deep down in my gut—to be true?"

Once we're in touch with our feelings, we need to choose how to express them. Emotional autonomy enables us to know when, how, and with whom to share our feelings. Autonomy is a difficult concept for women to grasp, because the term is often misconstrued as meaning independence to the point of being all alone. But being autonomous is different from being alone. Autonomy means that we have the strength to draw from internal and external sources. Being alone assumes that we have no one else to turn to, that we are so independent that we no longer need the love and support of others.

Although I'd never, ever want to see women aspire to this extreme level of independence, there are aspects of it we can learn from, especially from men, who are extremely advanced in the "art" of autonomy.

What Men Can Teach Us About Autonomy

I am constantly amazed by men's ability to live their lives as if everything is up to them and them alone. Almost every man I've ever known enjoys, and often even prefers, his own company. He rarely, if ever, asks for help, and seems perfectly capable of taking care of himself. Mens' general reluctance to seek help, comfort, or even information (try suggesting to a man that he ask directions, even when he's sixty miles off-course) is a stunning testament to their independence and autonomy. Most men cringe at the thought of needing anyone. They'd rather eat nails than expose their vulnerability, share their feelings, or depend on others (even their lover) for sustenance and support.

What is it about men that makes them adhere to such a rigid code of independence? Men are trained to stand alone. Cultivating autonomy is a essential part of the cultural transition from boyhood to manhood. In the necessary process of breaking his intimate tie with his mother, the boy separates and becomes autonomous. Intimacy is perceived as a seductive, dangerous, and potentially consuming trap to most men as a result. Men continue to long for nurturing and comfort available through intimacy, while fearing the possibility of losing themselves and compromising their manhood. It is a no-win situation, as evidenced by mens' ambivalence regarding intimacy in relationships. If they let go and allow themselves to be emotionally vulnerable, they risk losing their sense of self. If they remain armored, they risk losing the love they crave.

Women's training is diametrically opposed to men's. Everything in our upbringing draws us to intimacy rather than autonomy, which is why we have the edge on the former, while our partners have the edge on the latter. Like our brothers, our first source of love and nurturing is our mother. But unlike our brothers, we are encouraged to remain intimately bonded and, later on when we are older, to emulate a feminine model of emotional attachment. Consequently, we grow up to seek emotional fulfillment through intimate connection rather than separating from it in order to grow into womanhood. In contrast to men, who tend to withdraw into themselves, when we are angry, sad, or scared, we turn to our mate for comfort. Our impulse is to reveal ourselves, to share our insight, to process our feelings in the context of our relationship. But as we've seen, this impulse doesn't always serve us well.

The truth is that in some situations autonomy is called for, and other times intimacy is the healthier choice. It's a question of balance and an area where men and women have much to teach one another. Women would benefit from learning how to be more independent, resourceful, and capable of keeping our own counsel. Men have much to learn from women's ability to candidly share our emotions and expose our vulnerability. Sometimes sharing our feelings with our partner is an act of courage and a way to move our relationship forward. Many times our partner is the person whom we most trust. In many cases he is exactly the right person with whom to honestly share information or discuss mutually relevant concerns. But, other times our intimate partner is the last person with whom we should confide our emotions. He may or may not be able to respond lovingly or appropriately. For starters, he's emotionally invested, making it hard for him to be objective. Secondly, he feels responsible and therefore is likely to be defensive, especially in respect to any negative emotions we're sharing. He's only human; how can we expect to tell him we're lonely or angry or disappointed in our relationship without him taking it personally? In these instances we would be far better off if we revealed our feelings and did our healing with a skilled therapist, wise spiritual counselor, or trusted friend.

Using our resources wisely is both an expression and an outgrowth of self-possession. When we're whole unto ourselves, we make wise decisions about where to entrust our tender and vulnerable feelings. Using our resources wisely promotes our growth and healing.

Spiritual Foundation

A lack of self-possession keeps us wanting our partner to be there for us in ways that are neither healthy nor productive for either of us. Returning over and over again to what may be a dry well of emotion that we find in him keeps us from tapping other resources, especially the richest wellspring of all—our spiritual foundation. The roots we've planted, our relationships, commitments, beliefs, and values, form the basis of our foundation. They support us and reveal what we're made of, determining whether our well is rich and abundant and capable of quenching our thirst.

Cultivating self-possession asks that we create a firm spiritual foundation—strong enough to support us, sound enough to keep us secure, and safe enough to provide sanctuary from the storms. Each of us builds our own foundation made up of our unique and particular strengths. Our materials vary. We may see ourselves as courageous, flexible, determined, or resilient. We may include kindness, acceptance, or compassion among our gifts. Spiritual faith, perspective, solitude, even humor may reinforce our foundation. We likely have survived an experience or two in which we showed courage and fortitude, reminding us of what we're made of and how much we can truly count on ourselves.

Knowing what we're made of provides the roots of self-possession and greatly determines our capacity to stand on our own two feet. Here are two useful exercises to help explore what you're made of. The first invites you to list your strongest, most valiant qualities. If it's hard for you to "toot your own horn," try imagining how a close friend would describe you. There is nothing vain about acknowledging our strengths; it's a way of identifying the basis of our foundation. Complete the following sentence by writing down as many positive adjectives about yourself as you can:

I am proud that I am _____.

Remembering a personal act of bravery, a time when we were faced with a big challenge and rose to the occasion, also reveals what we're made of. We may have overcome an obstacle, survived a crisis, or triumphed over a personal battle that put our courage to the test. It needn't have been as dramatic as saving a drowning child. One woman recalls the guts it took to leave home and move halfway across the country in her early twenties, while another is proud of receiving her ten-year chemical-dependency sobriety medal, and another considers her decision to adopt a baby after a decade of infertility her greatest moment of courage. Recalling our personal story of bravery cements our foundation of self-possession.

Take a moment now to remember a time when you were tested. Recall the nature of the challenge, the fear you overcame, and, most important, what qualities in yourself made it possible for you to rise to the occasion. Now notice the qualities you listed and add any that are missing from the previous list you composed.

As we continue to cultivate self-possession, we draw from our well of inner strength. We stand firmly on our strengths, and for us to continue to rely on ourselves in this way we must keep ourselves strong with a daily spiritual practice. Life is distracting and draining; our focus and footing are easily misplaced amid the daily stresses of our overwhelming demands. For this reason, we must fortify our foundation with some form of regular spiritual nourishment.

Where we draw our spiritual nourishment from is highly personal. Some people turn to prayer or meditation as a way of maintaining serenity. Nature is an abundant source of connection to the universe. Art and other forms of creativity are deeply nourishing. Religious faith or any belief in a higher source, reminds us of the divine power and the bigger plan in which we are a small, yet integral part.

Spiritual practice is a way of continually refilling our well. When we become still and quiet within, we can find our inner core. Our inner core is the deepest source of our being, the source of our wisdom and energy. We can locate our core by closing our eyes, breathing calmly and deeply, and noticing the place in our body where our breath originates. Most of us experience the source of our breath in the center of our chest, right below our rib cage. This area corresponds to what yoga philosophy refers to as the fourth chakra, or heart chakra. Our core can also be reached through quietly hearing our inner voice or inner truth, what we sometimes call "instinct" and is the truth that guides us when we're lost or confused.

Marjorie Shapiro, a massage therapist and healer, compares daily spiritual discipline to practicing musical scales. She recommends that each morning, we sit quietly for fifteen minutes and do this imagery exercise: we close our eyes, get in touch with our inner strength, and slowly imagine it flowing throughout our body the way we'd slowly pour honey into a glass. She also encourages us to imagine our spirit guides or guardian angels and to invite them to attend and protect us throughout the day. My personal spiritual practice is somewhat similar. Each morning I spend a few moments sitting quietly in front of a mirror. I open my eyes and stare deeply into my reflection, focusing on the inner truth flowing through me until I feel totally connected with the deepest essence of myself.

Finally, solitude is the spiritual gift we give ourselves. It is usually the one gift we deny ourselves and that our loved ones are reluctant to allow us. To love ourselves we must give ourselves precious time for silence and reflection. Whether we commit to a half hour of daily journal writing, a bubble-bath with dimmed lights and locked doors, a weekend retreat or a solo vacation, solitude is an urgent requirement in our search for self-possession.

Dealing with Him

Most of us know we need more solitude, yet we often fail to make it a priority. We can't figure out how to squeeze it into our busy schedule or we worry about neglecting our responsibilities or relationships.

Your partner may or may not object to you taking more time to be by yourself. Some men welcome the break and understand the need for solitude. Others feel threatened, neglected, or ignored. We have no obligation to defend our right to solitude; however, we have a definite responsibility to negotiate it respectfully.

How we express our desire for solitude has a big effect on how it's received by our partner. If we say, "Goddamnit, I never get a minute to myself. I'm locking the bedroom door and not coming out for the next two weeks!" he'll rightfully wonder what he's done to incur our wrath. If, however, we share our need for time to ourselves and express our intentions—"I'm feeling overwhelmed so I've made a commitment to meditate every afternoon for twenty minutes," or "I'd like to attend a women's renewal retreat next fall so I can rest and relax"—you're likely to receive his support. Suggest that he do the same. Our partners are plenty stressed out and deserve solitude as much as we do. By encouraging him to give himself the gift of solitude, we can bring greater serenity both to ourselves and also our relationship.

We may also avoid solitude because we're afraid of going deeply into ourselves, of facing our emptiness or listening to our inner truth. Our busyness serves a purpose, for as long as we are going and doing and achieving and producing, we can effectively avoid feeling any void within ourselves and facing the truth. We intuitively know that within the void is a swirling vortex of truth. Whether we dive into the vortex or slowly, carefully immerse ourselves in it one toe at a time, we return to a warm womb in which we find our way back to ourselves, to our center, to all that is holy. When we shut out the noisy world around us and turn our attention to the inner self, we begin to know what's real. When we silence the clutter in our psyche, we can hear the ring of our own truth. When we nurture our heart's yearning for connection to that which is sacred, we can make sound emotional investments that are both loving and beneficial for ourselves and our mate.

Sound Investments

As we've come to understand, there's no such thing as loving too much. There is, however, such a thing as giving too much, which is exactly what happens when we don't love ourselves enough.

It's safe to assume that almost every woman alive has a serious problem with giving too much. We say yes when we should say no, or we say no, then feel guilty and capitulate. We expect ourselves to pick up our husband's shirts at the dry cleaners, host the baby shower, drive the carpool, spend forty-five minutes on the phone with an anxious friend, and look fabulous for our weekly date night when we'd rather pull on a sweat suit and watch TV.

Why do we continue to drive ourselves crazy and make ourselves sick by attending to every need but our own? Because, in the words of the slogan of the Indispensable Woman, a topic I've offered seminars on for the past ten years, we find ourselves saying over and over, "It's easier to do it myself." And in some ways, it is. The more we do, the more we give, the more in control we feel. We get to do it our way. But the costs are heavy, especially in the sphere of our intimate relationship. Being an Indispensable Woman or a Woman Who Does Too Much, in the end, does more harm than good. We infantilize our partner by doing for him what he's perfectly capable of doing for himself. We stunt his growth by having minimal expectations of him. It isn't loving to excuse our partner from doing his share, and it isn't loving to ourselves to pick up the slack. While we have a tendency to offer him a hand, we inevitably end up resenting our mate for accepting all of our assistance and depleting us of our energy. Worse, we create an illusion of ourselves as bionic. But we aren't robots. Despite our superhuman facade, we are fragile, breakable human beings who can only give so much without falling apart, which is why we must learn to ration our emotional resources in the right way.

Emotional Currency

Each of us has a certain amount of emotional currency in our checkbook. Our emotional currency is the sum total of our resources—the time, energy, insight, attention, affection, and caring we have within us to give. Being self-possessed means having full control over our emotional currency in three ways:

1. Spending wisely.
2. Being aware of our cash flow.
3. Religiously balancing our checkbook.

Wise Spending

Loving ourselves requires knowing how much of our emotional currency to save and keep for ourselves and how much we can afford to invest in others. Our inability to make wise investments is at the root of why women keep giving way too much of ourselves, without getting nearly enough in return. It's not so much that our partners are selfish or lacking in generosity (although certainly some are), the bigger issue is our tendency to either *splurge* or *scrimp*, rather than soundly investing our emotional resources.

We usually splurge when we're feeling anxious or upset. We find that it's a way to temporarily "fix" our feelings of emptiness through distraction and drama. Individuals who attend 12-Step Spender's Anonymous groups are well acquainted with this concept as it pertains to addictive shopping or spending, usually to attain material goods. Usually the item purchased is less compelling than the process itself. That's because of the drama factor, often called an addictive rush, that accompanies most addictive behaviors, whether the addictive substance is alcohol, chemicals, gambling, shopping, or loving.

When we splurge, giving too much of our time, energy, attention, or other emotional currency, we are engaged in the same addictive process as the individual who indulges in a shopping spree. We splurge for the very same reason she shops, to fill our emptiness by trying to buy love.

It never works. When we're conscious of how much "money" is in our emotional checking account and place appropriate value on our currency, giving is extremely gratifying. But just like the shopping addict, when we splurge emotionally, we eventually come down and face reality. Instead of feeling good about what we've given, we realize we've gone overboard. We feel empty, cheated, and resentful.

When we're in the splurge mode, we don't realize what we're doing. We're almost in a trance, carried away with the thrill and excitement of giving. We're on a mission, blinded by the single-minded pursuit of our goal. We're unstoppable. I found myself in just such a situation last spring, when, in a moment of inspiration, I personally experienced the high price of splurging my emotional currency.

Louis was leaving on a business trip. I wanted to surprise him with a care package to make his weeklong stay at the rather drab and minilist Days Inn a little more inviting. I spent two hours and almost a hundred dollars at a gourmet grocery store assembling an array of goodies: smoked oysters, Ghiradelli chocolate, imported cheese, English biscuits, pistachio nuts, a carton of Winstons, and several of his favorite magazines. A quick trip to the liquor store for miniature bottles of vodka and olives completed the package. I carefully wrapped each individual item in tissue paper, burying a pair of his favorite pair of my black panties between the oysters and the olives. My heart pounding in anticipation, I drove to his house and instructed him to close his eyes as I carried in the unwieldy carton. I insisted he open it on the spot. One by one he unwrapped each item; when he finished, he looked at me and said, "Thanks. But you really didn't need to go overboard. One candy bar would have been great." I was livid. I had expected him to swoon or weep or fall to his knees and propose marriage. I'd spent all day and all that money and for what?

For myself. Which is why it turned out the way it did. My impulse to send along a special treat had been sound, until my "addict" took over. In the end, I had given too much in order to dazzle Louis. But, if anything, my extravagant care package embarrassed him and made him worry that I was a spendthrift. I thought I was doing this out of love, but really, it was a thinly veiled attempt to get *him* to love *me* more.

The other side of the same coin is our tendency to scrimp. When we're feeling in need of love or approval from our mate, we splurge. When we're mad at him, we scrimp by withholding, withdrawing, or meting out our

emotional currency as if we're on the verge of bank-
ruptcy. We think we're loving ourselves by protecting our
resources, but scrimping is just another way we cope with
fear. Fear of scarcity, the worry that giving anything more
will put us in the red. Fear that we will run out of time,
energy, or love, we had better assume a survivalist mentality and start stockpiling our resources. Once again, we
end up hurting ourselves. We feel isolated and estranged.
We feel selfish, guilty, and stingy when what we truly
want is to give.

We can only give in a way that fulfills us and him when
we stop squandering our emotional currency, whether
through splurging or scrimping, and learn to invest
wisely. Being self-possessed enables us to know exactly
how much we have, how much we need, and how much
we can afford to give away. How much we have also depends on our ability to ask for what we need, another
challenge that becomes easier when we feel self-reliant
and have set some healthy boundaries.

Why Can't He Read My Mind?

I often hear women say, "If I have to ask, getting it
doesn't mean anything, anyway." We complain that our
partner doesn't give enough, yet we still haven't completely mastered the art of asking for what we need.
There are three primary reasons why it's so hard to ask
for what we want:

1. We resent having to ask in the first place.
2. We don't want to start trouble.
3. We have little faith in our partner's ability to deliver.

Each of these keeps us from getting what we want.
Each is within our power to change.

Granted, it would be divine if our mate could read our mind, if he knew what we wanted and provided it without our having to spell it out. We can spend the rest of our lives waiting for The Man Who Anticipates My Every Wish, or we can accept the fact that it's up to us to ask for what we want. Once in a while our partner may surprise us with unsolicited shows of affection, gifts, support, or appreciation, but most of the time, as one woman puts it, "He needs a flow chart with diagrams."

Our desire for our mate to read our mind is driven by a very human need, to be known and understood. We long for our partner to know us so well that he instinctively senses how to love and nurture us. But this level of insight only comes with time and experience. As we give him more information, he learns about what pleases us. With time, he discovers ways to meet our needs without us explicitly articulating them over and over.

We need both patience and the commitment to do our part, which means we have to relinquish our need for him to be a mind reader and be willing to put ourselves on the line.

Fear of Conflict

We hesitate to ask for what we want because of our fear of making waves. Asking can be thorny, especially if what we're asking for has historically been a source of conflict. For example, if every time we mention how much we'd like him to be more enthusiastic about our work, he gets defensive and says something like, "What do you want? A medal?" we're unlikely to savor the idea of having this conversation one more time.

Assuming he's not a total jerk, it may be that we're asking in the wrong way. Our commulative frustration may make our requests come out sounding like accusations or angry demands. When we say, "You know, I'm working myself to the bone, which I wouldn't have to do if you made a little more money. The least you could do is show some appreciation," he's bound to feel criticized and be on the defensive. If, however, we say, "I'm working really hard, and it would mean so much to me if you would notice and acknowledge my accomplishments," this gives our partner an opening to be supportive. We can affect his response by asking in a respectful way, which requires our willingness to do two things: State our need. Ask respectfully. No one is forthcoming when they feel attacked. Most people—especially our partner, who loves us and has a vested interest in our success and happiness—can come through when approached in a respectful manner.

Another reason we don't ask is we're cynical about what we have to gain. Our experience may have convinced us that even when we ask respectfully, our partner still doesn't respond in the way we hope for. Here's where the assertiveness training seminars of the eighties failed. We learned methods of asking for what we wanted, but we didn't learn one basic truth: just because we want something and just because we ask for something doesn't mean we are going to get it. We can want what we want, we can deserve what we are asking for, we can communicate effectively, but we still need to consider the possibility of our partner not delivering what we desire.

Asking is a bit of an emotional risk. We've made ourselves vulnerable by stating our needs, the possibility of rejection adds insult to injury. If what we've asked for reflects a deep, bedrock need, "no" is especially hard to swallow. Our urgency to have our partners support is in direct ratio to our need. The more desperate we feel, the angrier we become when our request is denied.

The more self-possessed we are, the better we become at asking without urgency, accepting "yes," "no," or "maybe" in stride. A physical metaphor is useful in thinking about this situation. Let's say we're starving and we ask someone for a bite of their apple. We haven't eaten in hours; our blood sugar is plummeting, and we're starting to feel nauseous. The person with the apple says, "Sorry, no." We're furious. If we could, we might grab the apple out of their hands. We may even vow to never share any future apple we may have with anyone. If, on the other hand, our stomach is full, we react quite differently. If we're well fed, we may want a bite of an apple, but it isn't an urgent matter of life and death. We can ask for what we want, without begging, threatening, or throwing a tantrum if we're refused.

But Can He Deliver?

Our level of confidence in our partner's ability to deliver is the third factor that affects our willingness to ask for what we want. If we strongly believe in his capacity to come through, we are more apt to ask for what we want. If, however, we believe that our efforts are futile, we can easily talk ourselves out of asking since we're skeptical of getting what we want from him.

There is a fine balance between expecting too much and giving up before we start. Measured optimism is a reasonable attitude to adopt: we hope for the best and are willing to accept less. Here's how this works. Let's say you want your partner to be nicer to your parents. Let's face it, he doesn't much like them and they're not particularly thrilled with him either. But they're your parents. You'd like him to, at least, be civil to them and show up occasionally for Sunday night dinner. So far, asking hasn't gotten you anywhere. You're tried convincing him, yelling at him, making him feel guilty, and reminding him that you're good to his aging mother just because you love *him* and because it's the right thing to do. Should you give up and assume he's never going to be a mensch, or do you give him the benefit of the doubt and keep hoping he'll rise to the occasion?

Measured optimism allows us to do a little bit of both. We can hope for the best and try approaching him in a new, more effective manner, while simultaneously preparing ourselves for the possibility of disappointment. One way to cushion the blow is by adjusting our expectations. We should first assess whether or not this issue is worth fighting about. Then, we need to ask for a little less than what we truly want, for example, being satisfied with his being polite on the phone but only asking him to come to Christmas and Thanksgiving. Meanwhile, we feel good about how and what we give without expecting him to do the same. What matters is to find a balance we can live with between holding our partner to our highest standards and making peace with an ever-changing reality.

Be careful to avoid confusing requests and tests. We may unwittingly set up our partner and ourselves by asking for things as a way of testing our mate. For example, we ask him if he'd mind taking an hour off work to drive us to the dentist's office for a root canal when we could get another ride, and when he can't, we decide he's not devoted enough. Or we ask sweetly for a back rub, and he say's "not now," which convinces us he's really as selfish as we thought. Once again he gets a failing grade. Testing our partner is bad for both of us. He senses that our request is loaded, that there's more on the line than what's on the surface, which makes him less willing to comply. We don't get what we want because our true need is subterfuged beneath our agenda.

Finally, it's important to consider whom we're asking in light of what we're asking. In other words, is our mate the best or right person to fulfill certain requests or is there someone else who is more willing and capable?

This is an areas in which it's useful to diversify our resources. Way too often we choose our mate as the person with whom we want to share our feelings when our best friend might be a better choice. Half the time he may be incapable of or disinterested in delving into our emotional terrain and, as a result, he struggles to meet our needs and will fail miserably. How many times have you spent hours trying to explain your feelings to your partner, who stares back at you with a blank look, and then given your best friend the two-minute version, which she totally got.

We want our partner to be the first person we turn to, but this isn't always the most productive option. He listens attentively for twenty minutes, then starts channel surfing or yawning. He asks us to cut to the quick or give him the clift notes. He downplays the issue or says we're making a big deal out of nothing. He seduces us into a dynamic I refer to as the Musical Issues Syndrome. It goes like this. You want to talk about something important that's bothering you. He reluctantly agrees. You think he is interested in your feelings and share them candidly. He cuts you off in one way or another. You tell him he's cutting you off. He becomes increasingly defensive and anxious about not responding to you the way you need. You start helping him sort through why this is so difficult for him. He feels better. You're angrier than you were when you started. After going round and round in a circle he's sitting down and you're without a chair.

What happened? This conversation was supposed to be about *your* feelings and you ended up attending to *his*. The message is, Talk to someone else—a close friend, your sister, mother, or therapist. The woman behind the counter at the dry cleaners. It's amazing how naturally women respond to our feelings when our partner can't or won't. Diversify and then go to the right source with different needs. This is another way of protecting our emotional resources.

How much we can give, and how much we need to ask for, depends a great deal on whether or not we're emotionally well fed. Nourishing and nurturing ourselves well is part and parcel of loving ourselves and taking responsibility for our lives. It is up to us to become as strong, full, and well developed as possible, the task we turn to in Chapter 6.

6

The Fourth Leap:
CULTIVATING STRENGTH

I n the movie *Fried Green Tomatoes*, actress Kathy Bates plays the character Evelyn, a shlumpy, overweight middle-age woman in search of herself. Her marriage is dying a slow death, her self-esteem is in the toilet, and her Neanderthal husband favors a TV tray over a candlelit dinner she's carefully prepared. She tries to talk to him about their marriage; he's clueless and asks her to quit blocking his view of the game. She stuffs doughnuts in her mouth to fill her loneliness, attends an eighties-style assertiveness training seminar (complete with speculum and hand-held mirror), and, in perfect Total Woman style, greets her husband at the door, gift-wrapped in Saran Wrap topped with a huge red bow.

We adore her, we pity her, and we're hoping against hope she'll get it together. And she does! We cheer as Evelyn takes charge of her life. She replaces the doughnuts with carrot sticks, buys exercise equipment, becomes a successful Mary Kay consultant, experiments with hormone-replacement treatments, and, perhaps best of all, makes a wonderful friend in an eighty-five-year-old woman, played by Jessica Tandy. By the end of the movie Evelyn has heroically transformed herself into Tawanda, a gutsy, warrior woman. Her husband is both baffled and intrigued. His timid, insecure wife has disappeared. In her place stands a formidable woman who commands respect.

The movie could have ended in one of two ways. Scenario One: Evelyn, aka Tawanda, leaves a Dear John letter decorated with the red bow, empties her checking account, buys herself a BMW convertible, and runs off with her personal trainer to live happily ever after, cooking macrobiotic meals on a beach in Hawaii. Scenario Two: She continues to lavish love and attention on herself, becomes a high-level Mary Kay director, teaches other mid-life women to develop themselves, and recommits herself to loving her husband and improving their marriage.

I'd choose Scenario Two. Although Scenario One appeals to my Thelma-and-Louise sensibility, Evelyn remaining in her marriage is a more powerful and ultimately, more fulfilling choice. Maybe I'm romantic. Although her husband needs a lot of work, Evelyn loves him and that counts for something. She owes it to herself to see how the changes she's making will affect their relationship. As long as her marriage doesn't interfere with her growth, why shouldn't she share the fruits of her labor with the man she loves and with whom she's already invested years. I, for one, want them to celebrate their fiftieth anniversary.

Strengthening Ourselves

Evelyn, aka Tawanda, inspires us because she's Everywoman. She's one of us, a normal, everyday sort of woman who's doing her damndest to work with what she's got. She meets the challenge of re-creating herself, which is what each of us must do in order to be big enough, strong enough, and evolved enough to success-fully love another human being.

Loving ourselves means nourishing, nurturing, and de-veloping ourselves to the fullest. This is one area where we consistently shortchange ourselves. We jeopardize our health by denying ourselves balanced nourishment, eating Cheez Doodles on the run instead of following a nutritious diet. We're too busy to exercise, too oversched-uled to make regular doctor appointments, too stressed to give ourselves the rest and solitude we need.

We are equally unkind to ourselves in the area of our emotional health. We forget to go outside and breathe the fresh air and admire the birds, trees, and other glorious gifts of nature that replenish our spirit. We squeeze in time with friends, our finest source of emotional support. We fail to get serious about our career goals. We postpone pursuing our hobbies, creative endeavors, and secret pas-sions, which can give our life meaning and purpose. Fi-nally, we deny ourselves life sustenance available through prayer, solitude, and spiritual fellowship.

It's time to start feeding ourselves. If we don't, we will starve. It's that simple. We have too many projects, too many dreams, too much love to give, too much we want to achieve in our lifetime to keep depriving ourselves of nourishment and nurturance. A car, no matter how ex-pensive or well equipped, can't keep running without regular tune-ups. The most breathtaking flower withers and dies without water. We know all this, yet we continue to put off getting a tune-up and ignore our thirst. Why, when we're so giving to everyone around us, do we con-tinue to neglect ourselves?

∽

Overcoming Our Resistance

At first glance, it seems obvious why we ignore our own needs. We're just to tired and too stressed to make ourselves a priority. On a superficial level, this is true. Our schedules *are* demanding; there's little time to make well-balanced meals, get to the health club, much less indulge in mud baths and massages at an expensive spa. Along with the stress in our lives, however, there are other, more fundamental fears undermining our commitment to our own health and well-being.

First, we are afraid of being too big, too powerful, and too strong. Even if our partner supports and encourages us to develop ourselves, we may unconsciously fear damaging our relationship by outgrowing our mate. We may hold on to those five extra pounds or put off getting our master's degree because we sense our moving ahead might threaten our partner or upset the balance in our relationship. He teases us about getting so gorgeous we'll end up having an affair, and we know he's not totally kidding. We know he's sensitive about never having finished college, and we wonder how he'd really feel if there were letters after our name.

We can be sensitive to our partner's insecurities, but we mustn't use them as an excuse to justify our fear of becoming all we can be. Real love requires an absolute commitment to each other's growth. A strong relationship thrives on each partner maximizing his or her gifts and fulfilling his or her destiny.

Second, we may limit our own strength because of our cultural conditioning. Even as we assume powerful positions in the workforce and even as we bench-press at the gym, we may still carry remnants of negative messages about "strong" women. Although, in truth, women are more physically resilient and live longer than men, our culture has perpetuated a positive image of women as fragile and weak. Femininity has long been correlated with physical frailty. Some of our grandmothers were taught to starve themselves, hold their breath as they squeezed into corsets, even to feign faintness or dizzy spells in order to appear delicate.

We all know better. Anyone whose ever given birth or attended a childbirth knows full well the amazing strength and endurance women are capable of. I can't wait for the day when I get to say, "Just breathe, honey" to a man while he's trying to survive the next contraction. But even as we know the extent of our own strength, we may have internalized cultural messages that make us ambivalent about commiting to the development of our physical stamina.

Third, we may neglect ourselves out of sheer laziness. Making the commitment to strengthen ourselves involves rigorous effort and energy. Our habits, however unhealthy, are deeply entrenched. We're fond of our familiar lifestyle, even when we know it's not serving us well. Getting on a program—whether it's eating nutritiously, joining a support group, or signing up for the art history class we keep talking about—requires a commitment to ourselves and the impetus to get off our butt and get going!

Fourth, we're afraid of seeming selfish. We feel guilty putting ourselves first when we have children, a partner, aging parents, friends, a career, and community involvements we've committed to. As one of my favorite quotes goes, "Show me a man who feels guilty and I'll show you a woman." It's pointless for me to try to convince you that guilt is a useless, pointless, needless emotion. I could give you ten reasons why what we call selfishness is more often a way of loving ourselves and taking ourselves into consideration, and you'd have a ready argument for each.

Instead, let's learn from those who have mastered the art of putting themselves first.

What Men Can Teach Us About "Selfishness"

Why is it that men can make plans to play softball on Thursday night, say, "No, I'm too busy to drive the Sunday school car pool," and call home to say they're working late without feeling an ounce of guilt? Why do men so easily put themselves first, while we agonize every time we squeeze in fifteen minutes for ourselves with the remorse of someone guilty of negligent homicide?

Are men genetically selfish? Or have they been taught to put themselves first or, at least, very high on the list? The latter is more likely. For generations men have been raised with a sense of entitlement—the belief that they are born to have their needs satisfied. Many of our partners were waited on by doting mothers who cleaned their rooms, covered their tracks, and jumped up to serve coffee while they lingered over a second helping of pie. Ex-girlfriends or ex-wives may have indulged our partner, reinforcing behavior patterns that are now ours to undo.

We can and must ask more of our partner when it comes to giving. But it's also useful to learn from his sense of entitlement, which, in it's best sense, is a form of valuing himself. Clearly our partner thinks his health is important, his time is valuable, and his needs are worthy of attention, all of which we both resent and envy. How dare he take so much for himself when we ask so little?

"When Steven and I decided to have a baby, I agreed to take on the major share of child care," says Beth, who works part-time at a consulting firm and is the mother of a three-year-old daughter. "Steven's a wonderful father.

He's great with Casey, and he watches her if I ask him, which is hardly ever because it always ends up being such a big deal. If he wants to go out at night, he just goes. If I want to have dinner with a friend, I have to explain and make elaborate arrangements, which doesn't seem fair.''

Beth is angry for two reasons. First, she agreed to something she probably shouldn't have in the first place. Second, she resents Steven's ease at taking time for himself when it's so hard for her to ask for the same consideration. Clearly, she needs to renegotiate a more equitable parenting partnership. But even more to the point, instead of resenting that Steven takes time off, she needs to afford herself the same luxury.

We will continue to neglect our needs until we're ready to value ourselves—until we're ready to receive as well as give.

What We Can Teach Men About Giving

Lest we give men too much credit for taking care of themselves, let us not forget the value of giving, something women excel at. Here is another example of what women and men have to teach each other. We can teach our partner the value of giving through our example and through encouragement.

We may think we're being a positive role model by the sheer amount we constantly give. But being a good example is only powerful when it's genuine, when we're not secretly being martyrs or resenting how much we're giving. We demonstrate true generosity when we give from the heart, taking both our partner's and our own needs into account, with no hidden agendas or strings attached.

We can also encourage our partner to give more by asking him to do his share and reinforcing him for his effort.

Too often we forget to say thank you, especially when our mate is doing only the bare minimum, even after several requests from us. But *thank you* is important. So is "good job!" The more we reward him, the more motivated he'll be.

Giving is good, as long as it's supported by a strong and healthy foundation. We can give freely only when we're healthy and well-nourished, when we're feeding our body, mind, heart, and soul.

Nourishing Ourselves

A confession: I'm probably the last person on the planet to advise anyone on the merits of maintaining a healthy diet since all too often my breakfast consists of three cups of espresso, a chocolate-covered graham cracker, and a couple of Marlboros. Not that I'm proud of it. I'm fully aware, as are all of us, of the importance of trying to improve our diet in order to improve our health. Here, the operative word is "trying." Our eating habits are an integral part of our lifestyle. The more stressed out we are, the more apt we are to eat on the run and ignore our needs for balanced nutrition. We needn't do a complete overhaul of our diet in order to make improvements; we simply need to try, to make an effort by taking a few positive steps in the right direction.

Some individuals have the most success by making sweeping changes. They make a dramatic shift from junk food to healthy choices, ridding their diet of sugar and caffeine, or taking a purist approach, by becoming a vegetarian or adopting a macrobiotic diet. But most of us find it easier and more effective to slowly and gradually improve our diet. We add whole grains or green vegetables to our menu. We lower our sugar intake and start reading the fat content on food packaging. We take a salad, apple, and granola bar to work instead of grazing at our desk.

The goal is to be more conscious of what we're putting into our bodies so that they run more smoothly and support the enormous energy output required by our numerous demands. Food is fuel and the energy that keeps us going. When we fail to replenish ourselves, we deplete our resources, diminishing our ability to operate at maximum capacity. When we eat right, we have more energy, a better attitude, and are far more capable of handling stress.

Here, again, we must be careful of our perfectionistic tendencies. We may find the idea of radically changing our diet so overwhelming that it may seem impossible for us to do anything at all. We don't believe that our "little" changes will make enough of a difference, or we just don't know where to begin. But little steps lead to big changes. For example, making the commitment to eat breakfast every morning, even if we continue our regular eating habits the rest of the day, can make a real difference. Replacing our midafternoon Oreo cookies with an orange or gradually decaffeinating has a bigger impact than we may expect.

In order to improve our diet, we need to start by honestly assessing how we're currently feeding ourselves. Next, we must examine HOW we might make a few reasonable improvements and, if we're willing to, commit to one or two WAYS of making those improvements.

This exercise will help you begin:

Nutrition Assessment

Choose the answer that most closely describes your diet.

Right now I'd honestly assess my eating habits as: LOUSY. FAIR. PRETTY GOOD. EXCELLENT.

⤳

Now complete the following sentences:

My personal weaknesses are _____.

⤳

What gets in the way of my eating right is _____.

⤳

I could improve my diet by _____.

⤳

Here's what it would take _____.

Answering these questions reveals areas in need of attention. Knowing what we need to do is the first step and
then making the commitment to follow through is what
makes real change possible. At this point, you may be unwilling, sort of willing, or totally willing to improve your
eating habits. Now it's time to make a real commitment
by completing the following exercise. Choose one way in
which you're ready to commit to improving your diet.
Make sure your goal is realistic and something you're able
to accomplish. Remember, any commitment is a worthwhile way to be more loving to yourself.

I will improve my diet by _____.

Keeping commitments is difficult. There are numerous
obstacles, including force of habit, laziness, stress, and
delayed gratification. We may truly want to break the
junk-food addiction, but there's a candy machine in the
office. It takes time to make a salad in the morning and
will take weeks, perhaps months before we notice a real
change in our energy and appearance brought about by
eating right. Because of this, there are two important

ways to up our chances of success: support and the reward system.

Ultimately we have to motivate ourselves, but it always helps to have a cheering section. Ask one close friend to support you in the commitment you've made. You might arrange to call them at the end of each day to report your progress or allow them to be your "crisis counselor" when you're about to slip.

Rewards are equally motivating. Although eating right is eventually a reward in itself, you might need to give yourself some special rewards to acknowledge your effort and counteract your feelings of deprivation. For instance, have your favorite dessert one night after each week of avoiding sugar, or indulge in gourmet fat-free snacks, or buy one new outfit in a smaller size. You've made a firm commitment to improve your nourishment; now make a firm commitment to reward yourself by completing the next sentence.

I plan to reward myself by _____.

Stretching Our Bodies

Judging by the proliferation of health clubs, one would think we've become a nation of exercise nuts. Yet many of us are still talking about exercising without making it a regular part of our life. We fail to follow through on exercise for many of the same reasons that we ignore our diet. We're too busy, or we don't believe our efforts will yield a dramatic enough outcome. "I'd love to work out, but I just can't fit it in," says Vicki, whose daily routine includes getting two toddlers to nursery school by nine, managing the dress department at a major department store, racing to pick her kids up by six, making dinner, bathing them, getting them in bed, and spending an exhausted half hour catching up with her husband during the ten o'clock news. Millions of women share Vicki's dilemma: How do we integrate exercise into our busy, busy lives?

There are a range of possibilities. If we decide that regular exercise is a priority, we can schedule an aerobics class or work out twice a week at a health club that offers child care. We can negotiate a once-a-week deal with our partner to watch the kids while we swim. We can also choose other forms of exercise that don't involve money or specific time schedules. A brisk walk around the block, lifting weights in front of our bedroom mirror, doing twenty-five sit-ups every morning, free and easy ways to build our stamina and tone our physique.

Again, we needn't become bodybuilders or Olympic athletes. There are a growing number of women who are fanatics about working out. While their effort and its outcome is admirable, this too can be an extreme way of pressuring ourselves rather than feeding ourselves. Finding a healthy balance is a way of asking the most of ourselves without pushing ourselves to the limit. The hardest part is getting going, but once we do, we almost always feel rejuvenated and great about ourselves.

The process of making a commitment to exercise is similar to what we did above in the area of nutrition. So here we go again. First, rate your current level of exercise.

Right now I'd rate my level of regular exercise as:
LOUSY. OKAY. PRETTY GOOD. FABULOUS.

Now complete the following sentences:

What gets in the way of exercising regularly is _____.

༄

The area I need to work on most is _____.

༄

I can improve my exercise plan by _____.

༄

This will require _____.

Now make a real and realistic commitment to improve how much you exercise in one way.

I commit to _____.

Regular exercise is another discipline in which both support and rewards help us to keep our commitment. The buddy system is a perfect source of support. Having a partner with whom you regularly exercise will keep you on track and that buddy may be your husband, a co-worker, or a friend. In the next space, name the person who can best support you in exercising.

My workout partner is _____.

If you can't find an exercise partner don't let that keep you from following through. A woman I know came up with a great idea. She suggested to her husband that they buy Nautilus equipment and work out together each morning. She loved the idea of a regular exercise date. She envisioned them sweating, cheering each other on, showering, and sharing muffins, coffee, and who knows what else? She tried to rouse her husband's interest, but each time she brought up her idea, he blew her off. He thought it was great for her to work out and was happy to finance the equipment, but it just wasn't a personal priority for him. So she let go of the idea, which was a shame. She let his lack of enthusiasm and participation get in the way of getting in shape.

Remember, you're doing this for *yourself*. Any support you gather is frosting on the cake. Once again, be sure to reward yourself for effort. In the following space make your commitment to acknowledge your progress.

I plan to reward myself by _____.

Regular exercise strengthens us, enhances our appearance, and increases our vitality. But best of all, it feels great, which brings us to the subject of sexuality, one of the best ways to love and feed ourselves.

Sensuality

Sex is highly underated. We need more of it, not to satisfy our partner, but to feed our deep, human need to touch and be touched. In my work with women I've become terribly concerned about how often we deny ourselves this basic form of nourishment. With some exceptions, the pleasures of eroticism and lovemaking are often delegated to the bottom of our priority list. We're too busy, too exhausted, too distracted to make the effort; shifting gears, getting in the mood, changing out of our terry-cloth robe into the sexy lingerie we bought on impulse just seems like more pressure, more work. It's easier to crawl into bed with a book; maybe by Saturday night the idea will hold some appeal.

We may also avoid lovemaking if we aren't getting enough pleasure from it. We may only get minimally aroused, be unorgasmic, or find that the whole process is frustrating or goes on far too long, more endurance test than enjoyment. He's too fast or too self-absorbed or too inept to know what gets us off. We may have settled into a pattern of satisfactory, but not necessarily fabulous, sex; it's good enough, but it could be a hell of a lot better. Or we're unsure of how to ask for what really turns us on. He handles us roughly when soft, tender caresses tap our erotic desires. Or the opposite, he handles us with kid gloves when we'd love it if he'd throw us on the bed and masterfully take us in a scene right out of one of our favorite "dirty" books.

We may also turn off our sexuality or put it on the back burner because we're angry at our mate. Tension and unresolved issues hanging in the air, often leave us unwilling to be open and receptive to sexual advances, much less take the initiative. If we feel hurt or distrustful, we're apt to sexually shut down or, in some cases, use our sexuality as currency, punishing our partner by holding out on him in this area.

Some of us are able to be sexual when we're not feeling intimate and we may even have angry sex as a way of getting back at him, but this exchange falls more in the category of combat than lovemaking. We may release tension, the sexual encounter may provoke a more honest exchange of feelings, but usually we just end up feeling more estranged. Hard sex rarely compensates for sweet lovemaking.

Whether we deny ourselves sexual pleasure because we're stressed or emotionally withdrawn or because our partner can't figure out the right buttons to push, the end result is self-deprivation. For many women this is a gradual and commulative process. The less sex we have, the less we want it. As lovemaking becomes less frequent, we forget about how good it really feels. How many times have we passed on sex for several days or weeks, then had a wonderful lovemaking session, after which we remarked to ourselves or our partner, "Wow! We should do this more often." Each time we're surprised by how relaxed and yummy we feel.

We simply and plainly need more sex in our lives. Intimate, passionate, satisfying sex. Not because it pleases our partner or would solidify our relationship, although these are good reasons, too, but because it feels good. Being sexual makes us feel soft, open, hot, juicy, and alive. Being sexual is one way we express our creativity, get in touch with our sensuality, and give ourselves pleasure that we richly deserve. We can live without it, but there's a cost. The less sexual we are, the more mechanical we become. Sex helps us shift our attention from external, worldly concerns to our deeper, more internal sense of ourselves. It's a fine way to release tension, revitalize our energy, and rediscover the gorgeous, sexy, creatures we are.

Just as we're responsible for every other aspect of our lives, we're totally responsible for our sexual needs. It's up to us to find ways to open ourselves to sensual and erotic pleasure. It's up to us to create the emotional space needed to shift from everyday stress to a sensual mindset. It's up to us to build trust and heal the rifts in our relationship that make us pull back from our partners. Even our orgasm is ultimately up to us. We have to decide how important it is and find ways to give ourselves or be given moments of ecstasy and transcendence.

We begin by exploring the question of sensuality. Our sexuality is composed of two separate but related elements: sensuality and eroticism. We experience our sensuality both within and apart from actual lovemaking. Every time we rub body lotion on our silky skin; slowly bite into a ripe peach and let the sweet juice trickle into our mouths; take a long, hot bubble bath; cradle a new-born baby in our arms; or enjoy our partner softly stroking our hair, we are in touch with our innate sensuality.

Nourishing our sensuality requires slowing down and deliberately choosing to spend some of our time in ways that are conducive to opening our senses. One woman schedules a monthly body massage. Another takes an aerobics class twice a week, less for the exercise than for the pleasure of stretching, toning, and feeling her physical strength. Still another says that sleeping in a black silk negligee, feeling the luxurious fabric against her skin makes her more aware of her body.

Getting in touch with our sensuality makes us feel more relaxed and comfortable with ourselves and with our partner. We're more at home with our body, and, as a result, we feel sexier and more attractive. We may find ourselves feeling significantly more interested in sex. As our sensuality blossoms, our desire for passion and eroticism grows.

Eroticism

Our eroticism is experienced both with ourselves and within the context of lovemaking. Pleasuring ourselves is just as important as finding ways to get more stimulated with our mate.

We may be shy or resistant to the idea of self-pleasuring or masturbation. We may have been taught that it's wrong, even sinful to touch ourselves. We may feel guilty, weird, or embarrassed about indulging our sexual appetite or engaging in private acts of self-pleasure. But pleasure is one of our birthrights. We're entitled to experience the full range of our physical senses, and touching ourselves is another powerful expression of self-love.

Some of us regularly pleasure ourselves. We may take a

late afternoon "break" or make it part of our ritual before drifting off to sleep. We may easily arouse ourselves or we may need a little help. Here's my personal pitch for vibrators: Every woman should try one. A vibrator can help jump-start our libido and enhance our orgasm. It can also be a lovely sex toy during lovemaking, although some men may be threatened by a battery-operated aid. (Note how he starts playing airplane with it.) Using a vibrator isn't a sign of sexual dysfunction, nor is it meant to take anything away from our partner's sexual prowess. As Lily Tomlin says in Jane Wagner's one-act play *The Search for Signs of Intelligent Life in the Universe*, "Just think of it as Hamburger Helper for the boudoire."

Erotic literature or videos are other sexual enhancers. Although some feminists are stridently opposed to any form of pornography as demeaning to women and promoting violence, other women, many of whom also consider themselves feminists, are quite comfortable with and find pornographic images arousing. As adults we get to choose what sexually works for us, as long as we're not hurting anyone else. I have a well-worn copy of Anne Rice's *The Claiming of Sleeping Beauty* at my bedside. Other women may find this highly erotic, somewhat sado-masochistic material offensive. We each have to explore and discover what arouses us and gives us pleasure. Our sexuality is extremely personal. We needn't apologize about what turns us on, rather, we need to pay attention so that we can give ourselves what we need.

Fantasies fall squarely into this category. Most of us have a cache of fantasy material that we can assess for masturbatory or lovemaking purposes. We may have one tried-and-true fantasy we can always count on or we may choose from a varied menu, according to our particular mood. Again, our tastes in fantasy material are highly individualized. One woman fantasies about her brother-in-law, another conjures up scenes involving a woman, another imagines herself tied up, while another creates a pornographic scenario in which she's the stakes at a men's poker game. Our fantasies rarely match up with what we'd care to pursue in reality, that's why they're fantasies. They exist purely for our pleasure. They're harmless, helpful ways of adding spice to our sexual diet.

We can also rekindle our eroticism by paying more attention to what makes us feel sexy. Dipping into our Victoria Secret collection of sexy bras, thongs, even garter belts with all the trimmings is a great way to fulfill our occasional forays into sluttishness. One woman I know gives herself the treat of regular manicures. "It's the one time when I just sit and let myself be catered to. And there's something about beautifully shaped, bright red nails that makes me feel incredibly sexy."

Anything we do to open ourselves up to eroticism is great. Playing out the role of goddess, whore, pinup, or girl-next-door is fun, exciting, and can do a great deal to rejuvenate romance with our partner. But, again, to grow we have to take risks, which means both being receptive and willing to initiate sexual interaction that will please us. Again, we have to overcome some degree of negative cultural stereotypes and judgments aimed at women who are sexually aggressive. As adolescents, most of us were taught that it was the male's place to make the first move. We were also taught that we had little, if any, responsibility in lovemaking other than to be willing and receptive.

Times have changed. Although there are certainly men who prefer submissive partners, the majority of our partners would welcome more initiative and resourcefulness on our part. One way to initiate is to show our partner what pleases us. He shouldn't have to guess or play hide-and-seek with our sexuality—"You're getting warm . . . warmer . . ." Showing our partner how we touch ourselves, how we bring ourselves to orgasm, is the best way to teach him how to please us. Lovemaking goes far beyond kissing, caressing, and intercourse. Taking turns watching each other is fun, erotic, and very educational. Plus, it removes some of that simultaneous orgasm pressure, so that we can each have all the time we need.

Of course, showing our partner how we pleasure ourselves so that he can make love to us more effectively involves emotional risk. We need to let ourselves be a little bit of an exhibitionist, which means overcoming any shyness and fear we might have. How receptive we are, and whether we're willing to make the effort to be more creative in our lovemaking, depends on the level of trust we have in our partner. Even if our libido is relatively healthy, our sexual relationship in pretty good shape, we still need to trust that our partner will treat our sexuality with sensitivity and tenderness.

Safety and Passion

A strong sexual relationship needs a healthy balance between passion and safety. We can swing from the chandelier only if we're sure we'll land safely on the mattress. We can let go and be as wild as our wildest imagination allows only when we know that our playmate is totally trustworthy.

Trusting our partner in bed is a little different from trusting him in other arenas. Making love, by definition, is an act of vulnerability. We expose our imperfect bodies, open our most internal recesses, our heart, becoming literally and figuratively naked. We let ourselves be physically scrutinized and emotionally X-rayed, which takes enormous trust. Ideally our partner has earned our trust. He does so by admiring our beauty, learning about what pleases us, being sensitive to our emotions, and consistently demonstrating respect. But everyone makes mistakes. Our partner may have hurt us at some point in the history of our love life. He may have said something negative about our appearance that ever after makes us want to turn off the lights during sex. He may have been selfish or inattentive about pleasing us, which makes us mistrustful about his level of love and commitment.

Once again, we're faced with choices. We can turn off, or we can heal our wounds and to move our sexual relationship forward. Shutting down and turning off our libido—or worse, punishing him by having an affair—are short-term, self-destructive measures. Although there are couples who swear that an instance of infidelity turned out to be the catalyst for improving their marriage, it's a desperate last-ditch attempt that rarely succeeds. Yes, an affair may inform us of our hunger, our longing, of what's missing in our relationship, but ultimately broken trust and betrayal is too high a price to pay. It's far more profitable, and far more loving to ourselves and our mate, to rebuild or repair the bridges that connect us.

Of all the areas of self-nourishment, assessing the health of our sensuality and sexuality may be the touchiest (pun intended). Sex may not rate high on our list of priorities. Past sexual trauma or ongoing body-image issues may make this area difficult for us to look at and assess the importance of honesty. We may doubt the likelihood of improving our sexual relationship with our mate. How do we open up a conversation about having more sex, better sex, more intimate and satisfying sex without sounding critical or making him feel inadequate? Wouldn't it be

⌒

simpler to just accept this one area of our relationship for what it is?

In some cases, yes. Some of our relationships are strong enough for us to introduce this issue; others are too shaky, in which case we may choose to wait. But either way, it's important to clarify where *we're* at, both in terms of our own sexuality and the level of eroticism in our relationship.

The following exercise reveals ways in which you are in touch as well as ways in which you may need to pay more attention to your sensuality. Remember, sensuality is about opening all our senses, in order to feel more alive. Complete the following sentences:

I am most aware of my body when _____.

⌒

I am least aware of my body when _____.

⌒

My most developed sense is my _____.

⌒

One thing that helps me get more in touch is _____.

⌒

I feel most shut down physically when _____.

⌒

Being more sensual would feel _____.

This exercise may help you discover what gets in the way of experiencing your sensuality as well as what might enhance it. You may find out that stress, a negative body image, or relationship conflicts contribute to your estrangement from your physical self. You may find that soft music, warm baths, back rubs, naps, or eating raspberries stimulates your sensuality. Contemporary life is demanding; its emphasis is on external concerns rather than internal senses. For this reason, we have to make a concerted effort to become aware of the loveliness of our whole physical self and allow our sensuality to blossom. In the following space make a commitment to one way in which you can enhance your sensuality.

I will become more in touch with my sensuality by _____.

Now we turn to assessing our sexuality. How sexual we are depends in large part on our interest level, creativity, and willingness to be both responsive and responsible for taking initiative. The next exercise reveals to what degree we're turned on, turned off, or somewhere in between. Answer the following multiple-choice questions:

1. Most of the time I feel (a) hot and sizzling. (b) luke-warm. (c) About as sexy as a piece of leftover pizza.

2. I think about sex (a) constantly. (b) about once a week. (c) when I have to.

3. Masturbation is (a) my favorite recreational sport. (b) an occasional necessity. (c) deviant.

4. I have sexual fantasies (a) while I'm doing the dishes. (b) when nothing else works. (c) almost never.

5. The thought of dressing up in sexy lingerie makes me (a) wet. (b) curious. (c) embarrassed.

6. Being sexier or more sexual strikes me as (a) fabulous. (b) a good idea. (c) too much work.

If you mostly answered *a*'s, your sexuality is fairly hot and happening; mostly *b*'s means you run hot and cold, mostly *c*'s is a sign that your libido is waning and in need of recharging.

Now let's turn to assessing your current sexual relationship. This exercise helps you explore the quantity and quality of lovemaking with your partner. Complete the following sentences:

On a scale of 1 to 10 I'd rate our lovemaking as _____.

We make love on the average _____.

I'd describe our lovemaking as _____.

My partner would describe our lovemaking as _____.

He initiates _____.

I initiate _____.

The best part of making love with him is _____.

I'd like more _____.

What gets in the way is _____.

I'd describe my orgasms as _____.

∽

I fantasize about _____.

∽

I long for _____.

You may discover that your sexual relationship is steamy, fluctuates from not-so-great to wonderful, or is on autopilot and requires more attention and creativity. How willing are you to improve it? Some women need to make more time to focus on making love. Some need to let go of inhibitions. Some need to develop trust and lower barriers. Others need to be more specific in sharing their sexual desires and asking for what they want. Now make a commitment to revitalizing your sexual relationship. You may commit to increasing the frequency of lovemaking, being more playful, wild, or imaginative, showing your partner how to touch you, or telling him what would make you feel more trusting and receptive. Make a commitment that you're willing and able to keep.

I will open myself to eroticism by _____.

We should celebrate our sexuality for our own benefit. It is a way for us to be aware of our bodies and increase the pleasure they give us and the respect we have for them. It is also a direct source of incredible energy. But I assure you, our partners will welcome our efforts with open arms. The more comfortable and open we are, the more they will receive from us sexually and how could any man not like that! Now here's one area where men most definitely have something to teach us. A recent roundable magazine interview with men corroborated what we already know. Sex matters to men. In fact, all the men interviewed said "good sex" was the single most important ingredient in their intimate relationship. What a surprise. But let's not let that get in our way. Perhaps there's something we can learn about how and why sex is so very, very important to men.

What Men Can Teach Us About Sex

I took this opportunity to ask my lover why sex is such a big deal to men. He answered, with this disclaimer, "Obviously, I only speak for myself, not for all men everywhere—but for me, there's few things I'd rather do. Sex is the most powerful area of intimacy, for me at least, because it's so natural. I feel competent, masterful, at my best. I mean, you get in bed with a woman and it's not a struggle. You don't have to talk about it; you just do it like all the other animals in nature. We can be gentle or rough; we can give and take; we can be soft or hard . . . maybe because it's one area of our relationship that isn't hard."

Lucky for me. Some of our partners are able to combine sex and intimacy. Others are more compartmentalized; some men's sexual organs are far less connected to their heart. It's an old saw that, most men can have sex without love, while most women need love in order to feel sexual. I doubt it's that black and white across the board. While men *do* seem quite skilled at getting it up even when they're not feeling emotionally loving or close, their egos are extremely vulnerable when it comes to sex. They want to be wanted, and often, we're not very forthcoming in this area. We forget that men need to be told how sexy and attractive they are, that we want them, and what terrific lovers they are.

There are pros and cons to men's capacity for separating love and sex. Sometimes it's great to just have sex for the sake of sex. At times it feels great to throw off our clothes and wildly ravish each other in purely animal fashion. Prior to the AIDs epidemic, a fair number of women say that some of the best sexual encounters were spontaneous one-night encounters in which lust was a fair trade for love. There's all kinds of ways to be sexual: soft sex, hard sex, fast sex, slow sex, crazy sex, deep sex, giggly sex, and sex where we find ourselves weeping. Even phone sex can be fun. One of my favorite sexual memories is a long, erotic phone message on my recorder left by my lover from a hotel room. I saved it for three months. Men, who generally are more diverse and less emotionally tied to lovemaking than women are, can teach us a lot about recreational sex. And then there are the times when sex and love come together, when we crave the feel of his fingers stroking our neck, tender caresses, eye-to-eye, heart-to-heart, soul-to-soul communion.

What We Can Teach Men About Sex and Love

Although I've known women who'd rather have sex with a stranger than make love with the man they adore, most of us prefer intimate lovemaking. For me, kissing is the best part. I know I'm not alone here. That instant when he takes my face in his hands, stroking my forehead while gently, then passionately running his tongue over my lips, sends shivers down my spine.

Our hearts are connected by a thin silver thread to the center of our being. Our sexuality is both external and internal: the petals of our delicate flower at the doorway of a deep, dark cave. We like to be seduced, teased, and taken; a slow tango, the slightest stroke or circular motion makes us want more. Sometimes we like being handled roughly, our wrists firmly grasped in his larger hand, our legs confidently spread, his telling us explicitly what he wants to do and how he intends to do it.

But whether we prefer a sensitive lover, caveman, or some combination of the two, the key to our sexuality is knowing what we want, when we want it, and how we want it. Being cuddled leaves us cold if we'd rather be thrown on the bed; likewise, getting laid when we need to be loved vastly diminishes our libido. Just as our partner needs to respect the ways in which we're emotionally wired, we must attend to his need for both sexual reassurance and more varied appetite. Dancing well together requires timing, the ability to both lead and follow, and, most of all, a finely tuned sensitivity to each other's rhythm.

Dealing with Him

Unlike other areas of our relationship, most men like to hear where we're at with sex. They want and need to know how to please us, how to make lovemaking more frequent, more passionate, and more satisfying for both of us.

Of course, our partner may be more reluctant to hear about our dissatisfaction or negative feelings about sex. Telling him that he's missing the spot, moving too fast, or that emotional estrangement is getting in the way can be hard to hear. Proceed with caution. Sex is always a highly charged area. Be sure to let your lover know how much you love him and that your goal is for the two of you to have a great sex life. Tell him what he's doing right before explaining what's missing or could be better. Instead of saying, "You're not . . . ," say, "I really like it when you . . ." or "I'd love it if you'd . . ." Invite him to share his honest feelings as well. Find out what's working for him and be open to hearing what it would take for you to be closer to his perfect sexual fantasy.

If you are concerned that your relationship isn't ready for a candid dialogue about sex, hold off until you feel more trusting. If you're willing to have a go at this, you may discover a whole new way to enhance your love-making.

Nurturing Ourselves

We've seen how nourishing ourselves—through a healthy diet, exercise, sensuality, and sexuality—is a powerful gift of self-love. Just as we require nourishment in order to strengthen ourselves, we need nurturance in order to flourish and grow.

What does it mean to nurture? We often speak of nurturing our children by helping them develop to their fullest, or nurturing our garden by lovingly tending our tomatoes or tulips so that they may ripen and blossom. So, too, we need to nurture ourselves—by tending to our interests, expressing our creativity, enjoying nature and beauty, and cherishing both our solitude and our friendships.

Nurturing is a form of soul food. It is the spiritual counterpart to feeding our physical selves. Without nurturing we wither inside, whereas when we are well nurtured, we prosper and grow more fully into ourselves.

Lack of nurturing is another way in which we have neglected ourselves far too long. Many of us have consistently exhausted our energy in the service of nurturing our children, our partner, our friends, and our aging parents, often with little attention to our own needs. We may have put hobbies and interests on permanent hold, tabling our creative urges and postponing fulfilling our passions until our children are grown or our career is well established. And, as much as we value our friendships, we may barely find time in our demanding schedule for close friends or community involvements.

Loving ourselves means making time for what we care about, for that which truly matters, for that which pleases and fulfills us. Often, it's in midlife that we begin to pay attention to what nurtures us. As Gloria Steinem says in her wonderful book *Revolution from Within* when speaking of midlife, "For me, it's the belated ability to ask, 'What do I want to do?' as opposed to what needs doing."

As we mature and ripen, we see the importance of making time to pursue our interests and in the process, discover whole new aspects of ourselves. One woman, a psychotherapist who had always dreamed of playing the flute, bought herself a flute and lessons for her fortieth birthday. Another took up sky-diving. My friend Maggie, after talking about it for years, created a studio space in her home and devoted one afternoon a week to painting.

Sometimes it takes until midlife or beyond to believe that we deserve to follow our dreams, whether they include trekking through the Sahara Desert, learning French, or becoming a mother at forty-two after spending twenty years in the workforce. Most of our mothers wouldn't have considered taking off two nights a week for a yoga class or going off on a weekend women's retreat. We must break through the generational barrier and those words that ring in our ears, "But you have children . . . But what about your husband . . . ?" and all the other continuing, duty-filled messages that keep us from making our dream a reality.

Self-nurturing is a necessity. Here, as in all areas of

our lives, we need to assume full responsibility for giving ourselves what we need. There are many different ways to nurture ourselves, and a good place to start is to explore the areas of creativity, nature, beauty, retreat and replenishment, friendship and community.

Creativity

As food is to our bodies, creativity is to our souls. We are hungry to express our creativity, whether through belly dancing, cooking, writing poetry, parenting, gardening, or any number of other ways. Creativity is our gift—to ourselves and to the world. Creative expression is a way of sharing our authenticity, singing our own, unique song, giving flight to the dearest, most passionate part of our being.

Over the years I have taught writing, usually to individuals who don't think of themselves as "writers," people who are shy to assume such a pretentious moniker having never seen their name on the cover of a magazine or book. I believe everyone can write because everyone has words, their own words, which, when expressed purely and powerfully, can move and inspire. Some of the best writing I've ever had the privilege of sharing has come from the pens of so-called amateurs. They can write because they believe they have something to say.

I suspect the same is true in most aspects of artistic expression. We may never be virtuosos—but expressing creativity is not about how good we are, it's all about how doing it makes us feel good inside. I play the piano by ear, but my drawings look like a six-year-old's stick figures. We needn't be professional artists in order to free our creative spirit. We create for our own pleasure, for the sheer joy of fashioning something that satisfies us.

The same is true of every creative pursuit. We bake bread for the sensual pleasure of kneading dough, savoring the fragrance, biting into the first, moist slice. We plant begonias, run marathons, knit, sculpt, or strum the guitar to express our originality and explore a little more of who we really are.

Being creative makes us feel richer, more vital and alive. The more we express our creativity, the fuller we become and the more we have to give to our loved ones, especially our partner and children.

Mothering

Giving birth has been called the ultimate act of creation. This is not to say that it is the be-all and end-all of every woman's existence. I have complete respect for women who, for reasons of necessity or choice, have remained child free; there are many ways to be creative beyond parenting. However, motherhood is ripe with opportunities for expressing our creativity, far beyond the moment of birth.

Being a mother demands constant creativity. The phrase "Necessity is the mother of invention" perfectly describes a mother's never-ending need to come up with new and imaginative ways of dealing with her children. Our creativity is tested through every stage of motherhood. We make up lullabies to croon our babies to sleep, decorate cakes with peanut-butter faces to get our kindergartner to eat, create the perfect Halloween costume (one year Zoe insisted on being a chair!), help our teenager get an A on his creative-writing assignment, all the way to adulthood, when we may help find ingenious ways to help our grown children furnish their first apartment on a shoestring budget.

Those are just the practical aspects. We're challenged to be even more creative on the emotional-psychological front. We must find alternatives to disciplining our unruly three-year-old when time-out doesn't work, strategize ways to get the "monster" out from under our eight-year-old's bed, answer our adolescent's questions about sex with savvy and sensitivity, and guide our college-age child in finding the right career path.

Sometimes our children's questions catch us off guard. We're unsure of ourselves and feel as though we are in over our head. We don't always have an answer on the tip of our tongue, and that's when we need to take a deep breath and give it our best shot, employing all the wisdom and creativity we can muster.

A few years ago my daughter went through a period when she was irrationally terrified of my imminent death. "If something happened to you, I'd die," she sobbed. "No, you wouldn't. You would be very, very sad, but you would be okay," I said. I told her to close her eyes and imagine my death, funeral and all. I asked her to imagine who was with her, helping her through. I suggested that she picture the various people in her life who would be there for her if I was gone. When she opened her eyes, she told me that she knew, even if something happened to me, she would always have her dad; her brother; her honorary big sister, Miriam; her grandparents; Auntie Faith; Jason's mom, Char; and my dear friend Jill. The creative exercise of imagining my death was difficult for both of us, but it reassured my daughter that she'd never be alone.

The creative challenges of motherhood are endless. Sometimes they're fun, requiring artistry and imagination, other times we're forced to reckon with painfully difficult tasks. When we parent well, we experience deep and abiding satisfaction. It nurtures us to nurture our children. We give and give, and then, suddenly, they do something loving and enchanting. Our child presents us with a hand-picked dandelion, serves us chocolate-chip pancakes in bed, or wraps his arms around us and says the magical words that make it all worthwhile, "I love you, Mom."

Depending on our individual lifestyle, pressures, and personal motivations, we may or may not currently be expressing our creativity to the fullest. Now is a great time to make a commitment to find the right venue for your artistic expression. You might decide to take up needlepoint, plant tomatoes, join the church choir, or read one good novel a week. In the following space make a promise you can keep.

I will express my creativity by _____.

Nature

Nature is, perhaps, the most basic source of soulful replenishment. In our busy lives we forget to go outside and breathe the fresh air, notice the everchanging seasons, and the hundreds of colors of blue in the sky. Appreciating nature brings us closer to ourselves and makes us more aware of our connection with the universe. We gain perspective and get a sense of the bigger picture simply by sitting quietly beside a tree. We are steadied and grounded by the firm foundation of the earth beneath our feet. Vast stretches of ocean, and magnificent mountain ranges remind us of the infinite reaches of the cosmos.

One of the best things about nature is that it's readily available. We needn't become mountain climbers, birdwatchers, or long-distance runners to enjoy nature's abundance. Having been raised as a city kid, until recently my relationship to nature was limited to dining at outdoor cafés. A few years ago, my friend Bonnie and I went on a Zen writing retreat in southern Minnesota. Off we went with our tent, sleeping bags, cooler, and of course, my makeup and hair dryer. For five days we lived outdoors, cooking meals over a fire, finding our way with a flashlight to the ramshackle outhouse. I felt as if I'd found my true home. Needless to say, the mascara never made it within a foot of my eyelashes, I never unpacked the hair dryer, and within twenty-four hours I forgot about makeup and deadlines. I even had to remind myself to occasionally call my children. I returned home in a state of total serenity. The circles under my eyes had disappeared, and I was so mellow I sounded like a Moonie.

In whatever way you find to be more attuned to nature, make it more a part of your daily life. One woman chooses to walk outdoors each morning before work; another plans a family trip to the Amazon rain forest. Our commitment needn't be grand, as long as it helps us feel more in touch with all that nature has to give.

I will appreciate nature by _____.

Being outside, with the wind in our hair, the sun warming our face, replenishes us and reminds us of why we're here. The more replenished we feel, the more relaxed and open we are in our intimate relationship. We can appreciate nature solo or spend time outdoors with our mate. What matters is that we consciously try to find ways to fill ourselves with nature's power and beauty. It will help us to create beauty in all aspects of our lives.

Beauty

We nurture our spirit by surrounding ourselves with beauty. Simple day-to-day things like a breathtaking sunset or a bouquet of fresh irises on our kitchen table can awe and inspire us. Adorning our living space with objects of beauty reminds us of the finer things in life.

We don't need an expensive interior decorator to create a beautiful environment. All we need is an awareness of our own aesthetic and a few carefully placed treasures. Beauty is entirely subjective. What delights our eye may not have the same effect on others. My mother and several of my friends questioned my choice to paint my living room lavender and my bedroom aqua. But my lavender walls are intensely sensual, and each night I fall asleep in my bed I feel as if I'm floating in the bottom of the sea. Likewise, the exquisitely minimalistic Japanese print, paper blinds with their scene of an outdoor Paris café, and the perfectly balanced, custom-made mobile that I have suspended from the ceiling bring me a deep sense of peace and joy.

We immerse ourselves in beauty as a way of lavishing love on ourselves, as a way of giving ourselves the pleasure we deserve. Bring more beauty into your life by making this commitment.

I promise to _____.

Retreat and Ritual

Our bodies need rest; our souls require retreat. Going on retreat, whether we take fifteen minutes in the morning to mediate, pray before sleep, or participate in a more formal spiritual get away, is a precious act of self-love.

Our ordinary lives are rife with tension. Our muscles tighten in response to stress, and our psyches are on overload from life's endless barrage of information and noise.

Retreat reconnects us with the sacred nature of existence. When we physically and psychically remove ourselves from the noisy freeway of our day-to-day lives, we can hear our inner voice, we can feel the magical, mystical power that surrounds us. Our perspective sharpens, our purpose is more apparent, and our gratitude for the opportunities our lives provide deepens when we let down and allow ourselves to be immersed in holiness.

On the seventh day God rested. Why shouldn't we? Many religious practices include rest and retreat as essential aspects of spiritual growth. In the Jewish religion, Shabbat, the holy day, is regarded as a time of rest and reflection. Many observant Jews set aside the time, from sunset on Friday until sunset on Saturday, as a structured retreat. This period is spent studying, napping, conversing, praying, and sharing meals with family and friends. It's a lovely tradition and a way of stopping the world for twenty-four hours in order to turn inward and sanctify life.

A retreat can be a spiritual vacation or just a time to relax and renew our energy. Giving ourselves this much-needed break is the single most important element to replenishing the energy we expend. We need to replenish the well if we are to be as creative, giving, and loving as we wish to be. Rest and retreat aren't selfish or self-indulgent; they're required ingredients that allow us to be healthy and balanced.

Another way we spiritually nurture ourselves is through ritual, symbolic acts that add meaning to our lives. Most of us experience ritual through formal religious participation, such as taking communion, watching our child be confirmed or bar-mitzvahed, and saying our wedding vows.

But, ritual needn't be limited to the sphere of organized religion. We can enrich our lives by creating our own meaningful rituals to mark important passages and celebrate significant events. Many women in midlife are participating in candlelit "crone circles" to sanctify the shift into a new stage of womanhood. A woman I know planted a rosebush when each of her children were born. I honor each new book I write by kissing the final manuscript good-bye and good luck before sending it off to my editor.

Rituals can also be incorporated into our daily routine and can include simple things like keeping a journal, lighting candles, or tucking our children in with the same special words or favorite song before we tiptoe out of their bedroom. Most nights, just before falling asleep, Louis and I whisper, "Meet you on the dream train." Whether I've had a stressful day or a wonderful day, these words comfort me as I drift away.

Our form of retreat and our rituals change as we change and as different aspects of our lives take on deeper significance. Take a moment now to think about how you might integrate retreat and ritual into your life. If it seems right, make a commitment to do so in any way that will bring you greater peace and serenity.

I commit to _____.

Nurturing ourselves through creativity, nature, and spiritual retreat helps us to maintain our mental health. Although we try to pay attention to our mental health, our demanding lifestyles create an enormous amount of stress sometime to the point of feeling as if we're on the verge of a nervous breakdown.

Anxiety often leads to self-destructive behavior. We may suck down caffeine, binge on chocolate, or turn to recreational drugs as a way to escape and alleviate stress. We may be in the throes of or dangerously close to chemical dependency or addiction—a warning sign that our lives are seriously out of balance. Stress-related illness is on the rise, and today more women are suffering from heart disease, stomach ailments, chronic back ailments, and migraine headaches than ever before. At last count over six million Americans are taking Prozac or other antidepressants, over eighty percent of whom are women.

Something's got to give. Our mental health is a barometer of how well we're managing all the competing demands and responsibilities we face on a daily basis. Seeing a professional counselor is one helpful way to assess mental health; if nothing else, we get a whole hour to sit still and just talk about what's going on with ourselves. An ongoing support group is another good outlet for sharing feelings in a safe environment. We can all use a little help and some extra caring and encouragement.

We may also need more serious medical attention. My brief bout with depression convinced me of the physiological factor inherent in many cases of mental disorders. I owe my recovery to the right blend of rest, emotional support, antidepressants, and hard work.

I found the hardest part of my depression was admitting that I needed help and asking for it. As we become stronger and more self-possessed, we may fall into the "infallibility" trap. We set ourselves up by creating a facade, by convincing ourselves and others that we are doing fine, and if we're not, we'll tough out the rough times alone. But it takes great courage to expose our vulnerability and allow ourselves to be taken care of. Nurturing our mental health—by taking an occasional mental-health day, by seeking emotional support, by receiving help from professionals, friends, and relatives—is another way we love ourselves and allow ourselves to give.

There are many different ways to nurture our mental health. Doing so, again, requires our willingness to make it a priority. You might choose to create more balance in your life, join a support group, confide in a friend, or see a professional therapist. Any step is a step in the right direction, as long as you're ready to make a serious commitment to your mental health and well-being.

I commit to improve my mental health by _____.

And now for my favorite way of nurturing myself— through the one thing that gives me the greatest support, pleasure, and joy outside of my children and my partner—the company of women.

Early in the process of writing this book, I was talking to one of my close women friends about how to improve our intimate relationships. This forty-something advertising maven and mother of two, who has been married five years to a man she clearly adores, confided, "Actually, the secret of making my marriage work is women." By the conspiratorial tone of her admission, you'd have thought she was talking about a lesbian affair. But no. What she wanted me to know was, "I just like being around women more than men. I love my husband, but frankly, if I didn't have my women friends, I don't know if our marriage would survive."

One-time *New York Times* syndicated columnist Anna Quindlen has said, "Women are the glue that hold our day-to-day lives together." I'd go a bit further. For me, women are the reality check when I'm lost and confused, the mother I need when I'm tired of being so big, the encouraging "You're doing great!" when I'm shaky, the "I know you love him, but yes he's being a jerk" when I'm frustrated, the, oh, so gentle "Honey, let's think about this" when I'm about to do something I may live to regret. Not to mention, my women friends are the only ones I can totally trust to tell me whether or not the jeans fit, the haircut's okay, or the extra five pounds are visible to the human eye.

Sisterhood is as powerful as ever. There's no richer, more dependable source of support. The intimate women in our lives provide a different and equally profound love that complements what's possible with our partner.

There was a time not so long ago when the company of women was considered second to that of men for most of us. As teenagers we broke dates with our female friends to go out on a date with a boy, and many of us were taught to view women as competition instead of valued companions. My mother tells me that when she was seventeen, if you didn't have a date on Saturday night, you'd dim the lights and lower the blinds so no one would know. Personally, I wouldn't trade my women friends for all my Saturday night dates past and future.

We've come a long way, baby. Ask most women whom they turn to when they're down, whom they trust and choose as their confidants, and most will name their closest woman friend. At this point in our lives we happily pay a baby-sitter or schedule time with our partner around a precious night out with the "girls." On a recent trip to Negril, I met two women who make this tropical paradise an annual shared vacation. Both are attractive and successful in their careers; one is happily married, the other is in the early stages of a promising romance with an available single, straight male. But neither wanted to talk about men. Instead, they went on at length about the women's bookclub they founded four years ago. They raved about the other amazing seven women in the group. They all meet monthly, not only to discuss books, but to support each other through life's ups and downs.

In contrast to contemporary times, historically women played a huge role in one another's lives. In primitive times, we cooked around a fire with our sisters, aunts, nieces, grandmothers, mother, and friends while our brawny counterpart was off making the kill. In most cultures over time, women traditionally spent the majority of their time together, often separated from the men. It was understood that women belonged together in certain ritualized circumstances. Preparing food, bathing, menstruating, giving birth, and raising children were done within a close community of women. The phenomena of nuclear families is relatively recent, forcing us to forge friendships with women in other ways. As the majority of women have joined the workforce, we've lost the casual "over-the-fence" comraderie so many of our grandmothers relied on. If we've moved far away from our birth family, we miss having our mother, sisters, or aunts casually sharing the benefit of their experience on a daily basis.

We have to make a little more effort today to connect with other women, whether it's through friendship or community involvement. Many of us, even with relatives close-by, have a number of "chosen sisters" we consider as near and dear as family. I give thanks for my sister, Faith, every single day, but I'm also blessed to have several women friends who have seen me through my dark days as well as my finest moments. There are other women in my life who I consider role-models and mentors. As we get older, we understand the value of having an older woman we can learn from, someone who has come before us, seen more than we have, and is willing to show her wisdom. In the same spirit, we can become mentors to younger women, enjoying our well-earned status as "wise woman" even as we continue to learn and grow. In the past year, my friendship with a number of my daughter's teenage friends has given me great joy. They are my teachers as I am theirs.

In the following space, either give thanks for the women in your life or make a commitment to nurture yourself in this special way.

I am grateful for _____.
I commit to _____.

If you have a close woman friend, offer up a prayer of gratitude. If you count a number of women among your ongoing circle of love and support, consider yourself fortunate. If women haven't played a significant role in your life up until now, ponder the possibility of letting at least one offer you the unique love and nurturing women are capable of.

Finally, nurturing ourselves includes taking responsibility for cleaning up our act. There are areas of each of our lives that could use some attention, if not a total overhaul. We need to improve or update our appearance, straighten up our finances, get serious about our career, or throw out the fast-food cartons that have accumulated on the floor of our car. Another way we make a statement about how much or little we value ourselves is how we carry ourselves, how we care for our belongings, and how we present ourselves to others, all of which affects our self-image and has an impact on our relationship.

Cleaning Up Our Act

Have you ever noticed how when a woman is going through a separation or divorce, she suddenly seems to get her act together? She's refused to cut the long hair she's been clinging to since adolescence, and now she shows up with some cool, new bob. She's lost ten pounds, is lifting weights twice a week and taking Spanish classes, has signed up for a women's Outward Bound trip, and says she's never been happier, healthier, or more excited about her life.

Must we wait until it all falls apart before we get it together? Separation or divorce is a serious wake-up call that galvanizes us to clean up our act. The possibility of being single is both scary and highly motivating, and when we consider it, we figure we'd better get busy on self-improvement, both to make ourselves feel better and to up our chances of attracting another partner.

We may as well wake up right now. Let's get busy cleaning up our act for ourselves and for the partner to whom we're already committed. Taking more pride in our appearance, our attitude, the overall quality of our lives is another way of saying, I matter, my life matters, I value myself enough to make the most of what I have.

No matter how "together" we are or appear to be, each of us knows there are ways in which we've neglected ourselves or could use a little improvement. My secret shame is that I'm a horrible slob. I wouldn't think of going down the street to the SuperAmerica without putting on lipstick, but the inside of my purse looks like a bomb site, my car is a survivalist's dream, my dresser drawers are crammed with mismatched socks and empty cigarette packs. It would take a team of organizational experts to clean my closet, my desk, the piles of books, papers, and random correspondence in cardboard boxes in the corner of my office.

For me, cleaning up my act literally means cleaning up and ordering my living space which, as I edit the final version of this book, I am proud to say I have done just that. Some of us are careless about our appearance; some of us may procrastinate; others may need an attitude adjustment or more commitment to following through on our goals. Whatever way we need to get it together, whether it's throwing out the ten years' worth of junk we've been unwilling to part with, making more quality time with our children, or regularly balancing our checkbook, this is as good a time as any to start.

This is a cleansing process, and, like all cleansing processes, cleaning up our act feels great. The hardest part is starting, which is why it's important to decide on specific tasks and commit to following through. Making a list and checking it twice is always a good strategy. But the most important factor is our willingness to sift through the piles, face the messes, and make a real stab at making a tangible difference where it counts. As the famous Nike ad says, "Just do it." What are you willing to do? In the following space, make a real commitment to clean up your act.

I commit to _____.

We empower ourselves by becoming bigger and stronger. As we get serious about improving our health, our lifestyle, and any areas that need cleaning up, our self-esteem soars. As our sexuality awakens, we experience the satisfaction of intimate touch and erotic excitement. As we nurture our creativity, reconnect with nature, deepen our spirituality, and surround ourselves with dear friends, our foundation is strengthened and our well replenished. We feel better about ourselves, and we feel better prepared to deal with our partner, to act instead of react, and to make wise and discerning choices, which we now move on to explore.

7

The Fifth Leap:
CULTIVATING DISCERNMENT

It's ten o'clock at night and I overhear my daughter, Zoe, on the phone with her boyfriend Will. They're talking about her upcoming trip to Vermont to visit her other boyfriend, Avram, over spring break. She's desperately trying to get Will, her shy, sweet seventh-grade crush, to tell her how he feels. She patiently explains the importance of honest communication. She teases, goads, and cajoles. She tries multiple choices: Are you Angry? Scared? Jealous? She threatens to break up with him since he obviously doesn't care about her. He insists he "doesn't have any feelings about it" and that she should do whatever she wants. He'd give anything to be out on the baseball diamond instead of being stuck in this excruciating exchange. Her voice rising to fever pitch, she replies, "You must have SOME feelings about this!" I pause at her doorway, motion her to put him on hold, and offer my motherly wisdom with words based on dozens of similar conversations with grown-up versions of Will, "Give it up." She hangs up and curls up with me in bed, asking me why she isn't getting anywhere. "Because you're using the wrong tool," I explain, knowing from experience that her efforts to engage her boyfriend are simply and plainly the wrong tack.

The famed psychologist Abraham Maslow once said, "If your only tool is a hammer, you think everything is a nail." This quote aptly describes one of the primary challenges we face, the need to add new tools to our toolbox that will help us to build a better relationship.

Our "hammer" is engagement, which means directly involving our partner in processing our issues. If we're sad, angry, or confused, we automatically reach for our tried-and-true tool. We handle our feelings by trying to command our partner's attention and raise his level of emotional involvement.

Disengagement is an important alternative to dealing with relationship issues. Depending on the circumstances, disengagements can be equally effective, yet we return again and again to our familiar approach, even when it isn't getting us anywhere.

We're too smart to keep wasting our time by reaching for the wrong tool. It's like trying to open a can of tuna with a wrench or change a tire with a can opener. So why do we continually try to engage our mate instead of trying some other, more appropriate means?

We turn to engagement because engagement feels like intimacy. Anytime we have our partner's emotional attention—and it needn't be a positive connection—we experience a compelling feeling of intimate connection. Whether we're arguing or having a wonderfully stimulating conversation, whether we're revealing issues in therapy or making love, simply being engaged reassures us that our partner is involved. We opt for engagement even when it creates anxiety and estrangement. How many times have we initiated a conversation about difficult feelings and it only made us feel worse? How often do we prematurely insist on conflict resolution or express anger before we're ready to forgive? There are times to engage and times to find other, more useful ways of approaching relationship issues. The key is *discernment,* the ability to make wise and mindful choices. This is another important way of being loving toward ourselves and toward our partner. Beating our head against a wall, repeatedly using strategies that don't work, is self-destructive. Doing so demonstrates a lack of self-respect. We squander our energy and our resources by making choices that only add to our feelings of frustration and powerlessness.

Making Discerning Choices

We show our love for ourselves by making discerning choices that further our goals and serve both ourselves and our partner. Discernment means knowing when to engage and when to step back, when to initiate and when to exercise restraint, when to take the lead and when to assume a more receptive posture.

Let's say, for instance, we're intent on getting our husband to take a more active role in parenting. We'd like him to occasionally help our children with their homework, drive the school car pool once a week, and generally be more involved and available. We've asked dozens of times. We've explained why it's important and how much we'd appreciate his cooperation. We've brought it up in therapy, and we've been honest about how angry and disappointed we are each time he fails to come through. None of this has made the slightest bit of difference. Well, okay, there was the one time we had to go on business overnight and he covered the car pool. And he *did* spend three hours making an erupting volcano out of papier-mâché for our son's sixth-grade science fair, which he brings up each and every time we ask for his help. But, in the end, all our expressed desire, explanations, ultimatums, and emotional processing really haven't made a dent in his resistance. Obviously he just doesn't get it. Or he doesn't really want to get it. Either way, we don't get what we need.

Loving ourselves enables us to make choices that further our goals and serve both ourselves and our partner. We have the clarity to know what we feel and what we want in any given situation. We have the integrity to act according to our values. We have the self-possession to remain solid and safe whatever the outcome of our actions. All of these qualities strengthen our intention—to improve our relationship—and our actions—making discerning choices as to how best to approach our mate.

We can remain chronically frustrated by continuing to use limited tools. Or we can learn to make discerning choices in our relationship. Clearly it's time to try a different tack. Personal-growth guru Tony Robbins says, "People only change for one of two reasons: Inspiration or Desperation." Either can be powerfully motivating. The more frustrated and hopeless we feel, the more open we are to trying a radically different tack. Although we throw up our hands saying, "I give up. I've tried everything and nothing works," we haven't actually thrown in the towel. We're simply out of ideas, which is precisely the point at which we're able to envision something new.

That's where inspiration comes in. When we stretch our imagination, allowing ourselves to entertain previously unexplored options, we may suddenly glimpse the possibility of things getting better. Imagine what a blessed relief it could be to stop struggling, stop fighting, stop doing anything at all to change our mate into the man we want him to be. What if instead of spending our precious energy being consumed with anger and frustration, we removed ourselves enough to look at our mate and say, "I love him. At times he will disappoint me. But I can decide whether or not to get bent out of shape over what he does or doesn't do."

We think we've been doing exactly that by working on our relationship in therapy, by starting soul-searching intimacy talks, by helping our mate find himself so that we can figure out what he's truly capable of. However, these strategies won't give us the information we're in search of. Nor will the opposite approach succeed. Giving up, going on "relationship strike," or bailing out are opposite sides of the exact same coin. Deciding he's just not worth it effectively backs us into a corner where we have one of two lousy choices—resentment or resignation. Both keep us imprisoned, unable to move our relationship forward.

Beyond Codependence

"Codependence" has become a household word. Millions of women readily use it to describe the unhealthy and addictive pattern of being overly engaged in another person at the expense of ourselves. There are many reasons why codependence is rampant. Traditional female conditioning has trained women to be caretakers, to put others' needs ahead of our own. We have been taught to depend on men for approval, which means basing our value on external feedback rather than reaching deeply within for the source of our self-worth. And, as we've continued to be intimately involved with men who may be limited in their capacity to give, we've attempted to get what we need by focusing on helping them instead of figuring out how to get what we need.

Falling into patterns of codependency is understandable and may, on the surface, even seem like a loving attempt to maintain and build intimacy. But it's not. Scratch the surface and we discover anger, resentment, and a desperate need to control our partner's behavior. We don't become codependent because we're weak or manipulative—we do it in order to manage our feelings of powerlessness.

With the help of 12-step recovery groups, personal growth seminars, and professional counseling, many of us have developed healthier boundaries and are learning to disentangle our emotional energy from our mate and refocus it on ourselves. But sadly, this hasn't been true for everyone struggling with the problem. Over the past decade, countless women have tried to recover from codependency by overreacting in the opposite direction. We've lowered our expectations, withdrawn our affection, and come to the conclusion that giving up on getting what we want is the only way to survive in our relationship. This posture of *angry independence* is the other side of *codependence*. Both are motivated by anger and disappointment. Both keep us barricaded behind a wall of bitterness that prevents us from giving and receiving love.

Whether we adopt codependence or angry independence, we will find either strategy is a poor substitute for intimacy, as the following woman discovered. Paula, a thirty-nine-year-old personal trainer had recently celebrated her third wedding anniversary when she began to wonder if she was "settling" in her marriage to Mark, a man she describes as "sweet, good-looking, trustworthy, and affectionate." In many ways Paula and Mark's marriage worked as well or better than most. They were excellent coparents, had devised an equitable distribution of domestic chores, enjoyed each other's company and supported one another's career paths. But Paula wasn't happy—at least not enough of the time to keep her from worrying that her marriage was becoming stale, possibly even dying. "Everything's okay," said Paula, almost apologetically, as if her marriage had too much going for it to complain about little things, especially if you compared the "little things" to some of the "real" problems her friends faced in their relationships.

Mark was devoted, involved, and clearly in love with her, of that Paula was sure. But there were things that bothered her. He had a limited attention span, especially when it came to listening to Paula process her feelings. If something was on her mind, she wanted his undivided attention and support. After fifteen minutes or so of listening to her talk, he'd change the subject, flick on the TV, or start puttering around the house. Romantic gestures were few and far between. Early in their marriage, he often came home with a bouquet of flowers or her favorite cannoli from the corner deli. She had come to treasure how affectionate he was. Just walking from the kitchen to the living room, he hardly ever passed her without pausing to kiss her neck or stroke her hair. But things weren't the way they used to be. Although she hesitated to admit it, their sex life had gradually eroded. In the first few years they hadn't been able to keep their hands off each other and their lovemaking was hot. They'd go at it in the kitchen, the bathroom, wherever they happened to be. Now their lovemaking was lukewarm and routine, once a week, at most.

None of these seemed like horribly serious issues to Paula, yet they were slowly causing her to emotionally withdraw. She was "pretty sure" she was still in love. But the magic was fading and the passion dwindling. If the truth be told, Paula was secretly terrified that unless something happened fast, she might end up like her mother—who'd spent too many years in a seemingly love-less marriage—or, worse, like too many of her friends whom she felt were staying married for the wrong reasons. Paula looked around her and saw women married because they feared economic insecurity or were scared of permanently scarring their children or were frightened of being alone and starting over. Paula was painfully aware that she had joined the ranks of women staying in their relationship because they were scared of making the mistake of leaving prematurely or of giving up without being absolutely sure that the relationship was untenable.

Paula wanted her marriage to work. She vacillated between codependency and resignation, between getting in there and fighting (by trying to fix Mark) and giving up and trying to accept that, in her words, "This is all there is. I may as well just live with it." She had tried everything. She'd convinced Mark to attend weekly therapy sessions, which he reluctantly showed up for and sat through sullenly and silently. When asked to share his feelings, he'd say, "I'm just here because Paula thinks something's wrong with our marriage." She'd arranged a romantic weekend getaway, bought Mark a copy of Robert Bly's *Iron John,* lost fifteen pounds so she'd be more sexually alluring, none of which seemed to make a difference. Her attempts to move her relationship forward met with classic male resistance. Mark was defensive about her intimations that their marriage wasn't up to par. He resented the expense of therapy, which he threw in her face one month when they struggled to pay the gas bill. He couldn't hear her comments as concern and commitment. In fact, it seemed as if he couldn't hear her at all, as evidenced by a dialogue they regularly engaged in.

PAULA: There's something we need to talk about.

MARK: Can we talk about it later?

PAULA: I really think we should talk about it now.
MARK: Fine. What's wrong?
PAULA: Nothing's wrong. I just want to talk about how we're both feeling.
MARK: I'm feeling fine.
PAULA: I've been feeling like we're getting more distant, like something's missing in our relationship.
MARK: I don't know what you're talking about.
PAULA: Are you really that detached that you haven't noticed that we're drifting apart?
MARK: Why do you have to make up problems that don't exist?
PAULA: Forget it.

Paula and Mark were stuck in this unsatisfying loop. Each time they talked about it, Mark was more baffled and began to wonder if maybe something *was* wrong. Each time they got into it Paula became more convinced that she may as well shut up and give up. Neither could hear what the other was saying. That's because both were masking their real feelings behind rhetoric instead of saying what they meant. Let's revisit their conversation, this time looking at the subtext.

PAULA: I need to talk.
MARK: Oh, shit, not this again.
PAULA: I'm at my wits end. Either we talk now or I throw a major tantrum.
MARK: Fine. What is it NOW?
PAULA: I am scared and this conversation is making me more scared.
MARK: I'm perfectly happy.
PAULA: Maybe we're not in love anymore.
MARK: I don't know what you're talking about.
PAULA: Are you retarded?
MARK: Why do you keep ruining everything?
PAULA: I give up.

Each time Mark's response—or lack of—disappointed Paula, a part of her would give up. She'd emotionally withdraw. Instead of engaging Mark in intimate discussions, she'd do a 180 in the opposite direction. She'd virtually stop talking to Mark about anything that mattered. She'd make sarcastic comments aimed at getting him to notice she was mad. She'd go on temporary sexual strike, forgoing her silk teddy for a flannel nightie. She'd decide that once, and for all, she was done doing all the work in their relationship. If Mark didn't care, why the hell should she?

Giving up didn't serve Paula any more than getting in there and fighting did. Both approaches yielded the same result: Paula felt isolated and crummy, thought Mark was hopeless, and wondered if it even made sense to keep trying. But the most tragic part was that this self-destructive pattern kept Paula from being someone she could be proud of. Instead of the warm, funny, loving, and affectionate woman Mark had initially fallen in love with, Paula's essential sweetness was being eaten away by lingering resentment and seething rage. She hated the rigid walls she had erected in order to protect herself. The sound of her clipped, defensive voice made her shudder and wonder if she was turning into a hard, bitter woman incapable of love.

Presence: A Powerful Alternative

Paula was stuck in an inner battle between codependence and angry independence, teeter-tottering between engaging Mark in useless intimacy dialogues and retreating into bitterness and blame. She was stuck in a position of dependency. Codependence (manifested as engagement) depended on her husband's responding to her unsuccessful attempts to engage him. Angry independence left her waiting for him to make the next move. The ball was in his court and he wasn't playing. Either scenario made Paula feel more powerless to effect the changes she was after. Both approaches reinforced her dependency.

Control is an attempt to assuage our feelings of powerlessness. We exercise control anytime we try to manage our feelings by manipulating another person's behavior. We're anxious, so we start a "What are you feeling?" conversation in order to get him to delve into his feelings and pay attention to ours. We're angry, so we serve an ultimatum, throw a mini-tantrum, or take our ball and go home in order to shake him up and get him to see we mean business. These strategies can be effective in the short-term. He reluctantly agrees to talk about his feelings and listen to ours. He takes the bait and responds to our issues and complaints. But this is a stop-gap measure, a temporary way to humor us and keep the peace. Ultimately, it's a no-win situation in which nothing really shifts. For the moment, he's off the hook, but we're left in exactly the same position of powerlessness, which is why, after years of alternating between codependence and angry independence, we still aren't effecting positive changes in our relationship.

The alternative is *presence*. Being present is a powerful stance. When we're present, we stand on a foundation of clarity, integrity, and self-possession. We know what we want, we're true to ourselves, and we have the inner strength to make wise and discerning choices. We needn't frantically try to engage our mate in order to experience intimacy nor need we withdraw into bitterness, because we are deeply connected to ourselves. We have the presence of mind, of heart, and of spirit to meet our needs without controlling our mate.

Dependency, whether manifested as codependence or

angry independence, relies on methods of control, whereas presence requires power. Control and power feel similar because both involve initiative and action on our part. But, control masquerades as caring when, in fact, it's inherently disrespectful. There's nothing caring about putting ourselves in a position of dependency. Even if our strategy motivates our partner to be more forthcoming, it's a hollow victory. When he responds the way we want, we feel momentarily reassured and hopeful; when he doesn't, we feel frustrated and despair over our dwindling hope in any real possibility of change. If we get the result we want, we still end up feeling weak and manipulative, plus we question whether his responses are sincere, since they're the result of our pushing, rather than a genuine overture on his part.

We free ourselves from dependency by trading control for power, as exhibited in the following chart:

CONTROL is	POWER is
reactive	proactive
manipulative	respectful
rigid	flexible
urgent	patient
driven by fear	driven by love

Let's return to Paula and Mark once more to see how replacing power with control might improve her chances of success. We've seen Paula react to Mark's unresponsiveness by pushing harder. Instead, she might take a more proactive role by simply stating her feelings without expecting him to reciprocate. Rather than continuing to manipulate Mark by engaging him in conversations to elicit his feelings, it would be more respectful of Paula to accept his feelings and his way of expressing them. Paula rigidly persists in exclusively relying on one of two tools, engagement or angry independence. Being more flexible by trying new tools—for example, affection, humor, or backing off for a while—might give her more power in the situation. Paula's urgency exacerbates the problem. Instead of giving Mark the message that their marriage is on the rocks, she can practice patience and create a time line she can live with. Finally, she can explore the underlying fear that's driving her behavior instead of trying to get Mark to convince her that everything is all right.

Assuming power requires our willingness to break free of our existing patterns, to see the possibility of taking another route. Paula mistakenly believed she had reached a dead end. But dead ends are actually crossroads, as we've experienced in other aspects of our lives. For example, we're driving down the road trying to reach our destination. It may be a fairly familiar road, one we've taken before. We're on autopilot, cruising along without paying much attention. So it is in relationships. We may operate on cruise control for months, even years, driving along at a comfortable pace without planning our itinerary, consulting a map, or choosing to turn right or left. And then there are times when we are forced to consider which direction to follow. We may hit a dead end, a crossroads where we can't keep going and we can't turn either way. Now we're decidedly in the driver's seat. We have choices to make. We can put it in park and sit there for a while, which is fine as long as we're not in any hurry. We can turn around and reverse our path. Or we can rethink our position, our path, and, most important, our destination, perhaps even charting an entirely new and exciting course.

Like many of us, Paula is ready to navigate a new course. Her intentions are pure; she loves her husband and longs for them to repair their relationship. She has everything she needs to move forward; all she's missing are the right tools.

∽

Filling Our Toolbox

We need more tools if we are to improve our relationship. We choose engagement most often because we are comfortable and competent at it. But disengagement is another, equally valuable tool. The terms *detachment* or *letting go* are often used to describe the concept of disengagement. Letting go means stepping back and emotionally detaching from whatever struggle we're engaged in. It doesn't mean we stop caring about what happens. It doesn't mean we allow ourselves to be treated poorly or stop going after what we want and trying our best to build a healthy and satisfying relationship. Rather, it means being so strong, so whole, that we refuse to allow another human being to determine our fundamental sense of well-being. It means we don't waste our precious life energy on things that are beyond our control. It means reclaiming our power by choosing what is and isn't worth getting upset over and getting on with what truly matters in our lives.

Asking you to detach, to let go of trying to change your mate, may seem like asking you to give up. But just the opposite is true. As long as we keep trying to fix him, we can be assured he'll withdraw, resent our interference, or, at best, make a token effort to please us, which is guaranteed not to last. Letting go and letting him be, however, makes two things possible:

1. We give *him* the chance to be who he really is, give what he's got to give, and grow in whatever ways he's ready.
2. We get to stop being the "bad guy" and direct our energy and attention more productively.

In order to cultivate emotional detachment, we have to be willing to let go of our belief that our partner's behavior is the cause of our discontent. We think he's driving us crazy with his stubborn unwillingness to meet our needs. But he's just being who he is, for better or for worse, imperfect as that may be. Believe it or not, he's not trying to aggravate or annoy us. Half the time he doesn't even know what we're talking about, much less what to do about it. Meanwhile we create our own anguish by getting all worked up over how he does or doesn't come through.

We have an alternative. We can actively decide to stop struggling and suffering, to think of ourselves as a mature oak tree, deeply rooted in the ground, impervious to the pounding rain and the driving winds, bending yet never breaking beneath the forces of the elements. We can take a firm and abiding stance, believing in ourselves, our love, and our commitment to our relationship, even when our partner falls short of our ideal.

Lasting change comes only when we let go of trying to control the outcome, when we're willing to adjust our level of emotional attachment.

Surrender: The Balance Between Attachment and Detachment

Emotional detachment is extremely challenging because it involves a mind-boggling paradox. Attachment and detachment seem diametrically opposed, extreme opposite ends of a continuum. Love requires both. We're asked to throw ourselves, heart and soul, into loving our partner without expecting anything in return. We're asked to be completely involved in his health, interests, career, and growth without having a stake in the outcome. We're asked to be totally and completely devoted to him while relinquishing any and all claim.

Eastern philosophy has much to teach us about the paradox between attachment and detachment. Whereas traditional Christian belief advocates salvation through grace, the act of giving ourselves over to God or a higher power, and traditional Judaism counsels salvation through works, the act of attaining divinity through good words and deeds, Eastern philosophy offers the spiritual concept of surrender.

This seemingly esoteric concept is perfectly demonstrated in a Buddhist tradition in which monks spend years painstakingly creating a mandala—a beautifully designed puzzle—using millions of individual grains of sand. The endeavor takes years, each grain of sand is carefully placed with love and artistry in it's proper place in order to create a work of art. When the mandala is complete, it is instantly destroyed in one stunning sweep of a hand. This symbolic act depicts the temporal nature of our attachments and the power of surrender.

Every time we're faced with a situation over which we have little or no control, whether it's illness, our loved one's idiosyncrasies, or being snowed in by a blizzard, we have three choices: to fight, to give up, or to surrender.

Most of us have spent years choosing one of the first two options, fighting the battles in our relationships or giving up through chronic resentment or resignation. We've seen that neither works. Surrender offers us a new option, letting go of trying to control things and trusting they will turn out for the best, which is very hard to do.

Overcoming Our Resistance

Letting go is difficult because our emotions are intrinsically tied to our attachments. The more we love our mate, the more emotionally invested we are. We worry when he's upset, hurt when he's hurting, care about his feelings and the quality of his life. As we should. Our attachment is a reflection of our love up to the point when fear takes over, making it hard to let go.

Letting go is scary on several counts. We're afraid if we back off, he'll think everything's okay. We're afraid that lowering our vigilance will be interpreted as tacit permission for him to slack off and stop trying. We're afraid that without our constant effort, nothing will change and nothing will get better. We are afraid that our relationship will stay stuck and we'll just have to live with it, which leaves us right where we started—loving him, wanting him, but scared of settling for less than what we truly need.

Letting go is also difficult because we associate surrender with defeat. In war, this might be true. But in relationships between human beings, surrender means something entirely different. It's the spiritual part of letting go, accepting the reality that certain things are beyond our control *and* having faith that the outcome will be exactly as it should.

Life offers us countless opportunities to exercise surrender. It's what we do when our child has the flu and we wish we had the cure. It's what we do when we need to make the best of difficulties in the workplace. It's what we do when we go home for the holidays and find ourselves having the same argument with our parents that we had when we were fifteen.

As mothers we have a great deal of experience in surrendering. From the moment our child is born, we begin the process of letting go. On the one hand, we're asked to completely and totally love and invest in our children. At the same time we're asked to completely and totally allow them to follow their own path and fulfill their own destiny. It sounds contradictory, but it's not. In order for our children to grow up, they need our absolute attachment and our total detachment. Our unconditional love enables us to do both. Every mother who has ever put her five-year-old on the kindergarten bus, waved good-bye, and walked away with tears in her eyes and a prayer in her heart for his safe arrival, knows a lot about surrender. We let go because we must. We let go because our love exceeds our fear.

The same needs to happen in our relationship with our mate. This requires a leap of faith, a deeper belief that the universe is unfolding according to plan. When we're in the midst of difficulty—whether it's a heated dispute in our relationship or a serious life crisis—it's hard to let go and trust that everything will work out in time. Yet, in retrospect, those times are often the riches, most positive experiences of all.

When my father had his first heart bypass surgery, I was frantic and terrified. Ten years later I see that the surgery—however grueling—gave him a whole new life. Being hooked up to IVs in the hospital during my pregnancy infuriated me. I felt victimized and wondered why this was happening to me. Five years later when my first book, *Expecting Change: The Emotional Journey Through Pregnancy*, was published, I understood why I had needed to go through that seemingly unnecessary ordeal. In the midst of my divorce I felt as if the foundation of my life were crumbling. I was lost, hopeless, barely able to make it through the day. Today I am grateful for my marriage and equally grateful for its ending. The woman I am now and the love relationship I'm creating in the present would have been impossible without what came before.

In retrospect it's easy to have faith. What's tricky is trusting the present and the future without any guarantees. This is especially true in our intimate relationships.

Letting go and leaving our mate to his own devices feels risky. For example, if we stop pushing him to help more, what's the chance he'll volunteer? If we don't initiate "meaningful talks" about what's missing, what's the likelihood he'll surprise us and say: "Honey, what's going on with you?"

I wouldn't bet the mortgage on it. But nagging him isn't doing any good. We have a better chance of getting what we want by backing off and leaving him alone. If he doesn't have to constantly defend how oblivious he is, he just may notice that he has no clean socks and do something about it. If he stops having to prove that he isn't intimacy impaired, he may be more forthcoming about his feelings and far more interested in ours. He may not deliver on our time frame or in a style that suits us, but it's likely that the less we push, the more he'll give. The less we impose our agenda, the freer he is to actively participate in maintaining the relationship.

Where does this leave us? It leaves us with lots of time, energy, and attention to focus on ourselves. Understanding how letting go affects *you* is far more important than finding out how your mate is affected. Granted, he may be more forthcoming once you back off and give him more space to be who he is. But the biggest reason to let go is because of what *we* have to gain. What do we get when we detach and take a vacation from our traditional means of engaging with our mate?

First, detachment is essential to our emotional and physical health. Right now our relationship is slowly draining our life energy. Each time we struggle with anger and disappointment, each time we try another strategy, initiate another dialogue, propose another alternative, we tap our inner resources and draw on them often to the point of depletion. It's one of the reasons we're so weary and stressed out; our relationship has become a full-time job on top of all of our other incessant demands. Temporarily resigning from relationship management removes one very large pressure from our lives. It's a relief to stop trying to get him to change. It feels amazingly liberating to back off and stop investing our energy in *his* growth, which empowers us and broadens our choices.

This is especially true when our disengagement takes the form of giving ourselves space. When we're in the midst of engaging our partner, we don't see any exit doors. We don't see any way to escape the fracas; physically or psychically removing ourselves rarely enters our mind. We feel compelled to stay, even if we're not getting anywhere. But in reality we always have the option to leave, to take a time out until we're in a better frame of mind.

"It never occurred to me that I could walk out of the room," says Megan, who spent five years playing verbal Ping-Pong with her live-in boyfriend, Ivan, before figuring out that she could extricate herself by simply taking a time-out. "Now when we start arguing over the same old stuff without getting anywhere, I tell Ivan I've gone as far as I can go, and then I leave for a few hours until both of us calm down. Sometimes I go grocery shopping, or I lock myself in the bedroom and call my best friend. Getting some distance almost always puts a new light on the situation."

Perspective enables us to choose whether to remain engaged or to temporarily remove ourselves. We can take a serious and earnest approach or find humor in the situation. We can seek immediate resolution or exercise patience, assume an active role or do absolutely nothing for the moment.

Doing nothing is incredibly difficult, especially for women. We pride ourselves on effort and place little value on silence and inactivity. But doing nothing is an active choice, not a passive form of settling. Doing nothing takes a huge amount of trust and sends the message that we can patiently wait, that there is enough love and commitment for our relationship to endure conflict, that our partner may be more forthcoming if we step back and give it a little time.

Measures of Discernment

Having more tools at our disposal increases our range of choices. Using our tools appropriately gives us a way to measure and make right choices—ones that will move our relationship forward. How do we decide when to keep struggling and when to surrender, when to engage and when to let go, what's worth working on and what we should try to accept?

Here's how to evaluate whether our tools, strategies, and approach are making a difference. We can measure the effectiveness of any choices by asking ourselves these two questions:

1. Is it helping?
2. Is it serving myself, my partner, and my relationship?

First we assess our choices by assessing whether they're making a measurable impact on the quality of our relationship. Each of us has attempted change in specific areas. We may be actively involved in building better communication between ourselves and our mate. We may be focused on fostering greater support, intimacy, or partnership. We've employed various honorable strategies—sharing our feelings, initiating issue-oriented dialogues, or brainstorming ways of solving problems and resolving conflicts. At times we may have resorted to more desperate and less respectful measures—cajoling, threatening, or manipulating our mate. Sometimes our efforts pay off; other times they leave us more frustrated than ever.

We have more than enough experience to judge what works and what doesn't. Most of us have volumes of evidence that make it easy to predict our mate's responses and measure the effectiveness of our approach. We might know that he's more approachable on weekends than right after work or more responsive when we're gentler than when we come at him full force. Maybe humor, teasing, or affection is the best way to reach him.

Our experience has given us a ton of information on what timing, style, and attitude facilitates the most fruitful exchange. For instance, we may have learned from experience that when we begin a conversation by expressing a complaint, our partner immediately withdraws. After trying this three or four times, it's safe to assume that this approach will consistently elicit a predictably negative response. In contrast, we may have found that every time we begin a conversation with the words "I love you; there's something getting in the way of our love and I want to talk about it," our mate visibly softens and allows—perhaps, even welcomes—our input. This tells us we're on the right track.

We need to use our intelligence. Being smart is another way of being loving toward ourselves. How do we know if we're investing wisely? How do we intelligently discern whether or not our efforts are paying off?

By rationally measuring the effectiveness of our actions. We can break down the question of effectiveness into four areas: the importance of the issue, how long we've been working on it, how many strategies we've tried, and what the outcome of our efforts is.

First, we decide whether the issue at hand is *our* issue, *his* issue, or a *mutual* issue. Then, we assess the relative importance of the issue. Some issues are urgent, demanding immediate attention; others can wait. Some issues reflect bottom-line concerns, whereas others are more negotiable. It's essential to identify which issues are potential relationship-breakers versus issues which have less bearing on the long-term viability of our partnership.

Second, we need to examine the degree of time, energy, and attention spent on any particular issue. Working on an issue for a few weeks is far different from spending months or even years hammering away at the same nail. Clearly some issues, by their nature, are more complex and require more time and attention than others. But, generally speaking, the longer we've been at it without seeing tangible results, the more reason we have to reexamine whether or not our efforts are well spent.

Third, we must examine how many ways we've tackled the problem. Have we tried only one approach or have we attempted a variety of strategies? If we've used only one approach, we may need to try another. If, however, we've exhausted our options, it's time to consider resigning from the job.

Finally, we need to evaluate the outcome of our efforts. Are we seeing positive results or are we merely spinning our wheels? Are we getting some, part, or all of what we're after? Is our partner making moves in the right direction? Is our relationship noticably improving? This questionaire will help you answer these questions. In this first exercise, list the three main issues you're working on in your relationship.

1. _____.
2. _____.
3. _____.

Next to each entry write MY ISSUE, HIS ISSUE, or OUR ISSUE. Now, on a scale of 1 to 10, rate the importance of each issue. Then, on a scale of 1 to 10, rate the urgency of each issue.

Once you've rated each issue, answer the following questions for each:

1. How long have you been hammering away at it?
2. How many different strategies have you tried?
3. Have you seen any positive changes? Describe them.
4. Have you seen any negative results? Describe them.
5. How long have any outcomes lasted?

Completing this exercise reveals whether we're focusing on primary issues or less central concerns, how much time, attention, and creativity we've devoted to making changes, and how successful we've been.

Our rational assessment gives us much-needed information, and our emotional perspective provides a different measuring tool. Exploring our feelings is another way to explore whether we're making smart, sound choices. In order to see where you're at emotionally, review your answers to the above questionaire. Notice any feelings of sadness, fear, or anger. Likewise, notice feelings of relief, satisfaction, and optimism. How you feel is a good litmus test, a revealing measure of success. If you're trying every conceivable strategy to improve your relationship and still feel frustrated, that's a sign to change direction. If your efforts are making you feel happy and hopeful, there's every reason to stay the course.

What Men Can Teach Us About Being Rational

Measuring our relationship in rational terms by asking if our strategies are working is a somewhat foreign concept for women. We tend to think in emotional terms, using our left brain rather than our right brain, making decisions based on how we feel rather than what we think.

The majority of men, on the other hand, seem to be wired in the opposite way. We can be in the middle of the most emotionally laden exchange, overwhelmed with emotion while he sits there cool as a cucumber. All we want is to tell him how we're really feeling, maybe even let down and cry. He just wants to know what he's supposed to do.

Although we tend to take a superior attitude toward men's rational approach, making patronizing comments like "Men are emotionally impaired," there's something to be said for their excellence at rational problem-solving. There are times when we need to apply a clear, objective mind when looking at the issues in our relationship. We needn't ignore our feelings, we just need to think them through or put them in a drawer for a while.

What We Can Teach Men About Feelings

In turn, we have much to teach men about emotional expression. Most women are highly evolved in the area of feelings. Our emotions are easily accessible; we have the exquisite gift of making other people feel safe and comfortable expressing their feelings.

Sometimes women's emotional sophistication is derided. We're criticized for being overly emotional, even hysterical, when in truth, we just feel a compelling desire to be honest and candid with our emotions. It takes courage to share our feelings, and we must never allow anyone to imply that our need for emotional connection reflects weakness when, in fact, it's a way in which we're extremely strong.

Sometimes our capacity to express our feelings threatens our partner. He feels overwhelmed, on the spot, or just plain out of his league. But he both needs and deserves the benefit of our emotional wealth. Just as we can profit from studying his rational approach, following our lead in the emotional sphere can complement and enrich his range.

Measuring our efforts rationally and emotionally tells us whether we're making intelligent choices that yield results. But there's another, far different way to explore this issue. We've asked ourselves, Is what I'm doing working? Now, we turn our attention to different level of measurement by asking the question, Is what I'm doing serving myself, my partner, and our relationship?

The Concept of Service

Service is the sacred purpose of being in a relationship. We serve our partner through guidance, nurturing, and healing. It's love at its best; the manifestation of our noblest intentions and actions.

We serve our beloved in both profound acts of devotion and everyday gestures. These may not strike us as particularly selfless, but they are. Every once in a while we have the opportunity to perform obvious acts of heroism, such as nursing him through a crisis or truama, unselfishly supporting him economically or emotionally when he's down, loving him when he's least loveable, and holding him up when he falters or stumbles. But there are countless, more ordinary ways in which we serve our mate. Every provision of help, support, comfort, and wisdom, every unconditional expression of love, is an act of service.

Serving another human being is far more complex than we think because it requires unconditional love. Service comes easily and naturally when it meets our needs and satisfies our agendas. When it doesn't, we face a difficult choice—whom to put first, ourself or our mate?

This isn't always a clear choice. We may think we're doing something in our partner's best interest, but he may not see it the same way. For example, we may truly believe that our husband's depression would lift if he'd start working out. We urge him to exercise, offer to run with him each morning before work, and surprise him on his birthday with a health-club membership. We're convinced we're doing this because we love him and know what's best. And we may. We get angry when he says he'd rather have a new watch than a membership to the club. We're hurt when he agrees he needs exercise but hits the snooze button when the alarm goes off at six AM.

Our act of service has been rejected and for good reason. If we're to be really honest, regardless of our good intentions, we're serving our own agenda, not our mate's. We want him to shape up and get in shape so he'll stop being a depressed couch potato. He'd probably be wise to heed our advice, but it's only a gift if he's willing to receive it.

There's nothing wrong with wanting what we want for ourselves, as long as we're honest and aboveboard about whom we're serving in any particular situation. We get into trouble when we're fuzzy about our intentions or agendas. And, to complicate the matter, even when our intentions are pure and our only agenda is our partner's growth, an act of service is only an act of service if the person we're trying to serve is receptive to our offering.

But what if our gift is valuable and needed? It doesn't

matter. We can offer our service, but if it's refused, we must graciously accept that refusal. The following three extremely diverse examples illustrate this point:

An Orthodox rabbi visits a dying man on Rosh Hashanah—the Jewish New Year. The rabbi informs the dying man that he's going to honor the ancient observance of blowing a ram's horn, called a shofar. From his deathbed, the man begs to rabbi to leave. He wants to be left alone. The rabbi, in a fashion, agrees to the man's wishes. He pulls the hospital curtain, and from the other side, blows the shofar. He considers it a mitzvah, or good deed.

Second scenario: A woman, married for one year, asks her husband to get a chemical-dependency evaluation. Although he maintains a career and isn't particularly abusive, he drinks daily and sometimes gets a little out of control. His friends and relatives worry about his drinking. His wife insists it's for his own good and for the good of their marriage. He refuses. She gives him an ultimatum: Get help or get out.

Third scenario: My mother desperately wants me to quit smoking. She calls me daily imploring me to quit. She tells me I'm killing myself and hurting her grandchildren by exposing them to secondhand smoke. She sends articles about lung cancer and the latest statistics from the American Cancer Society. I tell her I'm an addict. I promise that when I quit, she'll be the first to know.

Each of these scenarios includes a loving, caring individual trying to perform an act of service. In each case, their words and deeds fall on deaf ears.

As hard as it is, loving sometimes means accepting our powerlessness to give what we have to give. It means watching our partner make wrong or harmful choices. There's nothing more painful than standing by silently while someone we love hurts himself, knowing that we could, if given the chance, change the coarse of his action. That's when love requires the most courage, fortitude, and trust. We have to maintain our faith in our relationship even if our partner seems to be slacking or lacking motivation. We have to respect his privilege to follow his own destiny, in his own way. We have to trust in his ability to do what's right, and we have to trust ourselves to be loving enough to allow him to do so.

It's not always easy to discern whether our choices are serving ourselves, our partner, and our relationship. Here, again, there are ways to measure the effectiveness of our actions; in this case, the ways involve intention rather than outcome. To do this exercise, choose one way in which you're trying to improve your relationship that includes an act of service. You might choose something like helping him further his career, enhancing his quality of life, or healing one of his significant relationships. Identify your intention by completing this sentence:

I lovingly want my partner to _____.

Once you've identified a specific goal, answer the following questions:

1. What do you want your partner to learn?
2. How do you want your partner to grow?
3. How do you hope to benefit?
4. How do you hope he will benefit?
5. How do you hope your relationship will benefit?

Honestly answering these questions reveals our best intentions along with our personal agendas. No matter how much we love our mate, there are times when we're self-serving, just as there are other times when we have his best interests at heart. As long as we're honest with ourselves, we can perform acts of service when we're feeling especially generous and loving. Other times it's perfectly okay to serve ourselves.

There is no such thing as a completely selfless act. Our seemingly altruistic deeds are almost always somewhat self-serving, which doesn't lessen their power. We make charitable contributions because we have a vested interest in a cause. We help an elderly person because it makes us feel good and because we know that someday, we too, will be old and frail and need someone's assistance. Even as mothers, perhaps the most selfless relationship, our feelings of price and satisfaction are rewards for a job well done.

Service needn't be selfless; in fact, it's better when both parties benefit. I recently understood this seeing it through the eyes of my twelve-year-old son, Evan. Participating in a monthly service project was required in his fifth-grade class. Each child was expected to choose an activity—raking leaves, bringing canned goods to a food shelf, volunteering at a nursing home—as a way to learn the importance of service. Evan refused. Not because he's selfish or unwilling to lend a hand, but because he disagreed with the principle. "How can it be service if someone's making me do it?" he asked. His question stopped me in my tracks. I wanted him to see the value of volunteering his time and energy, but I didn't want to force him to do something meaningless or insincere. Besides, I agreed with him. So I asked *him* a question, "Is there something you'd like to do for someone else that would make you feel good?" Evan decided to spend every Friday afternoon with his eighty-year-old Nanny Jane, which delighted her and gave him a chance to hang out with someone who adores him.

Performing acts of service that benefit both you and your mate is one of the best ways to make a lasting change in your relationship. Here are a few examples of

〜

what women have tried: attending a weekend couple's retreat, sharing a hobby or avocation, opening up a mutual savings account for a dream vacation, auditing a college class together, taking turns watching the children and giving the other the night off, quitting smoking or drinking together, and creating a mutual vision and carrying it through.

Now it's your turn. Take a moment to review the primary relationship issues you listed earlier in the chapter. Next review the loving intention you previously identified. Taking both of these into consideration, make a commitment to one act of service you're willing to engage in that has the potential to make a positive difference in both your and partner's life. You might try using these words:

I lovingly commit to _____.

As you make your commitment, be aware of your emotions. Feelings of excitement, pleasure, and anticipation are signs that your intentions are well placed and your actions can powerfully affect the quality of your relationship.

Dealing with Him

So what *about* him? Here we are knocking ourselves out with good intentions and noble deeds, and meanwhile he's not winning any medals for service beyond the call of duty. So what? In all fairness, he's not reading this book, you are. Besides, the point is to become the finest human beings we're capable of being, regardless of his behavior.

Meanwhile, here's an interesting way to deal with him:

Conduct a time-limited scientific experiment, and for whatever length of time feels right—two weeks, a month, six months—assume he's fine just the way he is.

Hold on!!! Before you slam shut this book screaming, "You want me to just accept him?!" remember the operative words are "time-limited" and "scientific." Putting a time frame around this keeps it from being open-ended. You needn't do this forever, just for whatever amount of time you're willing to give him the benefit of the doubt.

Likewise, remember this is a *scientific* experiment. A scientist conducts an experiment with an open, objective mind and the goal of gathering information. That's your task, to relinquish your preconceived notions of your partner—"he's useless around the house," "he's uneducable," "he'll never get it."—and open yourself to the possibility of change.

You might be pleasantly surprised. It's amazing how much our partner can change once we stop pushing him to meet our expectations. It can't hurt. And it just may help.

Making discerning choices gives us the necessary tools to improve our relationship. Yet even when we're clear about what we want, are filled with integrity and self-possession, and have the right tools at our disposal, we may still find something stopping us in our efforts to create the relationship we envision.

Every relationship is broken in some ways. Unresolved conflicts, repressed anger, and unhealed wounds are the obstacles to moving ahead. We must learn to forgive ourselves and our partner so that we can move our relationship from the past to the present, where acceptance frees us and offers infinite possibility.

8

The Sixth Leap:
CULTIVATING ACCEPTANCE

Remember Mollie, the infatuated teenager who described her first love as "perfect"? It lasted all of a week. One night she came over to talk; Dan had called to say he was thinking about leaving Harvard. He didn't like his roommate, no one understood him, and he didn't know what he wanted to do with the rest of his life. In short, he was having the requisite eighteen-year-old existential crisis and leaning on Mollie to tell him it was okay.

She wasn't okay with it at all. His whining, neediness, and self-absorbed introspection turned her off. Where was the funny, confident, "older man" she'd fallen in love with?

Unlike in our earlier conversation, this time I didn't spare Mollie my wisdom. I explained that real love means seeing someone as they are, both their amazing gifts and their disappointing flaws, the ways in which they're magnificent as well as the ways in which they're broken. And I told her the story of the Velveteen Rabbit. This lovely and wise parable is about an earnest bunny rabbit who's recently joined the other stuffed animals in a child's nursery. He is befriended by an old, bedraggled Skin Horse who teaches him about what it means to become Real. Says the Skin Horse, "It's a thing that happens to you. When a child loves you for a long, long time, not just to play with, but REALLY loves you, then you become Real. Generally, by the time you are Real, most of your hair has been loved off, and your eyes drop out and you get loose in the joints and very shabby. But these things don't matter at all, because once you are Real you can't be ugly, except to people who don't understand."

Loving an imperfect man means accepting him for who he is—a real human being who is bound to fall short of our expectations. We may not always like him, he may hurt us, disappoint us, and make us crazy in ways that demand and deserve our attention. But these are the risks of love, the inescapable casualties of making ourselves physically, emotionally, and spiritually open. We can't change *him*. We *can* take responsibility for our own happiness by cultivating acceptance and forgiveness.

The little things are easily overlooked, and they may accumulate over time. The big betrayals, hurtful words or deeds, and seemingly unforgivable transgressions may leave lasting wounds that inhibit or prohibit us from loving and accepting our mate.

In order to create the relationship we want, we must be willing to get real, to love and accept our partner both in spite of and because of his flaws. It's easy to love someone when they're at their best. But it takes enormous patience, compassion, and devotion to accept the real person beneath the facade. It means helping each other face our demons. It means being willing to stick around when our partner is being weak, difficult, or incapable of meeting our needs. And it means being willing to sort through and clean up the emotional messes that are getting in the way of loving each other.

Each of us, unless we're still unwrapping the wedding gifts, has some lingering hurts, unresolved conflicts, and unhealed wounds hanging in the air and polluting our relationship. Even if our partner is incredibly sensitive, he may have, in a moment of anger, said something cruel or reprehensible that's still ringing in our ears. We may have one or two recurrent arguments that never get settled. Our partner may have let us down or failed to support us when it really counted. And some of us have sustained deeper, festering wounds—neglect or abuse, the trauma of infidelity, screaming fights when we look at the man we love and wonder, "Who in the world is this raving maniac?" or, worse, "Can I really live with this man?"

These are good questions. Real questions. And they're the questions and doubts that keep our relationship from moving forward. All the clarity, integrity, self-possession, strength, and powers of discernment aren't sufficient ammunition when it comes to getting beyond hurt. Our partner may do things that displease us, we may compromise and negotiate and get tons of support, but healing hurt is another matter entirely.

We respond to emotional pain on an instinctual level. We can rationalize, intellectualize, and try to talk ourselves out of it, but our survival instinct will always win out. When we're frightened or hurt, our animal nature kicks in. Just as a turtle withdraws into its protective shell, we, too, retreat when in danger. The same raw instinct that makes us flee fire or brace our child with an outstretched arm when we slam on the car brakes is operative when we feel threatened. My cat Isabelle normally affectionate to the point of being annoying, hid under the couch and refused to let me within ten feet when her little sister Cleo dethroned her from her two-year reign as Queen of the Castle. It took three days before she again felt safe and secure and rubbed up against my leg, allowing me to pet her.

Where we've been bruised, we are tender to the touch. Having made ourselves vulnerable and then getting hurt, we hesitate to trust. *Heartbreak,* whether it results from harsh words or insensitive acts, is exactly what it sounds like—a break or tear in our heart. We can love, live with, and even improve our relationship with our partner, but until we repair the tears in our heart, we lack the trust required to build a true and lasting love affair.

Cultivating acceptance requires guts and graciousness. It involves a number of different tasks, including accepting our partner's past and ongoing transgressions, accepting that he may continue to disappoint us, and accepting his efforts and his apologies.

Just as we've cultivated the previous five qualities as a way to free and empower ourselves, cultivating acceptance is a profound act of self-love. It hurts to barricade ourselves in bitterness. Anger eats us up inside, poisoning our hearts like the bite of a venomous rattlesnake. Our guard goes up; we become cautious and mistrustful. Our natural instinct to be loving is tempered by our fear of being hurt. We erect a wall of armor around our authentic, loving selves.

Permeable Boundaries

The term *boundaries* is often used in contemporary psychology to describe the emotional space we create around us to keep ourselves safe. Abusive relationships demand impenetrable boundaries because we must stay within the walls of our fortress so as to avoid harm. Most relationships, even those with chronic or serious problems, don't require this degree of protection. Our boundaries are meant to maximize security, not to push our partner away.

Permeable boundaries allow us more latitude. We can be flexible, adjusting the amount of distance we place between ourselves and our partner according to our level of trust in any given situation. Sometimes we're forced to temporarily put up higher boundaries. For example, our husband yells at us in front of the children and we know the best move is to shut him off and leave the room. A few hours later, he calms down and says he's sorry, it won't happen again. It's obvious he's come to his senses, so we lower our defenses and tentatively accept his apology.

Choosing when to be vulnerable and when to protect ourselves empowers us. We act in accordance with our feelings instead of reacting to our partner's behavior. We decide when, how, and under what circumstances to expose ourselves.

It's common for women to have shaky boundaries and to make ourselves more vulnerable than we should. We're driven by our desire to accommodate. Often, our need to for love and approval overrides our survival instinct. In general women aren't nearly as wary and self-protective as men, which both enables us to form intimate connections and puts us squarely in the line of danger. We may reveal more of ourselves than is necessary; we may expose our vulnerability when we would be wise to play it closer to the vest.

A man who knows me well taught me an important lesson, the distinction between vulnerability and availability. After an emotional exchange during which I'd bared my soul, then retreated in embarrassment, he gently suggested that it wasn't necessary to spill my guts all the time. I indignantly informed that I was just more honest about my feelings. But he was right. We can be available to our partner without putting ourselves too far out on a limb. Emotional availability means being open and receptive, while emotional vulnerability means rawly exposing our nerve endings, which isn't always safe, necessary, or called for.

We make ourselves overly vulnerable because of our yearning to be as close as possible to our mate. In an ideal world, we would each be so healed that there would be no need to protect ourselves from hurt. We aren't quite there yet.

Love doesn't mean stripping away all of our defenses; we reveal our naked selves only when it's safe and it serves us.

We let down our barriers a little at a time. Disassembling the wall we've erected requires us to be very, very big. To accept, we must be willing to face our hurt and express it honestly and respectfully. To forgive, we must develop compassion and trust, which takes both time and a huge leap of faith. There are both losses and gains inherent in taking this courageous step. Most of us will readily admit that we hesitate to accept and forgive even when we know how much we'd have to gain. Why is it so hard to let go of our anger? Would we rather be right than reconcile our differences?

Holding On to Anger

Deep down we do want to let go of our anger and heal our pain. But on the surface, it often appears as if we're unwilling to do what it takes. Fear is our obstacle, and, in this case, our fear may be well founded. For starters, we're afraid that forgiveness translates into letting our partner slide. How many times have we been hurt or disappointed and agreed to give him another chance, only to go through the same ordeal again? How often have we been accused of creating the problem simply by virtue of bringing it up?

Many of us worry that forgiving our partner is tantamount to telling him everything's fine and that we are unwilling to tolerate unacceptable behavior. If we're going to make another stab at it, we want our partner to know we mean business. We're not interested in excuses or empty apologies meant to temporarily appease us. We want him to understand, acknowledge, and make sincere amends. Most of all, we want some solid assurance that he's willing to change.

There is no guarantee that bringing up difficult issues will result in resolution. Only you can decide whether you have sufficient faith in your partner's willingness and capacity to rise to the occasion. Here, fear takes the form of cynicism. Cynicism is the opposite of faith; it's a lack of optimism about the likelihood of a positive outcome. "What's the point?" "Men are inherently limited," "I guess this is as good as it gets," are expressions of cynicism.

Although cynicism may seem like the safest and most realistic stance, in fact, it's just another way we protect ourselves from being hurt. We don't want to get our hopes up, so we stuff our feelings and lower our expectations, resigning ourselves to what we call "reality." But "reality" is very subjective. We, in large part, limit or expand our reality by how far we're willing to go, by our willingness to embrace optimism and vision. If we truly believe that this is as good as it gets, that our partner has reached his upper limits of capability, then we set parameters around our relationship that predetermine its growth. If, on the other hand, we're willing to risk hurt by holding ourselves, our partner, and our relationship to a higher standard, we can alter both the present reality and future possibility.

We may also be afraid of disturbing the equilibrium or pushing our relationship into stormy waters. It may feel dangerous to bring up problems when our relationship is going along relatively smoothly and even more so if our relationship is tenuous or on the rocks. In either case, we fear introducing an element of uncertainty and intensity. If we tell him we're still angry about the time he suggested we'd look better if we lost ten pounds, will he accuse us of being oversensitive or, worse, suggest we go to Weight Watchers? If we let him know that we're still smarting over his insensitive comment about our parents, if we inform him that the reason we haven't wanted sex is that we're tired of being ignored out of bed, if we inform him that his repeated emotional outbursts have us wondering if we should see a marriage counselor, will he retaliate or fly into a rage?

Cultivating acceptance doesn't necessarily depend on his participation. Each of us has to determine whether our relationship is sturdy enough to survive what it takes to heal areas of pain and estrangement. Some of us are fortunate to have only a few, relatively minor issues to deal with; other relationships are fraught with a long history of hurt, which the partners may or may not be able to deal with mutually. But the real purpose of healing is to heal ourselves—to release our anger and reconcile our pain so that we can be more peaceful, open, and loving.

We may have experience in this department with our parents. In the process of counseling, we may have discovered ways in which we were hurt growing up. Our parents may have wittingly or unwittingly damaged our self-esteem through neglect, abuse, or simply from not knowing how to love and nurture us. While some of us have found it useful and healing to directly confront our parents, many of us have chosen to work out these issues on our own.

Some twenty years ago I dragged each of my parents to therapy. My father showed up twenty minutes late and had little to say. My mother's opening words were: "Wouldn't you be disappointed if you put a cake in the oven and it came out a pie?" Neither of them meant to hurt me; they simply weren't in a position to share in my therapeutic process. Twenty years later, I have come to see how very, very much they love me. The work was mine to do, and it paid off in an unexpected way. For my father's seventieth birthday I created a video of his life. I spent hours poring over some three hundred photographs, interviewing friends and relatives, and editing the project. My relationship with my father has always been somewhat tentative. I yearned for his affection and approval in ways with which he wasn't readily forthcoming. I never intended the video as a therapeutic exercise, rather I approached it as an artistic endeavor, creating a composite with all the love and respect I bring to any of my work. The video was a classic rags to riches story, a tribute spanning nearly three quarters of a century, revealing the full measure of my father's life. For the first time I saw him as a real person, separate and apart from myself; he was a self-made man whose achievements reflected honesty, humanity, and hard work. And I thanked God for having him in my life.

The healing I experienced could never have occurred in a therapist's office. To my dad, it's all psychobabble; for me, it was patently unsafe. But in my own style, in my own time, I found my way to forgiveness, acceptance, and love. The gift I gave my father turned out to be a gift I gave myself.

So it is with accepting and forgiving our partner.

Throughout this chapter there will be many strategies and suggestions for healing the past, both with our partner and on our own. Certain aspects of forgiveness may be appropriate to process with him; others are private or best handled with the support of a counselor. As always, the purpose is to cleanse and heal ourselves internally so that we're freer to give and receive love.

Finally, we may hold on to our anger because we don't want to give up our edge. Being right affords us a certain degree of power and superiority. As long as we're the injured party, we can justify our self-righteousness. But we're fooling ourselves. Holding on to anger for the sake of being right is just a cover for self-protection. It's another way in which control masquerades as power. Grasping for control gives us the illusion of being in charge, of doing what we can to make ourselves feel better. We may temporarily ease our distress, but there's no real profit in controlling our pain and fear through arrogance and one-upsmanship. Relinquishing control in favor of working out our problems is the only true path to self-empowerment.

Eventually, we tire of being right. Nothing is more annoying than engaging our partner in an honest attempt to face difficult issues and hearing him say, "You're right. I'm a jerk." Personally, this response leaves me cold. Great. You're a jerk. Now what? When we overcome our fear, we're far more interested in getting to the heart of the matter, which requires looking squarely at ourselves, at our own part in whatever unfinished business remains between ourselves and our partner.

The rewards of cultivating acceptance are abundant. Letting go of our anger is a process of unburdening, getting the proverbial "load off our chest," only in this case, we lighten our heart. Releasing anger cleanses our spirit and frees our heart energy. Forgiveness softens us, penetrating the tough protection that keeps out the hurt. We become more open, available, and receptive to what's beautiful and joyous in our relationship. Holding on to anger keeps us focused on what's missing; healing our wounds makes us keenly aware of our appreciation and gratitude for everything we have.

When we let go of anger, we are able to move beyond the past. *A Course of Miracles* teaches that our fear exists only in the past and the future. This is a tough but extremely important concept to grasp. It means that every time we experience fear, we are actually remembering what has hurt us in the past or extrapolating what could harm us in the future. For example, six months after the excruciating exchange during which Louis had announced that he wasn't sure he was in love with me, I found myself angry at him over some relatively minor slight. I was under a lot of stress at the time, and I lashed out at Louis, accusing him of not being committed enough. Although objectively speaking he was being quite loving and attentive, I flailed around, testing him and trying to get him to prove his devotion once and for all.

Clearly, this was *my* issue, not his. I thought about the current status of our relationship and knew that I felt happy and secure. I tried to figure out what I needed in order to be reassured and immediately realized my fear was lodged in the past, frozen in that traumatizing exchange on my front porch. Then I fast-forwarded and saw how that incident terrified me about the future: What if it happened again? If I let myself believe in our love, would I end up betrayed and abandoned? This awareness clarified what I needed to do. I told Louis I was still angry and hurt and asked him to apologize one more time.

Then I asked him for whatever reassurance he could give me as to his future commitment. He went as far as he could, and the rest was a matter of my own confidence that our present relationship was worth risking the possibility that our love might not endure.

Healing brings us up to current reality, which is where our actual relationship exists and where change can take place. We relinquish our past anger and hurt in order to live in the present and be fully aware of the immediate challenges our relationship presents right now, today. We heal the past to prevent projecting worst-case, fear-based scenarios that may never materialize. Our relationship is dynamic, and we will continue to wrestle with new and different issues that arise. But to whatever degree we repair the past, we can approach the present with the attitude that "the past is the past; the future is yet to come; but today's a brand new day, a fresh start in which my relationship can be as wonderful as I'm willing to imagine and create."

Overcoming Our Resistance

Learning to vent our anger is a front-burner issue for many of us, as evidenced by the huge success of Harriet Lerner's book, *The Dance of Anger,* which offered much-needed permission for women to take off our kid gloves and start getting real about our rage. But we need to see the potential profit in order to take this risk. There has to be something in it for us.

Just knowing how much we have to gain through acceptance and forgiveness may not be enough motivation to push through our anger. There's a very good reason for this. Many of us have already tried, perhaps repeatedly, to express our anger to our mate in hopes of healing. We may have thought long and hard, some with the help of a skilled therapist, to name our anger and build up the courage to express it. We may have worked hard at pinpointing the exact origins of our anger in order to be specific about its source and not overwhelm our mate. We may have practiced or role-played, putting our feelings into the right words to avoid pushing him away.

If our efforts have failed or proved disappointing, we may understandably dread going through this exercise again. It's exhausting and heart-wrenching, and each time around we grow more defeated.

Going underground, militantly submerging our anger isn't the answer. When we do this, we just end up hiding in a self-made fallout shelter, gathering our provisions, and waiting for the bomb to fall. This is a very defensive approach.

Instead, we have to get in there and fight if that's what it takes. For many women, expressing anger is scary, even terrifying. As little girls we were taught to control our temper; as young women we were told that "nice girls" were docile, conciliatory, and forgiving. I can count on one hand the times I've actually ever gotten overtly mad. I get sad. I get scared. But rarely do I let it all out. Here's where we can learn from our younger sisters. Last summer I took my daughter and three friends on a camping trip. We roared down country roads, rock music blaring, digging being "four bitchy girls in a convertible." I was amazed by how much had changed since I was a teenager. *Submissive* would be the last word to describe this bunch. They were tough, out-there, bursting with attitude, confidence, and self-worth. They said "piss" not "pee," they fought like cats and dogs and made up with hugs and kisses; they even had me screaming "Fuck you" at the top of my lungs instead of "processing" a recent argument with Louis. I returned home determined to recover some of the guts and glory I'd lost somewhere along the way.

It's time for each of us to trade submissiveness for assertiveness, to let go of our fear of making waves in favor of the possibility of making peace. At this point in our path we've cultivated the necessary qualities to meet this challenge. We bring clarity, integrity, self-possession, strength, and the powers of discernment to the task before us. We need to employ each of these qualities in order to become effective peacemakers, which starts with getting clear about the issues that are up for healing.

Opening Our Wounds

Each of us has our personal laundry list of anger, disappointment, and hurt we've accumulated over time. It's essential to attend to these injuries if we hope to repair our relationship. The healing process can be broken down into four distinct steps:

1. Identifying the source of our anger.
2. Honestly revealing our feelings.
3. Asking for what we need.
4. Deciding how far we're willing to go.

Our past attempts at getting our anger out may have backfired because of failure in one of these four areas. Let's begin by exploring step one, identifying the source of our anger. The clarity we've gained will be useful in this stage of the process.

Identifying the Source of Our Anger

We may find it difficult to be specific about the source of our anger, to put our finger on exactly what's bothering us and separate past hurt from present issues. It's common, especially if we've been with the same partner for an extended period, for all our hurt to get jumbled up into one huge, angry wad. Some specific incidents may stand out more than others, but, for the most part, we're just plain mad. Cumulative injuries have piled up, and recent conflicts add insult to injury. For this reason, it's important to identify exactly which of our complaints are at the heart of our ongoing inability to accept and forgive him.

Getting clear is helpful in two ways: we deal with what's really on our mind, and we don't overwhelm our partner with a huge onslaught of accusations that he can't possibly process and respond to. Separating past and present issues makes the process of forgiveness more manageable.

Lumping old hurts and current conflicts into one big pile makes it hard to home in on and repair our feelings. An argument we have this morning may restimulate an old, unresolved anger. The littlest, most innocuous slight or hurtful gesture becomes monumental when it reactivates something traumatic we've stuffed or stored away. We're in bed with the flu, his mother calls, asks how we are, he says, "Fine," and suddenly we're furious about how he dealt with our extreme PMS five years ago when he kept telling us to stop making such a federal case out of it. He mentions that an unscheduled business trip will make it impossible to attend our son's school concert, and we get enraged over his having been out of town when we went into labor. When a minor interchange in the present triggers a huge emotional response, it's because the past and present have merged. We're suddenly right back there, flooded with intense pain that has yet to be healed, making it impossible for us to keep the immediate issue in perspective. Separating our pile of anger into "old junk" and "new junk" enables us to clean up the past and deal with the present in the present.

Keeping things separate helps us be concrete and specific should we decide to tell our partner what's on our mind. If we bombard him with years' worth of suppressed anger—with words like, "I've been pissed at you since our first child was born," or "I can come up with a million reasons why I'm mad at you"—we sabotage ourselves and put him on the defensive. It's like waging full-scale warfare and launching cruise missiles instead of attempting a negotiated settlement. If we can isolate specific issues and express them one by one, we stand a far better chance of reconciling our pain and having a productive exchange with our partner.

In order to clarify the source of your anger, start by listing unresolved issues that continue to come up for you. It doesn't matter whether they happened ten years ago or two weeks ago, as long as they continue to weigh heavily on your heart and mind. Whether or not he's apologized is also irrelevant; anything you're still angry or hurt about is worth examining. Try not to censor your feelings or tell yourself that these are "little things" that shouldn't bother you. Your pain is real, and you needn't justify it to yourself or anyone else. Identify old junk and unfinished business that's still hanging in the air by completing the following sentence as many times as you need to:

I still haven't let go of the time he _____.

This exercise may reveal old wounds we're unaware of or hesitant to delve into. Remember, this is just step one. Identifying the source of our anger doesn't mean we have to do anything about it. For now it's enough to just be

———————— ✍ ————————

aware of lingering pain that may be getting in the way of recovering trust and intimacy in our relationship.

Now we move on to exploring current issues. Depending on the emotional health of our relationship, we may experience frustration over little things that bug us, recurrent areas of conflict, or serious, ongoing destructive behavior or acts of abuse.

One woman's husband is chronically late, which infuriates her and makes her feel as if she's not particularly important to him. Another woman finds herself repeatedly struggling over her boyfriend's alcohol use; he goes for one or two weeks without drinking, then goes on a bender, becoming sloppy, sarcastic, and unpleasant to be with.

These are qualitatively different levels of injury. It's one thing to get irritated when he keeps bringing home two-percent when we've asked for skim milk; it's quite another to deal with his stubborn refusal to find a job, confront an addiction, or stop treating us like a piece of furniture. But whether our ongoing issues fall into the category of minor irritations, chronic issues, or potentially relationship-breaking behavior, naming them is the first step in dealing with them. In the following space, identify your existing issues in each of these three categories.

The little stuff that bugs me is _____.

✍

The chronic issues that trouble me are _____.

✍

The potentially long-term problems that make me question my willingness to remain in this relationship are

_____.

There is another, qualitatively different aspect of anger, which springs from our disappointment about those shortcomings of our partner's that don't directly inflict harm. There is a difference between our anger at things our partner has done *to* us, versus things *about* him we don't like or find difficult to accept.

This is a subtle but important distinction. We may be angry at our mate for reneging on agreements, hurting us, or acting out in any number of inappropriate or destructive ways. In contrast, there may be aspects of his personality or character we simply wish were different. For example, we may harbor disappointment over the fact that our partner isn't as smart, handy, financially successful, or sexually masterful as we would like. We may resent that he is a workaholic, a control freak, a football fanatic, or that he'd rather putter in his garden than go with us to garage sales. We may be frustrated that he's passive instead of bold, homely instead of a hunk, laid-back instead of exciting.

Every single one of us has trouble accepting certain things about her mate. It is up to us to decide what we can live with and whether or not we can reconcile the gap between who we wish he was and who he actually is.

I can't help but wonder how this dynamic operated in arranged marriages. In past eras it was customary, and still is today in certain cultures, for marital partners to be chosen by parents or community elders. Although this anachronistic custom seems unromantic and unrealistic—imagine living with someone you aren't in love with—it's instructive when it comes to understanding the concept of acceptance. There's something to be said for learning to live with the little things that bother us about our mate. Most of the arranged marriages seem to have survived. Whether they thrived, whether these couples were happy and fulfilled, is beyond my ability to evaluate. But one thing's for sure; for better or worse, these couples managed to find a way to live together, to develop mutual respect and love one another, over many, many years.

There's a lesson here. We can suffer over the ways in which our partner's imperfections annoy and anger us, or we can let go and learn to live with him and love him despite his limitations.

Something else we must come to terms with is any anger we have toward ourselves and our own behavior. It's painful to face our own feelings of shame, remorse, and regret. We have all, at one time or another, acted in ways we're not particularly proud of. No one reaches adulthood with a clean slate. As human beings, we're all subject to falling short of our highest expectations. At times we're impatient, intolerant, snotty, or downright mean. We may have fits of temper, bouts of depression, or simply so much stress that we find ourselves disintegrating into Sybil or the "bad seed." Usually our partner gets the brunt of our abominable behavior because of his proximity, as retribution, and, sometimes, because we know he's the one person who will forgive us for it.

It's harder to forgive ourselves. If we're to heal our relationship, we have to be willing to get in there and get our hands dirty. We have to clean up our part of the mess in order to accept and forgive our partner and ourselves.

We need to forgive ourselves both for mistreating our partner and for allowing ourselves to be mistreated. We may be angry at ourselves for the times we've been remote, mean, impatient, and unwilling to hear his side. We may be angry at ourselves for the times we've let ourselves be hurt, or disrespected. Just as we ultimately need to love our partner enough to forgive him, we need to love ourselves enough to say, "I'm human. I've made mistakes and I'm willing to make amends to myself and my partner." There's no sin in having failed; the only sin is in refusing to face our mistakes and grant forgiveness.

The integrity we've cultivated supports us in facing our mistakes and forgiving ourselves. Being true to ourselves also means being honest about the ways in which we haven't lived up to our own standards. This next exercise identifies the ways in which you have let yourself down by allowing yourself to be mistreated or mistreating your mate. Complete the following two sentences:

I'm angry at myself for allowing my partner to _____.

I'm angry at myself for hurting my partner by _____.

Honestly facing our mistakes is useful on two counts. First, we notice the ways in which we have failed to be our best selves. Second, we develop the humility required to put our anger at our partner into perspective. Both of these insights make it easier to heal our wounds and approach our partner in a spirit of forgiveness.

Expressing our Feelings

Knowing what's underneath our pain is both a comfort and a challenge. Clarity brings a certain measure of relief; it's reassuring to know we're not crazy, that there are tangible reasons driving our anger. In turn, this insight can be scary and overwhelming. It's painful to open our wounds, and it's tempting to sweep difficult issues under the carpet instead of directly confronting them.

Here's where timing is essential. We may be ready to

face some things and not so ready to face others. It took four years before my anger over my divorce from Gary surfaced. Up until then I was numb, all my energy was consumed in caring for my children and rebuilding the shattered pieces of my life. Our daughter's bat-mitzvah—a coming-of-age ceremony that poignantly symbolized the fruits of our union—evoked torrents of rage within me over buried feelings of betrayal that I had toward my ex-husband.

We feel our feelings when we're ready to feel them, a little at a time, peeling back the layers and slowly exposing our wounds. Healing doesn't usually occur in a linear fashion. More often, it comes in stages. We don't face everything at once or dive in deeper than we feel is safe. We test the temperature, gingerly putting in our big toe, then one foot at a time until we're ready to submerge ourselves.

Once we dive in and identify our wounds, we may or may not be prepared to take the next step which is honestly expressing our feelings. The movement from intellectual insight to emotional revelation requires a different set of tools. Thinking about past and current pain isn't quite as difficult as letting ourselves experience their emotional impact. For example, we may be able and willing to describe in detail how our partner missed our son's first birthday party without being ready to acknowledge the extent of our hurt. Letting ourselves feel the emotional intensity of our wounds may seem like an unnecessary exercise in inflicting pain on ourselves. But it is yet another act of self-love. The expression "No pain, no gain" comes to mind in this regard. Suppressing, repressing, or pushing down our emotions prevents the healing that frees and empowers us. Releasing our feelings allows the tension in our body to relax and our heart to open.

Most of us have had the experience of feeling tense and out-of-sorts. We're on the verge of tears, but we don't know what's bothering us, and then something opens the floodgates, such as understanding words from a friend, being held by our lover, or listening to a sentimental song. Suddenly the tears stream down our face like a summer rainstorm. Our shoulders drop, our fist unclenches, the free-floating anxiety melts as our pain moves lower and into the center of our being.

This process is similar to what happens during childbirth. Our instinct is to fight the pain and intensity of labor through steely determination, distractive techniques, and a survival mentality. When we surrender by allowing the waves of contractions to wash over us, we work with instead of against the forces of nature. Acts of healing are similar to the creative process of childbirth. We labor long and hard to push forth the pain in order to give birth to a freer, more whole and healed self.

Just as we prepare for childbirth, we must prepare ourselves for the process of honestly expressing our feelings in regard to old and current wounds. Expressing our feelings must be done with great care, for our own safety and the safety of our relationship.

Whether or not we are ready to share our feelings with our partner, we begin by acknowledging them to ourselves. We may do this internally, writing our feelings in a journal, or verbally, by confiding in a counselor or friend. The goal at this stage is to identify our feelings so that we can express them effectively.

The next exercise is designed to help you get more in touch with your feelings. To do this exercise, first return to the past injuries you identified earlier in this chapter.

———————————— ᗡ ————————————

Reread what you wrote, or think about what you thought, then complete this sentence:

These past injuries have left me feeling _____

_____.

You may be surprised by the nature or intensity of the feelings revealed. For instance, you may know that you haven't forgiven your husband for his behavior at that awful dinner party when he criticized you in front of friends, but you may not realize how furious you still are. You may remember perfectly the time he sided with your mother against you, but without your knowing that his lack of loyalty has caused in you a permanent breech of trust. Likewise, we may not be fully aware of our internal emotional pain due to ongoing unresolved issues in our relationship. We may think we're doing fine when in reality we are just coping, all the while carrying around a substantial amount of anger and pain. Take a moment now to look again at the three categories of current and ongoing issues you identified previously. Next to each category, express your feelings by completing these sentences:

The little things you do to bug me make me feel _____

_____.

ᗡ

The chronic issues in our relationship make me feel ____

_____.

ᗡ

Our serious long-term problems make me feel _____

_____.

This exercise, too, may uncover surprising feelings. You may say and believe that your partner's sarcasm is nothing more than an annoying habit when, in fact, it makes you emotionally retreat. You may be resigned to the fact that your mate refuses to join you in marital counseling, but deep down it shakes your belief in his love and commitment. You may genuinely believe that you can live with your partner's belittling comments in front of others when, actually, you feel ashamed and humiliated each time he does it. Acknowledging our feelings may hurt, but the hurt is there whether or not we bring it to the surface. It creates an invisible wall between us and our mates.

Burying our feelings is unfair to both our partner and to ourselves. Until we are willing to face them, we can't move ahead in our efforts to heal, which involves taking the next step, expressing our feelings to our mate.

Should You or Shouldn't You?

There are pros and cons to sharing our feelings with our partner. On the positive side, by expressing them we stand a chance of healing wounds and giving him the opportunity to make amends. But we also take the risk of making ourselves vulnerable and incurring his defensiveness or wrath. Whether or not to air your feelings is a judgment call only you can make. The two considerations in making this judgment are your level of willingness and your level of trust.

We may be skeptical about taking this next step. We may have been burned too many times to get near the flame. We may need more time to nurse our wounds and assess the extent of the emotional damage. Sometimes we need to sulk, rage, or make a list of EVERY REASON

HE DOESN'T DESERVE ME before we're ready to reveal our feelings. That's okay. Approaching our partner before we're ready to "deal" guarantees failure. When we do that, there's a good chance that we will point fingers, make accusations, and condemn instead of calmly communicating. We get to choose when we're prepared to express our feelings in good faith and we should think carefully before choosing to do so.

Our capacity to envision a positive outcome also influences our willingness to engage emotionally with our partners. Again, we take a calculated risk in assessing whether or not our efforts will pay off. There's no way to avoid the tension and discomfort that arises when we bring up past hurt. Peacemaking is an emotionally arduous endeavor; angry words and hard feelings usually precede the breakthrough required to build a better relationship. If we can envision the likelihood that expressing our anger will ultimately break down barriers and promote peace, we're naturally more willing to move forward. If we're convinced that there's no profit in putting our feelings on the line, we're more likely to keep our emotions in check.

Our level of willingness to say how we really feel also depends on whether we're ready to relinquish some of the perks inherent in holding on to our anger. Although we may genuinely want to accept and forgive, we stand to lose something in the process. Our status as injured party provides us with a certain amount of security and superiority. In this scenario, the roles are set; we're the victim, he's the defendant.

Our anger also justifies our feelings of superiority. We feel entitled to bask in our belief that we are far more loving and evolved, that we operate on a much higher level than our mate is capable of. Although this is nothing to be proud of, we may taunt him, patronize him, or just quietly enjoy watching him squirm. It's not that we're out for blood; we may have just been hurt one too many times to lay down our sword.

Then there's the "drama factor." We create drama as a way to counter feelings of emptiness. Many of us create drama and crisis to fill the void we experience as a result of unfulfilled lives or unsatisfying relationships. Unresolved conflicts are a dependable source of ongoing drama. Whether we suffer in silence, have screaming fights, or spend hours on the phone updating our best friend on the latest report from the front, the exhilaration of embattlement fuels our estrangement.

Trading drama for the possibility of detente requires our willingness to give up our urgency. If we are to sit down at the negotiating table, it must be with the clear vision and quiet confidence of a peacemaker. As Indira Gandhi said, "It's impossible to shake hands with clenched fists." Lasting reconciliation comes only when we give up militancy in favor of moderation.

Our level of willingness is directly affected by our level of trust. Even if the timing is right, even if we're ready to put aside our superiority and urgency, our lack of trust still may get in the way. The more hurt we've experienced, the less willing we are to trust. The wall we erect to protect ourselves is in direct proportion to the magnitude of our wounds. In order to honestly express our anger we must feel adequately assured that we can trust our partner to handle our feelings with care. We must feel secure that revealing ourselves won't leave us overly vulnerable.

How do we know whether we can safely express our anger to our mate? We determine our level of safety by evaluating two equally important issues: how much we can safely trust partner, and how much we can trust ourselves.

In the case of the first issue, this is another instance in which we can base our decision on experience. We have a pretty good idea of how much we can safely trust our partner based on how he's reacted in similar situations. If our past attempts to bring up difficult issues have been met with judgment, resistance, or offensive tactics, we need to prepare ourselves for a similar response. If our overtures have been treated with consideration and respect, we can safely assume that we're on solid ground.

Determining our level of trust is a calculated risk. Human beings tend to behave habitually, yet we also have the capacity to amaze one another. It's prudent to use past experience as a way to gauge our partner's response, but it's also important to give him a bit of the benefit of the doubt.

This is a good time to put on your white coat, go into your laboratory, and see how the scientific experiment you started earlier in the book is coming along. Let's return for a moment to the research you were conducting. The purpose of the experiment was to see what happened if you temporarily refrained from working on your partner so that you could concentrate on yourself. As objectively as you can, try to determine how your commitment to cultivating various qualities you desire in yourself has made a difference in your partner. Has he become more supportive, more forthcoming, more emotionally available? Has he demonstrated greater interest in his own personal growth or been more actively involved in improving your relationship?

As a result of our shifted focus, some of us may notice a marked difference in our partner's attitude toward himself, toward us, and toward our relationship. Others may see little, if any, discernable change. Any measurable improvement can make a real difference in how our partner responds to new initiatives on our part. We can take his past history into account, while factoring in the real possibility that he, too, is ready to make a leap.

In regard to the second issue, before expressing our anger, we must know that we can trust ourselves to communicate our feelings honestly and articulately. We should have a solid working plan and a fallback position and think how best we can find the right balance between making ourselves vulnerable and keeping ourselves safe as we express our anger.

Trusting ourselves is almost more essential than trusting our partner. I once heard actor Fred Rogers being interviewed on television by Tom Snyder. I was surprised to see that he was the same as his media character, Mister Rogers. He had the same soft-spoken rhythmic cadence, the same gentle, self-deprecating style, the same old cardigan sweater he wore on the show. At one point in the interview, Snyder rather snidely said, "Some viewers worry that you're giving children the impression that every neighborhood is as safe as Mister Rogers' neighborhood when, in fact, there are dangerous elements all around." Mr. Rogers smiled and softly said, "We don't have to teach our children *who* to trust; we have to teach them how to trust *themselves.*"

Trusting ourselves means knowing how far we can venture beyond our comfort zone without endangering ourselves. It means creating appropriate boundaries and knowing ourselves well enough, using our increasing powers of discernment, to make wise and judicious choices. It means having the self-possession and inner strength to protect ourselves regardless of the outcome.

We have more power than we think in affecting the outcome of any interaction with our partner. How we approach our partner—whether we bludgeon him with our anger or express it respectfully—will dramatically affect his response. The biggest error we make is in stuffing away our anger for weeks, months, or years until it erupts in a volcanic rage. There are better, more effective ways to communicate. We productively express our anger by carefully following four steps:

1. Rehearsing.
2. Setting the stage.
3. Expressing our positive intentions.
4. Communicating respectfully.

Four Steps to Productively Expressing Anger

I'm a big believer in the value of trial runs. Expressing anger can involve a wide range of emotion. Even when we feel ready to be calm and conciliatory, we may find ourselves trembling, crying, or lashing out in anger and frustration. A trial run tempers our intensity and diminishes the likelihood that we'll "lose it." Role-playing is a useful technique. We can rehearse beforehand by practicing what we're planning to say in front of a mirror or with a coach. A "dress rehearsal" helps us smooth out the edges, anticipate unforeseen contingencies, and steady ourselves so that we are less freaked out when we actually sit down and talk to our partner.

Setting the stage, the second step, involves carefully designing the right time and best atmosphere for a productive dialogue. Timing is everything. Knowing when our mate is likely to be most receptive stacks the odds in our favor. Cornering him the minute he comes home from work or when he's hungry, crabby, distracted, or about to fall asleep isn't prudent. How would you feel if he started a serious conversation just as you were running out the door, fifteen minutes late to an appointment?

Most of us are cognizant of the best times to approach

our partner. He may be most open and relaxed on the weekends, after finishing a nice meal, or in the dreamy state following lovemaking. Don't let your urgency dictate your timing; take your cues from your partner, trusting that the right timing will enhance his receptivity.

Likewise, it's worth your while to create a conducive atmosphere. Here again, past experience is a good guide. In the past, have your best conversations with your partner taken place over dinner, on walks, on the porch swing, in bed? Bringing up difficult issues in public places or while driving in rush-hour traffic may well spell disaster. Do what works, even if it means waiting until the right opportunity presents itself. This is *not* being manipulative; it's being smart and savvy.

The third step, knowing our positive intention—what we hope to accomplish—keeps us focused on our mission. Expressing anger isn't merely a release; it's the difficult but necessary prelude to making peace. What do we hope to accomplish? We must ask ourselves are we intent on clearing the air, putting the past to rest, becoming allies instead of adversaries, or finding a way to have a deeper, more trusting connection?

If our only objective is to vent our anger and punish our partner, our estrangement will grow. If reconciliation is our goal, we can make a lasting difference in the quality of our relationship, but we must keep this in mind and not let it get lost as we are letting off steam.

Our anger may cloud our awareness of our best intention. We can get in touch with it by delving beneath our anger to our feelings of longing. On the surface, we may feel angry or disappointed. But, if we go deeper, into the depths of our heart, we discover our yearning for tenderness, understanding, and intimacy. We long for our bitterness to dissolve, for an opening to reach out to our beloved and feel safe within his arms.

What is your positive intention? What do you hope to gain by honestly expressing your anger to your mate? With an awareness of your longing, complete the following sentence:

My positive intention is to _____

_____.

Fourth, we need to fine-tune our approach. In the past, we may have sabotaged ourselves by dumping our anger instead of expressing it respectfully. We blame our partner with words such as "You did" instead of taking responsibility by saying, "I feel." This is not about shifting blame from our mate to ourselves. It is about owning our feelings. By owning our feelings we aren't admitting culpability, we're simply framing the issue under discussion in a new, more empowering way.

Most of us are trapped in a traditional anger exchange, which keeps us victimized instead of enabling us to get beyond our pain. Typically, we express our anger through these two messages: Here's how you've hurt me, and what are you going to do to fix it? Although we may genuinely believe that our partner has behaved poorly and we may be right, this form of communication keeps us stuck. As long as we blame him, we put the ball in his court. For example, if we say, "You screwed up by forgetting my birthday," he can defend himself, rationalize away his lousy memory, or even go on the offensive, reminding us of the time we cut short our anniversary because of a conflict at work. If, however, we say, "I'm angry that you forgot my birthday," we're simply describing our feelings. Our feelings are our feelings, whether or not he agrees with them. Whereas his actions may be debatable or open for interpretation, the reality of our feelings is unassailable.

Saying how we feel, instead of telling him what a creep he's been, is also a strategic move. When we accuse our partner of having done something "bad," even if he's willing to cop to it, he's likely to experience shame. Like most human beings, he may cover his shame with defensive or offensive tactics. In contrast, if we tell him how we feel, especially if we're being genuine and open, he's likely to respond in a more sympathetic fashion. Although it may not be his first response, his natural inclination may be to reach out to us with comfort and reassurance, even if he feels guilty or responsible.

Stating our positive intention is another way we can express our feelings respectfully and foster goodwill. When we start right out with "You really blew it," our partner immediately braces himself and begins formulating his defense. Prefacing our feelings with "I want to tell you this because I'm hoping it will ease the tension between us," or "I want to clear up that argument we had so that we can get along better," diffuses his defensiveness and increases his capacity to hear what we have to say. Doing so also helps us stay on the high road. Our anger is placed within a context of conciliation, and we remember the positive reasons that motivated us to initiate this potentially difficult exchange.

Honoring Our Needs

Just as we typically express our anger by saying, "You did," instead of, "I feel," we usually follow our accusatory statement with some version of "What are you going to do about it?" Once again, we make our partner responsible for fixing our pain, which he may or may not be able to do. Saying, "Here's what I want," is a better, more empowering alternative.

One of the reasons our attempts at expressing anger have failed is that we've forgotten to factor *our* needs into the equation. It's not enough to say how we feel; we also have to *ask* for what we want and need in order for our anger to dissipate. I often hear women say, "I've told him how angry I am, but it didn't make me feel any better." They didn't feel better because they went only halfway; they expressed their feelings without asking for what they needed.

Let's return to the forgotten birthday example I mentioned above. As we've seen, saying, "I'm angry that you forgot my birthday," instead of, "You screwed up by forgetting my birthday," enables us to express our feelings without blaming our partner. Likewise, instead of saying, "How are you planning to make it up to me?" we need to figure out what would help. Do you want him to apologize? Do you want him to acknowledge how you were hurt by his actions? Would flowers or a gift make a difference? How about asking him to plan a special, albeit belated, dinner out to celebrate your birthday? Only we know what will alleviate our anger and pain. And we *must* be willing to ask for it.

Our anger remains until we honor our need for acknowledgment and amends-making. But we don't always see what we need to get beyond our anger and forgive our partner, as is illustrated in Alexis's story.

Alexis met Michael when she was just out of college and married him a few years later. She knew Michael's history well. His father had died in a car accident when he was twelve, and his mother had remarried, this time to a man who treated Michael and his sisters poorly. Although Alexis and Michael's marriage worked well in many ways, he often fell into regular bouts of depression. During these episodes he'd sulk around the house, filled with self-pity. At these times, he also had little interest in

Alexis, his libido would plummet, and he was very difficult to live with. For years, Alexis was extremely sympathetic. She'd listen for hours as Michael told her of his feelings of abandonment. She'd suggest therapy and try to be patient, knowing how deeply he was hurt and how much he needed to relive his memories to be rid of their pain. But after eight years of feeling pulled into Michael's ongoing drama and accommodating herself to his mood swings, something in her snapped. She insisted he get help and he did. Michael sought counseling and, with intensive therapy and a weekly support group, began to find ways to climb out of his despair and be more present in the relationship.

Alexis was relieved and grateful. Although she'd never given up hope, for the first time she felt optimistic about their future. Michael was doing great, their marriage was noticeably improved, but there was still something missing. It didn't take long for Alexis to figure out what it was. After years of focusing on Michael's feelings and helping him heal, she needed *her* feelings to be attended to. The experience had taken a toll on her, which she needed to have acknowledged in order to fully appreciate the strides that they had made together. She thought about what would help. An apology was in order, but equally important was her desire for Michael to really "get" how her life and her level of trust had been affected by his behavior.

Alexis carefully set the stage, choosing a time when she knew Michael was relaxed and could hear what she had to say. She made a point of telling him how excited she was about the changes he'd made and how much better she felt in their marriage, but that she needed something in order to continue to be fully committed. She asked him to listen as she honestly shared how difficult it had been for her over the years. She also asked him to recognize and acknowledge the ways in which his actions had directly or inadvertently hurt her and to genuinely make amends.

Closure is only possible when we state both our feelings and our needs. Return one last time to the previous lists you made identifying the source of your anger. Next to each item, add what it would take for you to forgive your mate. You may discover that what you want is for him to give you more time to get over your anger, or you may want him to demonstrate some tangible evidence of change—a letter of apology or a vow to honestly examine what's caused him to treat you poorly. Knowing what will help and asking for it accomplishes these two goals: We acknowledge and honor our needs, and we give our mate the opportunity to repair the situation.

Sometimes forgiveness is less complicated than we think. When it really comes down to it, what we're looking for is a heartfelt apology, and a genuine statement of intent. These ten "magic" words can work miracles: "I'm sorry. What can I do to make it better?" I'm amazed at how difficult it is for human beings to say "I'm sorry." We struggle so to utter these simple words that can do more healing than three hours of rehashing every hurt we've ever inflicted on one another. "I'm sorry" seems too easy. But we confuse simplicity with superficiality. A token apology *is* an easy way out. However, a genuine apology is a powerful admission of personal responsibility and can be the first huge step toward building a better relationship.

We may not realize the healing power of making a sincere inquiry into what our partner needs in order to relinquish anger. Asking "What can I do to make it better?" is an immensely respectful approach. We acknowledge the need for action and express our intent to repair our wrongdoing. In effect, we say, "I know that I've hurt you and I'm prepared to do whatever it takes to regain your trust."

Sometimes what we need is contingent on him. Other times what we need must come from ourselves. For example, following an angry torrent of words, we may need our partner to admit he was out of control and promise to get a handle on his emotions. On the other hand, we may need him to back off and give us some space until we're open to his overtures. And in many cases, we need time in order to see whether significant change has occurred.

Try to be clear and specific in communicating exactly what's needed. Men tend to be very concrete and are more capable of responding to our requests when given tangible, behavioral examples. Saying "I just need to trust you again," or "I just want to feel like you love and care about me," doesn't give him the sort or style of information he's best suited to hear. Telling him "A back rub would help," or "When you're mad, I want you to count to ten before you talk to me," provides him with a doable suggestion.

And what if he says "No," or "It isn't my fault," or, my personal favorite, "You're making a mountain out of a molehill"? This is a good time to remember that we have control over only ourselves. We can do our level best to express our feelings and needs carefully and respectfully. But how our partner will receive our anger and our request for healing is unpredictable. Ideally, he'll listen intently, apologize profusely, reassure us that it won't happen again, and we'll kiss and make up. More realistically, he may bend a little, make small stabs at looking at his part in causing our anger, or resist by pushing us away. Even if we rehearse, set the stage, and say our lines perfectly and respectfully, we can't completely orchestrate the scene. We are dealing with another person and entering very emotional and unpredictable territory here. We *can*, however, create the best possible scenario by anticipating some of the obstacles to his receptivity.

Dealing with Him

We can influence our partner's receptivity by taking his feelings into account. What will make him more open to hearing our feelings and responding to our needs? The single most important element here is usually our willingness to admit our own mistakes. When we make him the bad guy, the villain, or the designated patient, he naturally fights back. If we share the ways in which we, too, have faltered, we reveal our imperfections and level the playing field. If we take responsibility for our less-than-perfect behavior and welcome him to express his feelings as well, we make an important shift toward fostering equality and mutual respect.

Acknowledging the good things, what's working well in our relationship, also softens the blow. It's unfair to focus strictly on the problems; it gives our mate a skewed perception and makes him feel as if he can't do anything right. When we frame our complaints within the context of the whole picture, some things are good, while others need attention, we create a setting in which healing can occur.

Noticing and remarking on progress is another way to put difficult issues into perspective. We tend to be more aware of our partner's failure to meet our expectations than the steps he's taken in the right direction. This is another area in which we need to monitor our urgency. If we're insistent on total change, right this minute, our partner can't possibly deliver. It takes time and practice to alter habitual behavioral patterns. If we extend our time line and applaud any and all signs of progress, we give our partner the message that our relationship is worthy of our long-term investment—*as long* as we see tangible effort.

Touching can also go a long, long way. Words can heal, but they can also polarize and push each of us further into our corner. When we get trapped into intellectually debating who's right and who's wrong, there's only so far we can go. Taking his hand or embracing him at the right moment can be a miraculous healing agent, beyond what words can say.

As regards to the "mountain out of a molehill" refrain, it's best to gently hold our ground. This line of attack can be disarming. We're easily hooked by accusations of taking things too seriously. There's a time to persevere and a time to let go and stop working through our feelings. Here is another way in which we have something to learn from men.

What Men Can Teach Us About Keeping It Simple

I've come to the conclusion that men are relatively simple. Not stupid, shallow, or ignorant, just relatively less emotionally complex than women and therefore have a simpler approach to a relationship. I can't count how many times I've engaged a boyfriend, husband, or lover in an intimate conversation in which I'm prepared to spend hours, weeks if necessary, coming to terms. Fifteen minutes into it, they've reached their limit. They start yawning or staring off into space or getting frustrated over having to keep covering the same ground. I can see I've lost them.

Here's how to get them back. Get to the point as quickly as possible. Although we may want to give them an in-depth and elaborate map of our emotional terrain, all they need is an exact reading of our position. Even though we may need to go on and on about various ways to improve the situation, all they're looking for is a simple answer to the question, How can I fix it?

Whereas we are geared toward processing emotions, men are geared toward concrete action. Each has its place. When we go on at length, we reach a point of diminishing returns. But if we don't delve fully enough into our issues, we risk putting a Band-Aid on them without cleaning out the wound. Some women are more skilled at sensing their partner's attention span and tolerance for listening and talking about feelings than others. Some men are more patient and interested in excavating the hidden crevices of emotional intercourse than others. We need to find the right balance between getting into the issues we want to discuss and getting through it with our particular partner.

What We Can Teach Men About Emotional Processing

While men may have the market cornered on keeping it simple, most women are willing to go as deep as we can. It takes courage and perseverance to stick it out, to fully process our issues in hopes of getting to the bottom of them.

Our skill at emotional processing can best facilitate problem solving when we graciously teach instead of stubbornly push. If we're convinced that our way is the only or best way, he's less likely to listen to us. If, however, we can show him the benefits of processing by pointing out the progress it has brought about, he may come around to our approach.

Some of the following strategies create a more effective interchange:

1. Deciding on a set time limit before we begin. (A stopwatch can be a useful tool).
2. Agreeing to an agenda and sticking to it.
3. Focusing on one or two primary issues.
4. Taking turns instead of dominating the conversation.
5. Organizing our thoughts and ordering our priorities ahead of time so that we don't overwhelm our partner with too much at once.

Being intentional in our approach can enhance the discussion process, but our need to go further or deeper may still not be satisfied. In this case, we can turn to other avenues to express our feelings. Tell a friend or counselor. Write in our journal or compose a letter to our partner telling what we haven't been able to communicate verbally.

We can only go as far with our mate as he's willing or able to go, but we can do whatever we need personally and on our own to fully express the depth of our feelings.

The Nature of Forgiveness

Expressing our feelings prepares us for the final, most challenging step in the healing process, which is finding forgiveness. Even when we reconcile with each other over past hurt or current conflicts, we still have to go a step further by finding it in our heart to forgive the man we love.

We enter into this process with the understanding that not everything in life is forgivable. There are heinous acts of cruelty that exceed the limits of human forgiveness, but in most cases, the "sins" of our partner fall well within the realm of being worthy of forgiveness.

Amends-making is a process of releasing our pain and releasing our partner from his culpability. We forgive his wrongdoing and commit ourselves to moving on with a clean slate. But true forgiveness goes beyond the mere act of releasing and healing pain. True forgiveness asks that we rise to a higher level of love in order to accept and embrace our partner's imperfections.

The path we've been traveling has brought us to the point where we face the profound task of cultivating unconditional love. How do we accept our mate when he has and may continue to hurt and disappoint us? Even more challenging, how do we summon the enormous magnitude of love required to embrace his flaws—to love him even more when he is shaky, struggling, or less than the man we know he can be?

Compassion is the key. True acceptance occurs when our anger is transformed into compassion, when we put ourselves in our partner's shoes and feel the extent of his suffering. Each of us is broken in ways that cause us to inflict pain on others. When we are armored in anger, we see our partner as the "enemy" whom we're forced to fight or protect ourselves against. Where compassion exists, we sense our human connection to our partner and all people everywhere. We empathize with his pain, our heart aches for him and how he is hurting, and we realize the ways in which we, too, have caused hurt as a result of our wounds.

In the Sermon on the Mount, Jesus said, "Let he who has never sinned throw the first stone." Opening our heart to our partner's imperfections makes us highly aware of our own. We are humbled by our own humanity. Our impulse to blame and shame is transformed into a deep desire to heal ourselves and aid in our partner's

⟲

healing. We are touched by our mate's efforts to overcome his limitations. We see him as a fragile human
being trying to do his best.

He doesn't always succeed, nor do we. There are times
when no matter how hard he tries, our mate just isn't
very lovable. He's mean, high-maintenance or generally
difficult to live with. I used to tease my ex-husband by
saying, "You're no day at the beach." Accepting our partner means loving him when nobody can find anything
about him to love. At these times we remember that he's
acting out of pain or fear and we utilize some of the following strategies:

> When he's being a jerk: Protect yourself and try to not
> take it personally.
> When he's being a baby: Let him whine, while you find
> some other grown-ups to be with.
> When he's being a tyrant: Hold your ground.
> When he's being a fool: Let him figure it out by him-
> self.
> When he's being a coward: Remind him how to be
> brave.
> When he's being a terrorist: Remove yourself from the
> line of fire.

Likewise we need to accept ourselves when we're a
mess, when we're mean, snotty, or in a lousy mood. Here
are a few coping mechanisms for the times when you're
not at your best:

- Give your partner as much information as you can.
  Admit that you're not in great shape right now and
  tell him why, if you know.
- Let him know if there's anything he can do to help.
  The more information you give him, the more pa-
  tient and understanding he is likely to be.

- Give yourself some time and space. Our high standards get in the way of our compassion for ourselves.
  A time-out, nap, or heart-to-heart talk with a friend
  can help us recover our composure and be more lovable and appealing.

Love grows through acceptance. Our heart expands as
we embrace our own humanity and reach out to accept
and embrace our mate. We feel open, inspired, ready to
build a sweeter, more dynamic and exciting connection
with our beloved by tapping our creative resources, which
are the focus of Chapter 9.

9

The Seventh Leap:
CULTIVATING CREATIVITY

N ow comes the fun part. We get to use our creativity to make all sorts of positive changes in our relationship. The healing process has freed us from being stuck in the past. Now we must look to the ways in which we are stuck in the present.

Much of the dissatisfaction in our relationship can be traced to the ways in which we feel trapped in a habitual pattern that has ceased to be interesting, exciting, and fulfilling. We always sleep on our side of the bed. Our conversations may revolve around the same, old subjects. We spend too much time sitting in front of the TV, hanging out with the same one or two couples, going to the same neighborhood restaurant week after week. Saturday is designated "date night"—a movie and dinner followed by forty-five minutes of satisfying but predictable sex. So, when conflicts arise we attempt to solve them in the same routine mode.

It's time to improvise. Merlin the Magician says,

"When you're sad, learn something." When I'm sad or feel stuck, I *make* something. I make a phone call to a friend I haven't talked with for several months. I make my favorite chocolate-chip cookies, throwing in Reeses Pieces just for the hell of it. Likewise, when my relationship seems stuck or stagnant, I make a stab at doing something differently, adding a new ingredient to the recipe. Once, instead of going out to dinner and a movie as planned, I took Louis to Grand Slam, an indoor kids' park with skee-ball, bumper cars, and a batting cage. Another time, right in the midst of a heated argument, we took out our giant color crayons and drew. And on more than one occasion, I've shown up with massage oil and candles, wearing a new, sexy piece of lingerie under my jeans.

Breaking out of our familiar patterns keeps our relationship from getting stale. Whereas the healing process brings about reconciliation, the creative process leads to revitalization. Cleansing wounds from the past enables us to be fully present in the here and now. It's similar to cleaning out our drawers and throwing away the mismatched socks and faded underwear. We get rid of the old, accumulated junk in order to open a space for something new.

The something new is *creativity*; it is discovering exciting, innovative approaches to revitalize our relationship. We have the tools. The six qualities we've cultivated so far have prepared us to take this next big leap. We have the clarity to know what we want, the integrity to act on our best intentions. We're supported by a firm foundation of emotional and spiritual self-possession, strengthened by feeding ourselves a daily diet of nourishment and nurturing. We have the wisdom to make smart, discerning choices. Through healing and forgiveness, our heart has expanded, enabling us to recommit to our relationship with optimism and good faith.

Now we're ready to take action, to use what we've learned in the spirit of enterprise. It may seem as if we have enough information at this point to evaluate whether or not our relationship is good enough, whether the man we're with has what it takes to be our lifelong companion. Not so fast. We've come this far, and if we're to give our relationship a fair shot, we mustn't leave a single stone unturned. If we assume that the status quo is as good as it gets, we'll never know if that's all that is possible.

It's premature to judge the long-term viability of our partnership until we try new ways of approaching and interacting with our mate. Intimacy, romance, and love-making can be dramatically enhanced by expanding our repertoire. We make major breakthroughs in communication and problem solving when we experiment with creative techniques and inventive strategies.

But we have to take yet one more leap of faith by believing that our relationship is worthy of our creative energy and investment. How we respond to this challenge depends on how much our partner truly means to us. If we believe that our relationship is worth it, we will pull out all the stops, summoning all our creative energy for this next leap. More important, when we love and value ourselves, we refuse to settle. We have enough faith in ourselves and our partner to explore every possible avenue available to us. We value our investment too much to give up without trying to infuse it with new life.

Sometimes we feel as if we're fighting an uphill battle, summoning every ounce of energy just to maintain our relationship, much less come up with creative new strategies to keep our romance and intimacy fresh and spontaneous. It takes everything we've got just to get along and keep our relationship on an even keel. But the truth is, it takes more energy to plod along in apathy and frustration than it does to tap the deepest reaches of our creative resources. We have to find the energy and willingness to push through our very human resistance to change and give our creativity free range.

Overcoming Our Resistance

Pessimism is the biggest obstacle to cultivating creativity. It's the old "what's the point?" routine. Why should we bother to put our creative effort into revitalizing our relationship when it may not make a difference? Taking this next leap feels like yet another risk. By investing more we risk wasting our time and energy without due reward. And we risk even more disappointment by allowing ourselves to get excited and optimistic about what our creativity will bring about.

Once again we're faced with a challenge. Do we have enough hope, enough optimism to get in there and try something new without any guarantee that our efforts will bring about change? Consider the alternative. If we accept that this is as good as it gets, our relationship will remain static, which isn't all bad, as long as we're satisfied with the way things are. If, however, we want more, then our only real choice is to get busy making it happen.

Why is it up to us? We may resist taking the initiative because doing so feels like one more way in which we "do all the work." We resent always having to be the one who thinks of new ways to resolve conflicts and keep romance alive. Are women eternally doomed to doing the lion's share of relationship maintenance? Maybe, maybe not. The real question isn't whether it's fair, but rather, what do we have to give, and are we willing to give it? Again, we have to decide if it's worth it or not by considering these two factors: Does the idea of experimenting with creative new strategies interest and excite us? And what do we have to gain?

Taking action is empowering. It almost always feels better to *do* something than to sit around complaining about the way things are. Integrity dictates that we take whatever positive initiatives we can, regardless of whether or not our mate is making an equitable contribution. The saying "If you're not part of the solution, you're part of the problem," applies here. If we shrink from our responsibility to enact positive change, then we are, in effect, worsening the problem. If we seek creative solutions, we have the satisfaction of knowing we've given to the best of our ability.

Creativity is also its own reward. While we may be able to imagine all sorts of positive outcomes, the act of creativity is fulfilling in and of itself. Refocusing from worrying about the problems in our relationship to figuring out creative ways to approach them causes a shift in our energy. We stop feeling burdened and start feeling inspired. We feel intellectually stimulated and emotionally aroused, intensely focused on accomplishing our mission.

We've all experienced the excitement of engaging in a creative act—losing ourselves in an artistic project, devising an original approach to solving a problem at work, coming up with a new way to spice up meat loaf, or finding the perfect words with which to comfort a friend. We call upon our creativity every time we involve ourselves in a task that requires originality and innovativeness. Every time we tap our creative juices, we experience excitement.

Think about what it feels like to search for and find the perfect birthday gift for someone we love. First, we give some thought to who this person is and what they care about. Then, ideas begin to germinate. Our partner has mentioned that he used to write poetry back in college; he has four loose-leaf notebooks of his poetry tucked away in his filing cabinet. One Sunday morning after making love and reading the paper, he takes out the notebooks and reads us a few select poems. His birthday is coming up, so we peruse our favorite bookstore for a leather-bound journal and a beautiful ballpoint pen. We carefully wrap the gifts, enjoying our little secret and counting the days until his birthday. The day arrives and we're fairly bursting with anticipation. We watch intently as he opens the package. He's thrilled, or maybe he's just quietly pleased or moderately happy. But whether he likes, loves, or is ecstatic over our gift, using our creativity has given us a sense of purpose and joy.

The best way to combat our "Why should I make the effort?" attitude is to remember that we're doing it for ourselves, we are making an effort to experience the pleasure and excitement of letting our creativity carry us away.

This only happens when we overcome apathy. To some degree or another, each of us is somewhat prone to apathy. We're too tired and depleted to rouse ourselves. We have to force ourselves to get up and push ourselves out of our lethargy. It's easier to do nothing than to do something, even if that something would make us feel a whole lot better.

Optimism is the antidote to apathy. Getting our hopes up propels and compels us out of our stupor and stagnation. For example, we may know, deep down, that our relationship might benefit from something as simple as redecorating our bedroom or surprising our husband at work with a picnic lunch. We must be able to envision the rewards, curling up together between fresh new sheets or brightening the workday with a romantic interlude, in order to summon the necessary energy and effort.

Low expectations are another barrier to making change. We resign ourselves to how things are instead of reaching for a higher vision. I'm constantly amazed by human beings' high tolerance for mediocrity, by our willingness to live with chronic frustration, unsatisfying communication, and lukewarm sex. In order to rally, we have to believe in our heart that our relationship can be better and maybe even reach heights of fulfillment and ecstasy we've hardly dared to imagine.

Finally, we may not know where to begin. How do we go about becoming more creative in our relationship? How do we come up with innovative strategies and techniques? We begin by understanding the five elements of creativity: intention, initiative, inspiration, intelligence, and imagination.

Intention

Every creative act begins with intention. Whether it's building a birdhouse, drawing a picture, or inviting our partner to go roller-skating, our actions are inspired by our desire to make something happen. We want our backyard to be a hospitable environment for robins and sparrows. We want to recapture a beautiful image by depicting it on paper. We want to have more fun with our mate.

Intention is the drive that puts the creative process into action. *Inspiration* is the spark, *Initiative* is the means, and with *Intelligence* and *Imagination* we add our personal finishing touch.

A soup-making metaphor illustrates how these five elements interact. It's a snowy Saturday afternoon. The fragrant aroma of our grandma's vegetable soup wafts through our memory. Inspired by our tingling taste buds and sweet remembrances, we pull out pots and pans, carrots, noodles, and onions. We initiate the steps involved: lighting the stove, bringing the water to a boil, putting in the chicken, cutting up the vegetables. Scratching our head, we try to remember what the ingredients were. (Grandma never used a recipe; she just threw in a smidgen of this, a sprinkle of that). Common sense tells us to boil until tender, simmer, then skim the fat floating on the top. Then something occurs to us. What if we throw in a handful of curry powder, cabbage, lentils or rice?

Later we sit down to enjoy the fruits of our creative endeavor, which all began with our original intent—to give ourselves a gift. Our creativity was motivated by loving intention. Wonderful memories of our grandmother's cooking and a desire to comfort and nourish ourselves came together in act of creativity.

Creativity isn't something we learn; it's something we are. Every single one of us is bestowed with amazing creative powers that come from our divine connection to the cosmos. We are creative without even trying. Our innate capacity to use symbols, make pictures, and eloquently express ourselves through the melody of language and song is contained within the very essence of our being. Give any three-year-old a box of watercolors or a drum and we immediately see innate human creativity expressed. Only adults associate creativity with some standard of professional mastery. Children don't question their creativity; they boldly sing and paint and dance without the slightest inhibition or performance anxiety.

Our creativity is manifested in both profound and ordinary acts. For example, when we participate in the creative act of childbirth, we experience a profound sense of divinity. Tapping into the divine source transforms us into goddesses. But divinity also reveals itself when we use our creativity in ordinary ways. A close friend is bummed out because her boyfriend has fallen in love with someone else. We and three other friends show up unannounced with junk food and videos for a slumber party to diss him and cheer her up. Our toddler refuses to eat vegetables. So, we plug in the blender and voilà— carrot Kool-aid with a celery twist! We take these sorts of everyday initiatives for granted, but they, too, are products of creativity because they are products of love.

Creativity doesn't require talents or genius. It requires love. Love fuels our desire to give, to create beauty out of ugliness, order out of chaos, and joy out of misery. Love inspires us to want to make a difference, and it empowers us to believe that we can. Just as our love for our friend drives us to stop what we're doing and help her get through the night, just as our love for our child motivates us to concoct a healthy mixture, our love for our partner can inspire us to be creative in hopes of reaching him in a whole new way.

When we're acting out of love, our efforts succeed. If we're acting out of fear, the very same strategies will fail because of our need to manipulate and control. For example, in our attempts to "fix" our partner, we may have taken on the roles of mother, teacher, or counselor. We may have used clever and inventive approaches— coddling him, educating him, or counseling him—but our tactics backfired because they were motivated by our fear-based agendas rather than our love-based desire to give. Power can be used for the purposes of extending love or misused for the purpose of managing fear.

A powerful corporation can provide millions of jobs, produce useful goods and services, and support the community through charitable giving. It can also oppress workers, produce expensive and unnecessary commodities. A politician can be a mighty leader or dangerous despot. Parents can be mentors or terrorists depending on their personal balance of love and fear.

Fear is based on a projection of potential loss, while love is based on a projection of potential gain. The mother who uses harsh discipline as a means of control is frightened that without extreme intervention, her child may get into trouble down the road. The heavy-handed politician fears losing his following unless they're intimidated into compliance. Similarly, attempts at control strategies with our partner, however creative, are based on our fear of loss—the loss of approval, loss of security, and loss of love.

When we love ourselves, we have little to fear. We are whole enough to approach our mate strictly from a place of love. Our creative initiatives are motivated by our desire to give and an understanding of all there is to gain, not from our need for our partner to heal and make us whole. Remember the movie character Evelyn, whose fear and insecurity made her package herself in Saran Wrap in order to seduce her husband? It took self-esteem—a by-product of transforming herself into Tawandas—for Evelyn to find loving and creative ways to resuscitate her life and her marriage.

We, too, can tap our growing self-love and our growing capacity to love our partner in the service of creativity. We start by experiencing the depths of our love, then expressing these feelings in the form of a statement of intent.

Here's how it works. First, take a moment to feel your love and affection for your partner. Next, think about one way in which you are lovingly intent on improving your relationship. You might want a more cooperative division of labor, more social time together, the possibility of a romantic vacation in the foreseeable future. In the following space, make a statement of loving intent. Remember, the objective is to translate your feelings of love into a positive intention.

My loving intention is to create more _____
in my relationship.

Initiative

Translating intention into action is the next essential element of creativity. We can feel incredibly loving, but until we take action by *doing* something, we have little power to bring about change.

Here again, little things go a long way. The handpicked daisy or Mother's Day card decorated with pasted-on Cheerios is as good as it gets. We needn't invent groundbreaking strategies, brilliant initiatives, or creative masterpieces for changes to occur. Once, many years ago, when I was crabby and out-of-sorts, my then-husband, Joey, took my hand in his and asked, "Do you want to color?" I burst out laughing, tickled by his originality.

Initiative doesn't need to be manifested on a grand scale. What it takes is effort, leadership, and, once again, love. We must be willing to make an effort, even when we're dubious about the results. We must be willing to assume leadership by being an active agent of change. We must channel our love by remembering that both we and our partner are worthy of any and all positive steps that can potentially improve our relationship.

Taking initiative is another way we empower ourselves. Too often we give up before we start. We'd rather complain about what's missing than create something new, or we lack the confidence that we're smart enough or ingenious enough to make a worthwhile contribution. A

man I once dated chronically complained about how boring other people were. When we'd go out to dinner with
friends, he'd sit silently and sullenly, rarely contributing
to the conversation. Afterward, he'd go on at length about
another wasted evening spent with unstimulating people
who had nothing interesting to talk about. While I basi-
cally agreed (their conversation usually revolved around
the weather or the latest new restaurant), I had little
sympathy with his passive approach. "If you're so bored,
why don't you bring up a topic you're interested in?" I'd
challenge him, and he'd inevitably reply, "It's not worth
the effort."

We can fall back on any number of excuses to justify
remaining bored, frustrated, or unhappy. Or we can take
the initiative to introduce something new into the situation. Emma, a woman I met while traveling, shared a personal experience in which she discovered the value of
initiative. "Year after year I've dreaded going home for
the holidays," she said. "Even though my family is scat-
tered throughout the country, when we get together all
we do is eat, argue, or make small talk. After one day of
this, all I want to do is take the first flight home.

Last year Emma promised herself she wouldn't subject
herself to another miserable family reunion. She wanted
to share the holidays with her parents and siblings but
was determined that this time it would be different. She
envisioned her fantasy family reunion: catching up on
the real details of each of their lives, healing old rifts instead of resorting to power struggles, laughing and crying
and loving each other, and everyone acting grateful just
to be together.

Emma sat down for Christmas dinner and noticed how
immediately the conversation turned to trivial gossip and
lighthearted bickering. At the first opening, she shared a
piece of important personal news: she had given notice

at work and was going back to graduate school. To her surprise, each member of the family responded to her announcement with questions, caring, and concern. Her brother asked whether a master's degree would up her value in the workplace. Her father, clearly enthusiastic, admitted he'd always felt bad that she hadn't finished her dissertation. Her mother, the family worrier, wondered how she would support herself and offered to help.

Emma was able to dramatically alter the traditional dynamic by bringing something new to the dinner table. Surprised and pleased by her family's response, she said, "It was the best Christmas I've ever had."

Take a moment now to consider one creative initiative that might potentially alter the dynamic of *your* relationship. You might, for example, decide to take your husband's soiled dress shirts to the dry cleaners, get acquainted with the playing record of each of the Chicago Bulls, or find sleep-overs for the kids so you can spend the weekend together in bed. Initiative requires commitment, so be sure that you are willing and able to deliver. In the following space, identify your creative initiative:

I will actively initiate by ————————————————.

Inspiration

Intention and initiative enables us to put the creative process into motion. Inspiration is what keeps us moving in a creative direction. It's the fire beneath the boiling soup kettle, the spark that ignites us when energy flickers or fades. Following through on initiative is hard. How many of us get a glimmer of an idea, start on a project, and then come up with countless reasons to put it aside? We're too busy, too tired, or too pessimistic to get the job done. That's when inspiration kicks in.

On countless occasions I've been well into writing a book when I've suddenly run out of steam. I drag myself to my computer as if I were going to the gallows. I stare at the green screen, feeling lethargic and brain-dead, and utterly devoid of the slightest creative impulse or urge. This is often referred to as writer's block, but I experience it less as an obstacle and more as an overwhelming loss of inspiration.

In my earlier days as a writer I struggled to push through the pain—and believe me, it's agonizing. I'd fairly chain myself to my computer chair, typing the same sentence over and over. I'd whine to my friends, struggle to figure out why I was stuck, and deride myself for having the hubris to think I was capable of writing a book.

No longer. Now, when inspiration flees, I go looking for it in different places. I've learned that willing myself to create makes me feel angry and trapped, which does nothing to help me write. So I turn off my computer and take a nap, play the piano, shop, read a novel, or sit on my porch swing and stare at the sky. If I wait patiently and receptively, inspiration invariably strikes. My original thesis comes back to me. I suddenly understand a missing piece that was leading my narrative astray. Exciting ideas appear as if to say, "Good. Now that you're relaxed, here are some good ideas."

Each of us has our own sources of inspiration. Music, art, or literature may free our creative urge. We may be inspired by nature, religion, our career, or other human beings we look to as role models. Once again, love enters in. When we hear a great symphony, read a moving memoir, or listen to an inspiring sermon, we often feel a surge of love for the emotion conveyed and the feelings evoked. Likewise, love is at work in the moments of inspiration that fuel and maintain our ongoing creative initiatives in our relationship.

What inspires you? When you feel apathetic or unmotivated, what keeps you focused on doing what you've set out to do? In this next space, name the sources of inspiration that keep you excited and on track:

I'm inspired by _____.

At this point we've explored how intention, initiative, and inspiration motivate us to be creative. Now we turn to explore *what* actual elements are essential in the creative act itself. It's one thing to make a commitment to being more creative in our relationship, but it's another thing to come up with original and innovative ideas. In other words, how do we go about introducing new strategies and techniques into our relationship? We do so by calling on our innate powers of intelligence and imagination.

Intelligence

We are intelligent creatures. Our ability to think, to reason, to fathom mysteries and construct complex concepts is one of our richest natural resources. Intelligence takes many different forms, including common sense, intuition, wit, and logic.

Some of us are blessed with good, solid common sense. We can size up a situation and figure out the best way to handle it in no time flat. Common sense allows us to glean wisdom from experience; remembering what's worked in the past informs our choices about the future.

Whereas common sense has long been seen as a "normal" manifestation of intelligence, the role of intuition is just beginning to be understood. Intuition refers to our inner sense of knowing, often experienced through gut feelings or hunches containing seeds of truth. We may rely on intution to guide us in knowing the right words to say when our child is hurting or the best moment to bring up a sensitive subject to our mate.

Wit is a form of intelligence that helps us be sharp, vigilant, and savvy. It's sometimes called street smarts— the unique combination of knowledge and experience that helps us know how to handle ourselves in high-risk situations. Cleverness is another form of wit. We may employ clever tactics to trick our partner into taking out the garbage, giving us a back rub, or talking about something he'd rather avoid.

If we use our intelligence to manipulate our partner, our efforts may backfire. He's bound to see through our charade and resent our agenda. But if we judiciously employ wit as a creative means of enhancing our relationship, our efforts will be well spent.

Our reasoning power is, perhaps, the best use of our intelligence. Looking logically at the problems in our relationship allows us to figure out where we're stuck and what to do about it. Logic helps us sort out the various factors that come into play: *after working overtime for a month, of course he's uncommunicative; our toddler's kept us up for the past few nights, no wonder we couldn't be less interested in sex.* Logic is an extremely useful tool with which to approach both minor problems, such as solving the Kitty Litter dilemma by buying a white blend that matched my bathroom floor, and bigger issues, like understanding the link between our father's rage fits and how intimidated we get any time our partner yells. Putting this piece of the puzzle in place reveals a possible solution. We explain to our partner why his yelling upsets us and ask him to address us in a gentler, more even tone of voice.

Imagination

Using our head enables us to be strategic. Using our imagination allows us to let our intellect run wild. I like to think of imagination as the playful part of our brian, where ingenious ideas, extraordinary concepts, and interesting new connections emerge. We've all had the "Aha!" experience, when we suddenly see things in a brand-new way and are struck by amazing insights or brilliant realizations appearing out of nowhere. The "Aha!" opens up whole other worlds of uncharted territory. We find ourselves "pushing the envelope" of our mind and extending our intellectual reach.

Imagination has a magical quality about it. Doesn't it seem to come from a far-off, mystical source, like a gift from the magi? Every once in a while I feel the muse on my shoulder while I'm composing at my computer. The words flow fast and furiously, as if I'm channeling wisdom instead of laboring to write. As these experiences are few and far between, I've had to learn how to tempt the muse by exploying my imagination.

Although imagination seems to come from sources beyond us, in fact, it comes from inside us and we can help it along by sharpening both our intellect and our perception. There are many ways to give our intellect a workout, including reading, doing the crossword puzzle, or taking something apart and putting it back together. Exercising our mind expands our consciousness. Our clarity, comprehension, and creativity grow in direct proportion to our imagination.

Imagination is heightened by increasing our field of vision, by altering our preception to imagine fresh, new possibilities. Perception is totally subjective, even though it seems like objective reality. Consider how often two human beings see the very same thing through very different eyes. A cumulus cloud looks to us like a marshmallow, while our six-year-old insists it's a white cocker spaniel holding a hot dog in its paw. Who's to say? What we see is what we see because we see it from behind our own eyes.

Our perception affects how we see both tangible objects and emotional issues. The same "myopia" that makes it impossible for us to perceive the puppy in the sky limits our capacity to see our relationship objectively. For example, our view may be that our mate is closed to intimacy, but our marriage counselor sees it differently through her professional perspective. What appears to us as resistance looks to her like fear. As she helps our spouse push through his fear, we begin to see his genuine desire for closeness and intimacy. Or let's say we're convinced that we're doomed to financial insecurity and too many years of struggling to make ends meet have created this perception. But our partner has an entirely different outlook. He's optimistic about his recent promotion and the fact that all our bills are paid up. Through his eyes we start to see our economic reality in a better light and commit to keep working hard and whittling away at the debt.

What we can envision, we can undertake. What we undertake can create infinite change. The sky's the limit, but there are only so many pages in a book. So, for the sake of brevity, here are ten innovative strategies for creatively revitalizing your relationship. Each one involves taking on a new role or replaying an old role in a new, more loving, and respectful manner. Although some may be more useful for you than others, consider each one carefully, applying whatever is personally useful. Remember, you're experimenting, trying on a role to see how it suits you.

Your Role: Teacher

My Fair Lady is a musical comedy about a poor, ignorant cockney street girl who is discovered by a British professor of linguistics. She's a diamond in the rough, and he bets that he can remake her in six months and pass her off as a duchess. She agrees to the experiment, but his approach is abominable. He intimidates, shames, and belittles her. He tries to mold her into his image of a respectable lady, and the words of his solo, "Why can't a woman be more like a man?" say it all.

Like Professor Higgins, too often we shame instead of teach, ridicule instead of lead. Granted, it's frustrating to watch our diamond in the rough refuse our efforts to polish his edges. Why can't a man be more like a woman? Why can't our man be more like us?

He can't and he shouldn't be. It's neither responsible nor respectful to try to remake our partner into a male version of ourselves. Nor is it appropriate to approach teaching like a stern taskmaster or towering Catholic nun wielding a ruler every time he talks out of turn.

Instead, we can be loving mentors. Our best teachers are the ones who recognize our innate gifts and dedicate themselves to bringing out the best in us. Being a mentor is a step beyond being a teacher. The curriculum is based on developing his unique talents and interests, not on our own academic agenda. We can lend a gentle hand in helping our mate develop *his* potential, teaching through inspiration and example.

A personal experience brought home to me the importance of mentoring. A man I once loved couldn't stand my horrible habit of misplacing my car keys. He'd rave and rant or just shake his head in despair, muttering about how disorganized I was. "How can someone as smart as you be so stupid when it comes to taking care of your stuff?" he'd snarl. "Why don't you help me instead of making me feel dumb?" I'd respond.

Two relationships later, I still have trouble finding my keys. I casually toss them among the pile of newspapers on my bed or slip them in the pocket of a jacket I hardly ever wear. My current boyfriend isn't any happier about this than the old one was. But he has the mentor role down to an art. He came up with an ingenious way to help *me* help myself. He made me an oversized key chain, using a piece of wood from our Cape Cod campsite, brilliantly attaching an alligator clip to the end so that I could hook it to anything, preferably myself. It's too big to miss in the bottom of my purse and, more important, his creative initiative inspires me to pay attention. If he cared enough to go to this much trouble, I can make the effort to keep track of my keys.

The Hindi word for *teacher* is "guru." Being a guru in our relationship is another creative way to share our knowledge and wisdom. Although this term often refers to a cult leader, spiritual teaching is the true essence of being a guru.

Gandhi comes to mind as an example of an individual whose deep spiritual beliefs enabled him to bring about global political transformation. But we must do the same on a micro-level within our relationship. We do this by staying true to our own spiritual path and sharing whatever wisdom we've learned along the way. We also do it with humility. We've seen the horror that can occur when a self-proclaimed guru like Jim Jones gets carried away with grandiosity and power. We've also seen the healing that comes about through the gentle love of Jesus or Buddha. True spiritual leaders bring about change because they have no need to impose their vision in order to create a mass following. Likewise, we bring about change in our relationship by continuing to spiritually evolve, lovingly sharing our wisdom with our mate.

Use *your* creativity now to come up with one way in which you can be a teacher, mentor, or guru within your relationship. You might help your partner learn how to keep his things neater and more orderly. You might teach him how to rock your baby to sleep or how to help your teenager with boyfriend problems. You might teach him ways of being closer to his mother, more assertive in the workplace, more in touch with his spiritual beliefs, or more intimate in your relationship. The key is honoring what *he* wants or needs to learn, not what *you* need or want him to learn. If you're not sure where to start, ask. Your opening line might be, "Is there anything I can help you learn?"

I want to teach my partner how to _____.

Your Role: Student

In the movie *Awakenings,* Robin Williams plays the part of Dr. Oliver Saks, a shy, eccentric neurologist whose patients suffer from a rare viral disorder. Catotonic zombies frozen in time, they are literally statues, unable to move, speak, or minimally care for themselves. All efforts to reach them fail until Dr. Sacks takes over the caseload. He's as lost as all the other doctors and nurses, but instead of continuing the regimen or prescribing new treatment, he watches, listens, and waits. He begins to learn some amazing things. Clara, a woman approaching seventy who thinks she's a young, beautiful twenty-year-old, begins to walk forward like a wind-up doll. Observing this miracle, Dr. Sacks looks down and notices the diagonal black-and-white tiles on the floor and realizes Clara can move when propelled by the pattern. Another patient, Richard, can feed himself when jazz is played on the record player. Every time the music stops, his hand is stuck in midair, and when the playing resumes, he brings the spoon to his lips. The doctor's otherwise catatonic patients can even play catch if someone else puts the ball into motion.

Dr. Sacks watches, listens, and asks in order to unravel his patients' mysterious condition. He's a student and a miracle worker. As a result of his observations and with the help of an unorthodox treatment, his patients briefly recover and come back to life.

Most of us would rather teach than learn. But being a good student in our relationship is as important, if not more, than being an educator. For one thing, we have a great deal to learn from our mate. If we strictly assume the teacher role we miss out on benefiting from all his areas of expertise. We also create an inequitable balance of power by always assuming that we're the one who knows best. No one enjoys being consistently cast in the role of relative ignorance and each of us needs to know that we have something valuable to give.

Our partner can only teach if we're willing to learn. Being a good student requires an open and inquiring mind. Oftentimes we insist that our minds are open when, in fact, they're closed. We pretend to listen or listen with half an ear. We debate instead of communicate. We draw conclusions before weighing all the facts or construct our rebuttle instead of carefully considering our partner's point of view.

Our conviction that we are right prevents us from tapping into our partner's rich storehouse of knowledge and experience. Here are a few strategies for becoming a better student:

- LISTEN. Make a concentrated effort to pay attention to what your partner is saying instead of drifting off or composing your response. Satirist Fran Lebowitz says, "The opposite of talking isn't listening. The opposite of talking is waiting." We hear our partner's message much clearer if we stop waiting for our turn to talk.
- ASK QUESTIONS. The purpose of inquiry is to get more information, not to gather ammunition. If our partner feels as if everything he says can-and will-be used against him, he's sure to censor himself. If he senses our genuine interest he'll open up. The key is to inquire, not interrogate. It is learning to ask because we really want to know.
- BE TEACHABLE. Open your mind and be willing to say, "I don't know." A teacher can only teach if a student is willing to learn. We stymie our partner's attempts to teach when we act as if we have all the answers. If we're willing to reveal the gaps in our knowledge, we give our mate a place to start.

The whole point of being in a relationship is to learn. If we can't learn, we might as well be alone. And, in some ways, we are just that. When our ego triumphs over our willingness to receive what our partner has to offer, we end up alienating ourselves and pushing him away. The dubious reward of self-rightousness pales against the deeper satisfaction of learning something new.

Being humble doesn't mean putting ourselves down or diminishing our self-respect. It means having so much respect for ourself, our partner, and our relationship, that we gracefully go back and forth between being teacher and student.

What can *you* learn from your partner? You might want him to show you how to change a tire, garden, or sail. He may be skilled at negotiating or adept in social situations, parenting, or communicating, more capable than you are in any number of ways. Next, come up with one or two lessons you'd like to learn. If you'd like to, share this information with your mate.

I want to learn more about _____.

Your Role: Inventor

Both classical and contemporary theater invoke the theme of invention. Just think of Frankenstein's monster and H. G. Wells's time machine. The movie *Back to the Future* centers around the invention of a car that can travel back and forth in time. It's a terrific fantasy device that crates all sorts of interesting setups. The characters are transported back some twenty years. Once they come to their senses and realize where they are, they encounter a number of situations in which their awareness of the future informs the choices they make in this imaginary "present."

Just as we are naturally creative, all of us are inherently inventive. We're inventing all the time without even realizing it: We do it when we slice open an envelope with a pen or scotch-tape the hem of our dress because we're running late and can't find the thread, or improvise lyrics when we're crooning our children to sleep.

Our inventiveness can be well utilized in our relationship. Being an inventor is one of the best ways to solve problems and combat stagnation. In fact, this is exactly why inventors invent. Out of necessity. Every problem we face can be perceived as an obstacle or challenge. Inventors see every potential problem as an invitiation to create something new.

Our couple, Rick and Phoebe, were always fighting about who was responsible for what, especially when it came to household tasks. So they brainstormed and came up with an inventive solution. They divided the twenty-six letters of the alphabet right down the middle. To ensure fairness, they assigned specific chores to certain letters ahead of time. Each month they traded off doing tasks beginning with their half of the alphabet, then traded the next month. When it was Phoebe's turn for the first half, she took out the garbage, while Rick raked the leaves. Sounds strange, I know, but it worked for them.

Another couple invented this creative form of conflict resolution. Whenever they disagree, instead of arguing or stonewalling, they take out an imaginary scale. Each partner individual examines the intensity of their own feelings on a scale of 1 to 10, 1 meaning it isn't that big a deal, and 10 meaning they're willing to fight to the bitter end. The rules are that each partner has to be absolutely honest about how critical the issue is without second-guessing or manipulating the other. They share their findings, then whoever has a lower number graciously yields.

The beauty of this inventive technique is that it requires trust and trade-off. Each individual has to implicitly trust the other to represent themselves honestly and fairly. And, whoever "wins" this time knows that next time it will be his or her turn to compromise. There are no power struggles, no "gotchas," and no sulking in the corner. Everyone gets their way some of the time, which is perfectly reasonable and fair. Best of all, when it's over, "Thank yous" and Your welcomes" are exchanged.

Inventing ways to take turns is bound to improve your relationship, whether in practical or emotional terms. I once heard Marlo Thomas and Phil Donahue on television answer the question "To what do you owe the success of your marriage?" Marlo laughed and said, "We have a rule that only one of us gets to be crazy at a time." By "crazy" I imagine Marlo means the times when either partner in a relationship is struggling, hurting, or being less than their best self. Louis and I have revised this rule to read, "Only one of us can be little at a time. And the other has to be twice as big." I can honestly say that this rule has been the single most useful tool in our relationship. When I'm crabby, Louis goes out of his way to be cheerful. If he's confused, I give him all the clarity I've got. When we're both a mess, we go our separate ways.

Now it's time to get inventive. You might create a new job-sharing system, a game you and your partner can play when tension rules, or a secret code word to say when you and your mate are in the middle of an argument. In the following space, complete this sentence:

I'm busy inventing _____.

Your Role: Empathic

My favorite character on *Star Trek: The Next Generation* is Data, a computerized android with human features, who is perfectly programmed to know everything and feel nothing. But when it comes to relationships where emotions run rampant, we're better off with Deanna Troi at the helm.

Counselor Deanna Troi is an empath. Her vast powers of empathy enable her to intuitively sense the innermost feelings of any and all human beings or alien creatures. Her uncanny ability to empathize, to get inside and under other beings' skin, allows her to reach out in a way that truly makes a difference.

There are few things more frustrating than those times when we just don't know what to do. We can tell our partner is hurting or confused, but we haven't a clue how to help. We ask what's wrong. "Nothing," he says. He shrugs off our suggestions and rebuffs our hand on his shoulder. So we give up. We leave the room worried, wondering how in the world to break through.

We can't read minds, and we certainly can't expect ourselves to instinctively know what our partner needs. We can, however, make an effort to develop more empathy.

Being attentive is the simplest way of becoming more empathetic. Have you ever noticed how every mother has a sixth sense when it comes to her own child. Within forty-eight hours most new mothers can tell the difference between an I'm-hungry cry, I'm-tired cry, and a hold-me cry. Do mothers have supernatural power? More likely, our empathy arises out of our attentiveness. We "get" what our baby needs because we stand over his or her crib staring! If we spent the same amount of time scrutinizing every last nuance of our mate's personality, we'd be a whole lot more aware of how to respond to him.

Paying attention helps us know what works and what doesn't. When our efforts at communication, conflict resolution, or peacemaking fail, that's our first clue to try a different approach. This is harder than it seems because we tend to rely on whatever is most comfortable and what we're good at.

Janet, a therapist who works with inner-city youths, prides herself on her counseling skills. Ira constantly complained about being bored, unappreciated, and underpaid at his job during the six years he and Janet were married. Janet would respond by falling into her therapist role, using her counseling skill to help him get a handle on his feelings. Her techniques were useless; if anything,

Ira would get angrier, usually at her. Eighteen months after their divorce, Janet ran into Ira at a party. He'd fallen in love and started a wonderful new job. Although he appeared happier, Janet could tell he hadn't undergone a complete personality change. Out of curiosity, she asked Ira what his new girlfriend did when he went into his "poor me" routine. He casually replied, "Oh, she just tells me to shut the fuck up."

Janet ruefully chuckled to herself, realizing how she'd blown it, despite her good intentions, not to mention her professional expertise. What worked with her clients had failed miserably when it came to her husband.

Another woman, Liz, made the wrong move while trying to do the right thing. "At one point while my husband was in psychotherapy, he told me that he was really 'getting into' early childhood memories," explains Liz. "He shared some pretty vulnerable feelings going all the way back to the crib." Liz wanted to support her husband and facilitate the therapy process. So she went to a department store and bought him flannel jammies with feet and a flap, along with a half-dozen stuffed animals. Hoping to surprise him, she waited until he was brushing his teeth, then carefully arranged the purchases on his pillow. Surprised wasn't the word; horrified was more like it. Mortified, Liz's husband turned bright red and rushed from the bedroom with Liz running after him apologizing.

Sometimes we get it right and sometimes we blow it. When we blow it, it's usually because we've misread our partner's signals or don't know him as well as we think. Developing empathy helps us understand our partner's preferences. It helps us know how to speak in a language our partner can understand. And it helps us to listen, to hear both the spoken and the unspoken, to sense the meaning in the silence between the words.

Are there ways in which *you* can more fully develop

your powers of empathy? How well are you able to sense your partner's needs? To grasp his feelings? To read between the lines?

Consider one or two ways in which you might be more consciously attentive to your mate. Then, complete this sentence:

I will pay more attention to _____.

Your Role: Social Director

Didn't you just love Julie, the nauseatingly cheerful and perky social director on *The Love Boat*? She had the perfect "up" attitude, the perfect pageboy hairdo, the perfect activity for everyone age six to sixty-nine. Bingo, shuffleboard, sing-alongs—name your favorite recreational pleasure and she'd find at least two or three other captive passengers as playmates. (The only reason I know all this is because I spent the better part of my second pregnancy sitting on the couch trying to not throw up and watching every single episode.)

Julie knew how to play and she also knew the value of getting everyone else to play along. Playfulness is becoming a lost art. One of the casualties of contemporary life is that we've forgotten how to play together, especially with our partner. We're too immersed in the responsibilities of grown-up life to make time for one of the best ways to revitalize our relationship, which is having fun.

In the past few years, the ironic expression "Are we having fun yet?" has come into vogue. It's a good question. I suspect that in too many relationships this question isn't even asked, much less answered affirmatively. As working on our relationship has assumed greater and greater emphasis, the importance of playing together has taken a backseat. We may do a great job supporting each other's careers, coparenting, and working toward mutual goals, but we're just not having enough fun.

When was the last time you and your partner played together? When have you spent a whole afternoon or evening doing something fun and relaxing instead of sorting bills, talking business, or handling household concerns? We went bowling recently. I love bowling. I enjoy taking five or six practice frames, lacing up those ugly red and green suede shoes, stomping my feet over gutter balls, and jumping up and down when I get a strike. It's pure, clean, unadultered fun—a great break from worrying about the endless adult responsibilities that dictate my life.

Playfulness reduces stress and helps us blow off steam. Serious discussion isn't always the best way to ease tension or break through a seemingly unresolvable conflict. Getting down on the floor to wrestle with our partner or challenging him to a competitive game of hearts rechannels energy. When we do it, the tightness in our chest lightens and laughter bubbles up like a fresh spring.

I'm convinced that the most successful relationships are those in which laughter is present. Trading smiles of amusement when our child does something funny or laughing hysterically over a silly inside joke goes a long way toward building bridges and creating intimacy. Knowing that some of the same things bring us pleasure or make us giggle reminds us of our compatibility.

Being the social director in our relationship might not be anything new. Perhaps for years we've taken responsibility for coordinating social outings with family and friends. And sometimes we've resented it, especially if our partner is unenthusiastic or unappreciative of our effort.

Now we have the chance to play social director in a

new, creative way—by making plans for what might be mutually enjoyable or by taking turns introducing each other to new ways of having fun. He takes you skydiving. You invite him to your favorite art gallery. And by making the overture with these delightful words, "Can you come out and play?"

How can you and your mate have more fun together? Do you enjoy cooking together, perusing garage sales, or packing a picnic lunch and driving out to the country? In the next space think of one fun play date for you and your partner. Now complete this sentence:

Would you like to play with me? How about _____?

Your Role: Seductress

Hopefully, lovemaking falls into the category of fun in your relationship. Sex is one of the best ways to play because it includes many of the elements that make up fun, including playfulness, pleasure, adventure, laughter, and even exercise!

Some of us are perfectly happy with our sexual relationship, satisfied with the frequency and content of lovemaking. We look forward to playing in bed and are constantly discovering new ways to please ourselves and our partner. Sex may be one of the best things about our relationship and the realm in which we feel happiest and most connected with our mate.

But at least as many women out there I know are bored, dissatisfied, or disinterested. Our partner's technique leaves us cold. We make excuses to avoid lovemaking or put it off whenever we can. Fantasies are the only way to get aroused. We fake an orgasm just to get it over with.

Ladies, it's time to get creative and take charge of our sexual needs. We may have to overcome some cultural taboos in order to get started, such as "Nice girls don't initiate sex, make noises, or act out their fantasies." Phooey. The adage "Most men want a lady in the parlor and a whore in the bedroom" is more like it. Somewhere along the line we may have gotten the idea that all we have to do is lie back and "think of England." In fact, the majority of men are dying to be seduced; they dream of their lover being wildly aroused and getting down and dirty.

A recent slew of movies have promoted images of of women as seductresses or dominatrices. We saw Glenn Close giving a blow job on a warehouse elevator in *Fatal Attraction,* Demi Moore using her seniority to sexually harass Michael Douglas in *Disclosure,* and Linda Fiorentino in *The Last Seduction* manipulating men in a female version of Wham, bam, thank you, ma'am.

These are not particularly pretty pictures. Images of women using power to sexually use and abuse men are just as disgusting as their traditional male counterpart. But if we can get beyond our discomfort and disgust, there's a positive message and that is that our sexual desires are meant to be satisfied.

There's a vast menu of ways to expand our sexual repertoire. We can talk dirty, seduce our mate with a slow striptease, make love in front of a full-length mirror, experiment with different positions, take a bath with him, give him a full body massage with oil, lick his toes and work our way up. A bag of tricks—and even some toys to go with it—makes lovemaking more fun. These are just a few of the ways we can spice up our sex lives. Plan a field trip to an adult sex shop if you like; the shelves are full of erotic videos, provocative lingerie, and devices to enhance lovemaking.

Some women like to be very daring and adventurous in bed while others take a more conservative approach. There are plenty of ways to get more creative in bed without doing things that make us feel uncomfortable or out on a limb. We can be verbal without using four-letter words, and we an experiment with new positions without contorting ourselves like Chinese acrobats. Our goal is to take the lead, at least some of the time, in making our lovemaking a more creative and exciting endeavor.

How far are you willing to go? Think of some new ways you're willing to be more sexually assertive and expressive, then complete this sentence:

I'm ready to try being more _____ in bed.

Your Role: Parent

You might shy away from the idea of taking on the role of parent in your relationship, especially if you've ever heard this accusation, "Stop acting like my mother!"

But, remember, there are all kinds of mothers. There are nurturing mothers, domineering mothers, controlling mothers, pushy mothers, and intrusive mothers. There are also the kind we all wish we'd had: kind, understanding mothers who gave us our first and, perhaps most abiding, experience of love.

Years ago there was a wonderful television series called *Family*. The mother, played by Sada Thompson, epitomizes the sort of mother I'd like to be. She never lost her temper and intuitively knew what each of her three children needed. She was funny, nonjudgmental, and achieved the perfect balance between authority and flexibility. Her three children could tell her everything and did, trusting that nothing they could do would risk endangering her devotion.

Some of us have the good fortune of having been parented well; others of us missed out on the unconditional love that, ideally, parents would provide. If we've been seriously neglected in the parenting department, we may lean too hard on our partner to give us the loving we didn't get. Romantic intimacy is no replacement for the experience of good parenting; seeking this puts far too much pressure on our partner and places our relationship in jeopardy.

There is, however, a place for reparenting in our intimate relationship. All of us yearn for understanding, nurturing, and tenderness, no matter how well our early needs were met by our parents. As adults, we still occasionally need to be held, stroked, encouraged, and reassured. When hurting or in doubt, we need to hear "There, there," or "Everything's going to be all right," or "It's okay, baby." (Notice how often we use the endearment "baby" in addressing our beloved.) When our partner rocks us in his arms or tucks the blanket tightly under our chin, we recover some of the lost feeling of safety and security of our childhood.

Being a loving mother toward our partner is extremely tricky business. We want to cuddle him without coddling him, hold him without smothering him, envelope him in affection and love without making him feel vulnerable and exposed.

How do we do this? First, by doing our best to avoid repeating the ways in which his own mother inadvertently neglected his needs. Be careful not to act controlling or dominating. Respect his need for privacy and fight the temptation to push or interfere in his life. And most of all, be very sensitive about his need to maintain his dignity.

The first mistake we make when it comes to mothering our mate is going too far, too fast. He gets a little vulnerable and we dive into the depths of his psyche. Tears come to his eyes and we urge him to cry his heart out instead of allowing him to feel and express his emotions in his own way. The second mistake we make is in assuming that vulnerability breeds more vulnerability. It works just the opposite way. When our partner lets down all his defenses and allows us to mother him, he usually needs some space afterward to regain his personal power and equilibrium. Finally, we make the error of forgetting to let our partner return the favor by giving us some of the parenting we need. We need it every bit as much as he does. Once again, reciprocity creates balance and equity. Taking turns being loving parents enables each of us to give and receive.

Think of one or two ways in which it might be appropriate and loving to parent your partner. Now, complete this sentence:

I can lovingly parent him by _____.

Your Role: Cheerleader

A fifteen-year-old in Alabama desperately wants to make the cheerleading squad. It's been her lifelong dream, and she practices her cheers and routines and splits until she's ready to drop. She doesn't make the cut, losing out to an acquaintance at school. It's not the first time. The other girl, her nemesis, beat her out for the title of Homecoming Queen and has been spotted flirting with her boyfriend. The jilted cheerleader is devastated—but not as devastated as her mother. In an act of revenge, she pays a hired gun to murder the other girl. She's caught and given a twenty-year suspended sentence.

As this story proves, truth is stranger than fiction, and

this news item was turned into a made-for-TV movie. Two things fascinate me about this story, each aspect equally horrifying in its own bizarre way. First, we have this mother whose drive for her daughter to be a cheerleader (something the mother obviously wanted to be) leads her to contemplate murder. And then we have this seemingly innocent girl who just wants pom-poms and a way to fit into the in crowd and instead ends up a humiliated outcast.

It's a stretch, but I'm willing to give the mother the benefit of the doubt. Clearly her drive to help (read: push) her daughter created a psychotic break. Although few of us go to such desperate lengths, we sometimes go overboard in our desire to cheer our partner on. When something matters to him, we want to do everything we can to help him reach his goal. But sometimes our enthusiasm gets out of hand. He's up for a promotion so we surprise him with five-hundred-dollar suit that's way out of our budget. He signs up for a men's weekend retreat, and we show up with homemade cookies for the entire group.

There's a thin line between cheering on our partner and pressuring him to score. Remember, a cheerleader's place is on the sidelines, not on the field, rooting when the team is winning, rooting harder when they're behind.

What's one way you can channel your enthusiasm and energy into cheering your partner on? Once again, be sure that you're rooting for something he wants to achieve. Sometimes it's best to just say, "I believe in you," "I know you can do it," or, "Give it all you've got." In the following space, complete this sentence:

I can cheer my partner on by _____.

Your Role: Healer

Resurrection is one of my all-time favorite movies. It's the story of a woman named Edna, played by Ellyn Burstyn, who experiences a near-death experience after a devastating car crash, complete with the tunnel and white light. Following a protracted recovery in the hospital, she returns to her childhood home, where she begins to experience strange healing powers. She stops a young, hemophiliac girl's nosebleed by holding her and laying on hands. With the help of her mysterious healing powers, a deaf man regains his hearing and a woman confined to a wheelchair takes a step. Threatened and infuriated, the minister of this God-fearing Bible Belt community demands to know the source of her power. All she can point to is love.

The source of all healing is love. Consequently, each of us has the power to heal. Throughout history, the role of healer has been assigned to individuals with mysterious, mystical powers. In contemporary times our definition of healers has expanded to include practitioners of wholistic medicine with a conscious understanding of the mind-body connection.

But healing isn't the exclusive domain of mystics or massage therapists. There are countless ordinary examples of healing at work in our daily lives. We see it when a cancer patient uses imagery and positive thinking to diminish pain, and when a mother "makes it better" by kissing her child's skinned knee. Within our relationship we can bring the same healing powers to bear by radiating love and energy, by "laying on hands" with an embracing hug and by taking a wholistic approach to life, reminding our partner to balance work with play, to rest when he's tired, and to exercise and eat nutritiously when he's stressed and overwhelmed.

—————————————— ∽ ——————————————

We can also heal by honoring our limits. We are not God. Even as our love grows, we must respect that our resources are finite. One more scene from *Resurrection* serves as a cautionary note. A team of research scientists from Berkeley, California, invite Edna to demonstrate her healing power in front of their colleagues. The "guinea pig" is a woman suffering from an acute form of muscular dystrophy. She lies curled up in a fetal position, her limbs painfully contorted, twisting with uncontrollable seizures. Edna climbs up on the gurney and cradles the woman in her arms. We watch in horror and amazement as the two women merge in a total body-meld. As the patient's toes slowly uncurl and her twisted torso relaxes and is released from its prison, Edna stiffens and writhes in uncontrollable agony.

We can empathize to the best of our ability, but when we lose ourselves in another by becoming overly identified and enmeshed, we risk harming ourselves. For instance, we may exhaust ourselves staying up all night helping our partner through a crisis. We may get so consumed in his issues that we neglect our own. The love that empowers us to heal must be tempered by loving ourselves by both extending and protecting our energy and by loving our mate without taking on his pain.

How can you harness your love, energy, and empathy as an instrument of healing in your relationship? Complete this sentence:

I can offer healing through ————————————.

A Bittersweet Eleventh Act

What if you try every creative strategy I've mentioned, along with a few of your own, and nothing gets better?

What do we do when we have cultivated these qualities and put them into practical use in our relationship and there hasn't been any tangible improvement?

Some relationships are meant to flourish and blossom into lifelong romances. Others are meant to end. If we've devoted every ounce of love, energy, and ingenuity to no avail, we may have reached a sad but necessary crossroad. This may simply be as far as we can successfully travel together with our current partner. Our purpose is fulfilled, having taught and learned everything we can.

If, deep in your heart, you know that this is as far as you can go, then leave your relationship with dignity and grace. Tell the truth. Let your partner know how he's enriched and sweetened your life and take all the gifts and lessons of your relationship with you as you move on to meet the next challenges that await you.

At the end of act 2, scene 2, in *Romeo and Juliet*, we hear the poignant words, "Parting is such sweet sorrow." Every parting is sorrowful. But there is lasting sweetness in knowing that we've given our best.

More likely our story has a happy ending. We experience a rebirth in our relationship as a result of our creative initiatives. Desire is awakened, romance rekindled, and issues are resolved, filling us with excitement and gratitude. Through our own courageous willingness to travel a new path, we have reached our destination—a holy mecca where we rediscover the sanctity of our love.

10

The Eighth Leap:
CULTIVATING REVERENCE

ong before Oprah and Sally, I was an avid reader of the *Ladies' Home Journal* magazine column "Can This Marriage Be Saved?" It is a voyeur's paradise. Month after month I'd eat up the agonizing details of troubled relationships awaiting the professional verdict. Included were the typical marital issues: bored housewives, wandering husbands, couples whose sex life had dried up and couples who had nothing left to say to each other. Rarely, if ever, did the counselor advocate divorce, usually offering fairly pat advice for how to patch up the relationship under discussion.

As is often true of vicarious pleasure, reading this column usually left me empty. I was addicted, but my appetite wasn't satiated. Even as a teenager, I sensed there was something missing from the professional feedback. I wanted more. I wanted these couples to stop talking and start praying. Although I couldn't have articulated it at the time, I wanted the RX to go beyond practical advice to exploring the meaning and purpose of their union.

Fulfilling our destiny challenges us to love one another despite our imperfections. Our capacity for unconditional love is repeatedly tested as we strive to be more godlike in our lives and our relationships, a difficult task given that none of us are fully evolved. This is why we clash, argue, and sometimes treat each other like shit. How do we love someone whose imperfections drive us to distraction? Why would anyone find *us* worthy of love?

Deng Ming-Dao, an interpreter of Tao teaching writes, "Once you've seen the face of God, you see that same face in everyone you meet." The essence of God—apart from any particular religious deity—is that part of ourselves that is the best and most beautiful. When we are godlike, we are kind, noble, and compassionate. We treat ourselves and others as precious objects and cast everyone in the brightest possible light. We are filled with reverence and gratitude and our hearts overflow with love.

Each of us is made up of an equal mixture of human and godlike attibutes. We are both fearful and brave, weak and strong, imperfect and perfect. Our imperfection makes it extremely challenging for us to love another human being. Our perfection reminds us that somewhere, deep in the core of our being, we are capable of this awesome endeavor.

And so we carry on, sometimes supremely confident, other times seriously questioning whether we have the requisite courage and strength to continue on in our relationships. In our moments of confidence we are deeply aware of everything we have. In our moments of doubt we wonder if it's worth it to go on. Then it's time to get down on our knees and pray—for patience, for gratitude, and for a sign from the universe that our relationship, however challenging, is exactly where we're meant to be.

Ultimately, our sense of destiny is what keeps us committed to our mate. We can solve problems, improve communication, and rekindle our romance. But unless we truly know that our partner is an integral part of our destiny, none of the rest means beans. There are dozens, perhaps hundreds of people in this world with whom we can hang out, have fun, make love, and share lots of exciting and interesting adventures. We may have already met some of them along the way—past boyfriends, lovers, or husbands—who permanently enriched our lives. But there is only one person—hopefully our present partner—who is destined right now to be our teacher, helpmate, and spiritual guide.

The whole purpose of being in an intimate relationship is to facilitate our spiritual growth, to help each other evolve into more loving, self-actualized beings. When two people dedicate themselves to loving each other, something magical occurs—the sum becomes greater than the parts. When joined, the love we give each other has a synergistic effect, creating an energy all its own.

I once had the pleasure of meeting a couple who taught me about the Catholic concept of sacramental love. They saw their relationship as a vehicle to serve Christ, a love triangle in which God was the third essential partner. Although as a Jew, Trinitarian metaphors aren't part of my religious upbringing, I was moved by this couple's powerful connection. Their love for each other was palpable, a painful contrast to my then-disintegrating marriage. Although they'd been married nine years, they seemed like newlyweds, constantly touching each other, jumping up to fill a half-empty coffee cup, and each bragging about the other's accomplishments. Each one's eyes lit up whenever the other walked into the room. If this was what happened when spirituality enters a relationship, I wanted the same.

When our union is illuminated by purpose and meaning, the power of our love reaches far beyond the parameters of our relationship. Love is magnified when used to serve a greater good, such as serving God, raising children who will make a significant contribution, or working politically to create a safe and peaceful world.

Most of us are still learning how to come together in a way that will maximize the power of love. Sadly, our relationship is rarely an instrument of healing. It is more often a way to meet our own needs, not necessarily even those of our partner, much less our community or our world. When the primary purpose of our relationship is to serve only our best interests, we objectify our partner, or worse, see each other as adversaries instead of comrades and allies. We get angry when we don't get what we want. We bring out the worst instead of the best in our mate. We diminish each other's self-esteem through criticism, and we force ourselves and our mate into isolation because of our inability to accept and forgive.

It's easy to see why more couples in America divorce than stay together, extricating ourselves from our partner to put ourselves out of our misery. But we miss the point. Unless we're involved in an abusive or dangerous situation, it's usually not our relationship that's the problem, it's our understanding of how to love and be loved.

In Chapter One, these three pressing questions were posed:

- What's reasonable to expect in an intimate relationship?
- Should I back off and try to accept him as he is?
- Is there anything more I can do?

As we reach the conclusion of our journey, we are in a much better position to answer these questions. How much can we realistically expect from our partner? If we've learned one thing, it's that we are responsible for our own happiness. Our happiness depends on our ability to make conscious choices based on our love and respect for ourselves. Throughout the course of this book we have examined our expectations and replaced them with respectful requests based on our bottom-line needs. We have learned when to push and when to let go, how to creatively initiate change, and how to meet our needs both within and beyond our relationship.

We have evolved to the point at which there is absolutely no justification for remaining in a joyless relationship, no excuse for staying stuck, settling, or compromising our authenticity. If we choose to be with our mate, we must love and accept him for who he is. We've come too far to waste any more energy complaining about him or waiting for him to change. He may continue to disappoint us and he may amaze us as he continues to evolve into the man we know he can be.

Having said all this, is there anything more we can do? YES.

Are you ready to take the final leap of faith? Cultivating reverence is the ultimate, most profound act of love and commitment to ourselves, our mate, and our relationships.

Cultivating an attitude of reverence enables us to see our mate as our spiritual companion and to view our relationship as sacred and holy. In this state, we regard our partnership as a privilege and our mate as a gift. It becomes obvious that our union is no mere accident of fate but that our mate has been sent as an instrument of God to help us fulfill our potential.

When we revere something, we see it in a very special light. Normally when we look at something, we notice all its flaws and imperfections. We admire a painting, all the while pointing out where the texture seems uneven or the hue a bit off. Similarly, other people are perceived through our critical lenses. Our child is smart but a little too chubby, our husband is terrific but could use a little touch up here and there.

Reverence alters our vision. It's not that we put on rose-colored glasses, rather, the inherent perfection in people seems more apparent than their flaws. We're struck by their radiance, their individuality, their irresistable smile, or their amazing ability to know just the right thing to say. Their flaws haven't disappeared; they just fade against the glow of love that we've projected onto them.

Being in a state of reverence causes a profound shift in how we experience life itself. We are vividly aware of the beauty in everything and conscious of the sense of purpose and meaning in everday occurances. We take far greater care in how we treat ourselves, others, and everything around us.

Maintaining a state of reverence is no easy feat. Everyday stress conspires against the pursuit of the serenity necessary for reverence to develop. The struggle to make a home, make a living, and make our way through the labyrinth of adult responsibilities makes it difficult to experience the sanctity of our relationship. Our necessary focus on everyday demands makes our mate seem more like a colleague than a cosmic traveling companion and our partnership seem like a joint business venture rather than the spiritual adventure it's meant to be.

So, we must make a conscious effort to create reverence in our relationship. There are moments when it just happens. When we're sitting together holding hands enraptured by the sunset, witnessing your child take his first step. Trembling with awe when lovemaking approaches communion.

Making Our Relationship a Sanctuary

These are rare glimpses of heaven. We create more such moments by seeing our relationship as a sanctuary, a safe haven where we can rest when when we are weary, learn the lessons we need to learn, and where we can afford to reveal our human flaws without hiding any part of who we are. We create a fertile garden in which trust abounds and gratitude is ever-present. We try to be kind and gentle and forgiving of each other's imperfections in order to create an environment in which love can blossom and grow.

Consider how a church or synagogue or sanctuary is designed to evoke an atmosphere of reverence. Music sets the mood, helping us shift our attention to a more meditative state. Ceremony and ritual, inspirational words and the power of communal prayer, remind us of our connection to the divine universe of which we are an integral part.

We make our relationship a "place of worship" by removing ourselves from our normal surroundings, spending reflective time together in settings that bring us closer to each other and to our spirituality. One couple's lake cabin provides such a retreat, another spends Sunday afternoons at their favorite art gallery, while another couple has created a special corner of their den where they curl up on pillows, quietly sharing their thoughts.

Lynn and Michael realized how much of their time was spent at their kitchen table staring at dirty dishes or piles of bills. They agreed to spend at least an hour together in their bedroom each night, devoting this time to simply being together, without watching CNN or discussing domestic issues. They designated the bedroom as sacred space, making a shrine on their nightstand with their wedding photograph, candles, and incense.

We create an opportunity for reverence in our relationship by designing a setting in which we feel free to express our spirituality in the presence of our mate. Spirituality takes many different forms. We may offer up formal prayers to God or however we define our higher power. We may find spiritual sustenance in less traditional ways—by studying inspirational works or through music, dance, and other artistic expression. Some of us simply say thank you to the grass or a tree or the sky.

Opening our spirituality to our mate is a way to share our feelings of wonder and awe. We allow him to know what touches us and moves us, our secret longings and our deepest sense of gratitude. There is something extremely powerful about people coming together in blessing and prayer. Whether we do it with our mate or within an organized religious community, the act of joining hands, hearts, and spirits elevates and uplifts us.

We also heighten feelings of reverence through ritual and ceremony. So much of our relationship revolves around the necessary but mundane tasks of life. When we infuse ceremony into our regular routine, we bring our relationship to a more spiritual plane.

Most of the ritual in our relationships occurs in the context of traditional life-cycle events. We celebrate birthdays and anniversaries with parties and presents.

But how often do we take these opportunities to reflect on the meaning of the passage? Do we grab a Hallmark card off the shelf, or do we take the time to consider what it has meant to spend five, ten, fifteen years with our mate? Do we buy our partner socks for his birthday, or do we find a gift that reflects an important aspect of his personality or character?

One of the best gifts I ever received was a conga drum. One of the best gifts I've ever given was a song I wrote for Louis. Marking a passage with a meaningful gift gives our partner the message that we know who he is and we know what will please him.

Ritual can also be a part of our everyday lives. Early in my first marriage I met a couple in their seventies. For almost forty years they had read each other poetry aloud before going to bed. I met another young couple who always showered together in the morning. Whatever else transpired throughout the day, they had always started it together, naked, scrubbing each other's back. Any ritual initiated with the purpose of deepening our connection brings a sacred quality to our relationship, whether it's sharing morning coffee or saying bedtime prayers.

Ritual enhances our conscious appreciation of ourselves and our partner. We acknowledge both the ordinary and extraordinary ways in which our relationship is worthy of celebration.

Being a Blessing

Early in our relationship we may have participated in a ceremony in which we formally vowed our mutual devotion. We were blessed in the presence of family and friends with music, prayers, and wishes for a long and prosperous union.

A wedding ceremony, no matter how elaborate, takes at most, a half hour. Hopefully the blessings we receive sustain us for years to come. The reverence we felt then can endure if we bring the same spirit to our relationship as we brought to our wedding day or whatever day we pledged our love. We felt somber as we pondered what it would mean to make a permanent commitment. We felt inspired to live up to our promises, excited and exalted as we gazed into our beloved's eyes.

We continue to be a blessing in our relationship by maintaining the state of reverence in which our original commitment was made. We do it by remembering our promise to love and honor our mate, by reaffirming our pledge, saying "I love you" whenever and however we can.

Intentional Acts of Kindness

One of the ways we say "I love you" is by doing nice things for our partner. A beautiful little book, *Random Acts of Kindness* reminds us of the importance of spontaneous loving gestures. There's nothing quite so wonderful as feeling inspired to give someone something special *just because*. But we can also make a point of performing intentional acts of kindness in our relationship, such as surprising our partner with perfect little gifts, doing something to help him when he's overwhelmed or overworked, or showing him how much he means to us with kind words and thoughtful gestures.

Intentional acts of kindness have a tenderizing effect in our relationship. When I first fell in love with Joey, he gave me his old, weathered baseball glove. I used to sleep with it under my pillow. Three years later, on the day he moved out of our duplex, there was the glove, back under my pillow, a poignant gesture of our short-lived love.

It's the little things that go the longest way. When all
is said and done, they're often what we remember and
treasure the most.

Intentional Acts of Gratitude

We have so much to be grateful for. As we wholeheartedly
recommit to our relationship, we recover an appreciation
for all the ways our mate has and continues to make a
difference in our lives. When we focused on his shortcomings, we may have lost sight of how lucky we are to
have him at our side.

Each of us gives thanks for the special gifts of our partner—for being there when we need him; for supporting
us, encouraging us, taking care of us in so many ways; for
loving us when we have trouble loving ourselves; and for
being a loyal husband, devoted father, passionate lover,
and steadfast friend.

There will always be things about our partner that aggravate and annoy us. But as our appreciation grows, we
find it increasingly easy to accept his imperfections. We
take pride and pleasure in who he is and what he has to
give instead of measuring him against an unattainable
ideal. Appreciation melts our bitterness and anger, free-
ing us to give and receive love.

Human beings have an awful habit of taking each other
for granted. We jump on our partner when he screws up
but forget to say thank you when does something right.
As we grow comfortable and complacent, we often stop
noticing all the wonderful things about him and expect
them as our due.

Why are we acutely aware of what's missing and so
unappreciative of what we have? For the first four years
of our marriage, Gary never let up about how much he

despised my smoking, the overflowing ashtrays, the lingering stale smell of smoke. He screamed and yelled, reasoned and lectured, threatened and shamed. When I made a valiant attempt to quit, he hardly said a word. I expected a ticker-tape parade, and all I got was an occasional "Keep up the good work."

The presence of pain is impossible to ignore, and the absence of pain is easily forgotten. We suffer our partner's imperfections like a throbbing abscessed tooth—once the tooth's extracted, we stop thinking about it and go on about our lives.

Sometimes it takes the possibility of loss to fully appreciate how much we have. When something occurs that potentially threatens our partner, we suddenly realize how much he means to us. If he were suffering from a life-threatening illness, all the little things that bother us would seem irrelevant. We'd make deals with God; we'd make lists of all the times we weren't nice to him and vow to be more loving. Women who've been widowed often say they wish they'd appreciated their partner more when he was alive. With time and distance, some divorced women become more keenly aware of what they loved about their ex.

We avoid future feelings of regret by taking time to appreciate our partner in the present. None of us are guaranteed anything beyond this moment. Hopefully our mate will grace our lives for a long, long time, but nothing is forever.

Now is the time to count our blessings and to reflect on everything about our partner that makes us eternally grateful for his presence in our life. We may think he knows how much he means to us; after all, if we didn't love him, we wouldn't be with him, right? Besides we tell other people how great he is.

Tell him! Tell him every single thing about him that

you admire. Feel free to elaborate and go on at length. Make sure to mention specific qualities that you respect and attributes that you appreciate. Silent admiration has a certain amount of mystique, but yelling it from the rooftops ensures he'll get the message.

A relationship needs nurturing, and one of the best ways is by openly, intentionally expressing our gratitude. Make it part of your daily routine. At least once a day let your partner know how much you love him—with a love letter, a flower, a kiss, or a kind word.

Intentional Acts of Celebration

Another way to nurture a relationship is by celebrating our love. Over time, we may stop paying attention to opportunities for celebration. On the occasion of our first anniversary we spent all day making a romantic candlelit dinner and dessert was the top layer of our wedding cake that we'd kept in the freezer for a year. But our fourth anniversary went largely unnoticed; we vaguely remember a harried dinner out at a neighborhood fast-food joint with our two-year-old making a disgusting concoction of ketchup and sugar.

We must take advantage of every opportunity to celebrate. One couple always makes love on the anniversary of their first date. Another throws a "parents' birthday party" for themselves on each of the children's birthdays. Still another affirms their commitment by saving for and making one mutual purchase each year—season tickets to the opera, a new VCR for their bedroom, or rosebushes to plant in the backyard.

Celebration is a way to honor the importance of our relationship. In recent years, many couples have participated in recommitment ceremonies in order to update and reaffirm their vows. A formal ritual on our fifth, fifteenth, or fiftieth anniversary is a powerful statement of our ongoing commitment, but we needn't wait until then to mark important passages in our relationship. We can celebrate our love in simple ways by worshipping each other every single day.

We usually associate worship with God. Or movie idols. Or rock stars. We reserve the term for individuals or icons who inspire in us an overwhelming, sometimes obsessive, feeling of adoration and love. But who is more deserving of our adoration than our mate? Why limit our worship to deities or strangers when the one person we love more than any other is so worthy of praise?

Worshipping our beloved doesn't make one of us higher, the other lower. Rather, our love for each other elevates each of us our highest place where our godliness can grow. We worship our partner by expressing our adoration, by loudly praising their accomplishments, and by gently encouraging them when they fall off course. We worship our relationship by serving each other and our love.

When we're feeling particularly loving, we may serve our mate breakfast in bed. We can serve each other in so many other ways. We can do it by being a useful helpmate when there's an opportunity to lend a hand, by being thoughtful and considerate, by anticipating ways to ease our partner's struggles, lighten his load and brighten his day.

We are here to serve each other so that we may become everything we are capable of becoming. So that we can learn to love ourselves and each other. So that we can spread love in our families, our communities, in our world.

We have the power. And now we have the tools. We are big enough, strong enough, whole enough to continue the journey of loving our imperfect selves, our imperfect mate, and our imperfect world.

May you find peace and joy along the way.

Afterword

I am certain that there are writers who have full knowledge of their subject matter prior to writing a book, however, I do not include myself among them. This book began as a mere inkling of an idea, the slightest glimpse into a possibility I could barely imagine, much less speak about with confidence and certainty.

I conclude it having gained a far deeper understanding of what it means to love myself—and be a stronger, more empowered partner in my intimate relationship. Like you, for me this has been an extremely challenging learning process that has required a great deal of self-searching and personal healing in order to be whole enough to assume the task of real love.

So I thank you for being my traveling companion. Hopefully, the journey has inspired you to remain on the path of loving, respecting, and strengthening yourself. But the path is far from complete. It's common to be momentarily inspired by reading a book, hearing a lecture, or participating in a seminar. We get excited and motivated. For a day, a week, a month we walk around thinking, "Wow! This is great! I'm ready to change my life!" And then real life intervenes. Slowly but surely the glow wears off as we fall back into our regular routines.

Here's what I've learned from my spiritual teachers: Lasting change requires daily discipline. What this means is, we have to practice what we've learned—each and every day—if we are to truly benefit from the insights and work we've done so far. What this *doesn't* mean is that we have to dramatically alter our regular life, shedding our responsibilities and joining a spiritual monastary. On the contrary, the lessons of this book are designed to be practiced within the context of our lives and our relationships. Each day we can go a little further in cultivating the spiritual qualities presented—making sure we are clear about what we want, being true to ourselves, knowing we can stand on our own two feet, nurturing and nourishing ourselves, making smart choices, respectfully resolving conflicts, initiating creative strategies, and, most of all, living in a state of reverence and awe.

At times we will falter; at times we will experience the exuberance of knowing we are being our biggest, brightest, best selves. This is all anyone can ask of themselves or anyone else. If there is one gift of this book, may it be the enduring message that each of us is a divine spark, an integral part of the greater design. It is absolutely incumbent on us to discover our destiny and play it out to the fullest.

We can only do so if we are brave enough to stand up tall and say aloud what every woman knows: Love is the answer. It's always been the answer. And, thank God, women know how to love. We may never be perfect, our partner may never be perfect, our world may never reach perfection. But we have the wisdom and guts to bring it a whole lot closer if we're willing to put our best energy to the task. We must work toward this in our individual lives, as well as collectively, in the spirit of sisterhood. This is my hope and my prayer: That together we may pave the way for a safer, more peaceful and joyous world.

ABOUT THE AUTHOR

Ellen Sue Stern has more than a half-million copies of her books in print worldwide. She has appeared on national talk shows, including *Oprah, Sally Jessy Raphael, Maury Povich, Jane Whitney* and *Jerry Springer*. Thousands of women have attended her seminars, and her articles have been published in *New Woman, Woman's Day, Expecting, Self, Parenting, Working Woman* and *American Baby*. She lives with her two children, Zoe and Evan, in Minneapolis.

For more information on Ellen Sue Stern's books, tapes, seminars and speaking engagements, contact:

Ellen Sue Stern
5115 Excelsior Blvd., #248
St. Louis Park, MN 55416